The Gatekeepers
of
Psychology

The Gatekeepers of Psychology

EVALUATION OF PEER REVIEW BY CASE HISTORY

E. Rae Harcum and
Ellen F. Rosen

PRAEGER

Westport, Connecticut
London

Library of Congress Cataloging-in-Publication Data

Harcum, E. Rae (Eugene Rae).
  The gatekeepers of psychology : evaluation of peer review by case
history / E. Rae Harcum and Ellen F. Rosen.
      p.   cm.
  Includes bibliographical references and indexes.
  ISBN 0–275–94514–6 (alk. paper)
  1. Psychological literature—Evaluation. 2. Peer review in
psychology. 3. Psychology—Authorship. I. Rosen, Ellen F.
II. Title.
  [DNLM: 1. Peer Review—methods. 2. Peer Review—standards.
3. Psychology. WM 21 H257g]
BF76.8.H37 1993
150′.72—dc20
DNLM—DLC   92–48980

British Library Cataloguing in Publication Data is available.

Library of Congress Catalog Card Number: 92–48980
ISBN: 0–275–94514–6

First published in 1993

Praeger Publishers, 88 Post Road West, Westport, CT 06881
An imprint of Greenwood Publishing Group, Inc.

Printed in the United States of America

The paper used in this book complies with the
Permanent Paper Standard issued by the National
Information Standards Organization (Z39.48–1984).

10 9 8 7 6 5 4 3 2 1

Copyright Acknowledgments

Excerpts in Appendix A reprinted with permission of the Helen Dwight Reid Educational Foundation. Published by Heldref Publications, 1319 18th Street, N.W. Washington, D.C. 20036–1802. Copyright © 1989. Harcum, E. R, Rosen, E. F. & Burijon, B. N. (1989). Popular vs. Skinnerian views on the relation between human freedom and dignity. *Journal of Psychology, 123,* 257–267.

Excerpts in Appendix B reprinted with permission from *Psychological Reports.* Copyright © 1990. Harcum, E. R., & Rosen, E. F. (1990). Perceived dignity of persons with minimal voluntary control over their own behaviors. *Psychological Reports, 67,* 1275–1282.

Excerpts in Appendix C reprinted with permission of the Helen Dwight Reid Educational Foundation. Published by Heldref Publications, 1319 18th Street, N.W. Washington, D.C. 20036–1802. Copyright © 1990. Harcum, E. R., & Rosen, E. F. (1990). Perceived dignity as a function of perceived voluntary control of behaviors. *Journal of Psychology, 124,* 495–511.

Excerpts in Appendix D reprinted with permission of the Helen Dwight Reid Educational Foundation. Published by Heldref Publications, 1319 18th Street, N.W. Washington, D.C. 20036–1802. Copyright © 1992. Harcum, E. R. & Rosen, E. F. (1992). Perception of human dignity by college students and by direct-care providers. *Journal of Psychology, 126,* 27–36.

To our first teachers, John Bare and Stanley Williams,
steadfast advocates of integrity and excellence in research

Contents

Preface

This book documents in an unusual way several weaknesses in peer evaluations of research that has been submitted to psychological journals for publication. Complaints about the validity of the peer-review process are not unusual. The unique aspect of this book is its method of documenting multiple deficiencies in the evaluations. It presents actual copies of the original submissions to different journals of several manuscripts on a similar topic. Quoting the specific comments of the evaluators on each submission, it permits direct comparisons of the comments with the actual manuscripts. Readers of this book will thus be able to make their own judgments about the appropriateness and propriety of the editors' and evaluators' comments.

This particular evaluation procedure has not been used previously. Although Cummings and Frost (1985b) did describe two specific cases of evaluations, the papers were written by different authors for a single journal. One submission was successful and the other was unsuccessful. The small size of the samples of both research submissions and evaluators precluded any conclusions about possible biases with respect to specific subject matter. Moreover, the generality of the particularistic view of the process in these two articles was limited by the apparent personal acquaintance of the chief editor with both authors.

The present direct method is the only way to answer definitively the ubiquitous charge that the complaints of rejected authors reflect nothing more than personal psychodynamic mechanisms, such as denial and frustration-aggression (Roediger, 1987). The overall result of the present documentation and discussion is a clear indictment of certain aspects of the journal peer-review system. The reviews are shown to be, in general, neither competent nor conscientious, and often imperious in style. We present several suggestions for strengthening the evaluation system.

The cases discussed here are examples of the system in apparently normal operation. The major issue is whether the current system needs revision to keep up with changes in sociological development within the scientific community. The current editorial system, for example, was developed for a small community of scientists who knew each other and shared training and experiences, not for the current large, often relatively anonymous megacommunity of modern scholars. We focus on the specific scientific and professional issues and the review styles of these evaluators, rather than on the final editorial decision.

We think that the quoted responses of the editors and consultants are representative of the attitudes and interpretations of the scientific community of psychologists, particularly social psychologists. Therefore, a summary rebuttal should foster a rethinking of those beliefs and the attendant responses. On the basis of these examples, we conclude that the system needs serious reworking. We do not think that the problems that this book describes are specific to the social/personality area of research, based on our more general experiences. Harcum (1992) used a similar case-history procedure to document the same difficulties in the context of perceptual-cognitive research. We trust that this book will have a positive effect on the peer-review process.

Although action editors have the decision power, of course, in our experience they rarely decide against the consultants. The so-called peers who review manuscript submissions are trusted lieutenants of the editors, who, as gatekeepers of the science, hold in their editorial hands the keys to the door of the storehouse of scientific knowledge—published research. These editorial teams, these editors and their consultants, therefore control both the rate of progress and direction of scientific efforts.

We are assuming some personal and professional risks by writing this book. We incur the risk of alienating a large number of editors and evaluators to whom we may later submit our research results. Yet, we believe so strongly that the current review process needs to become more compatible with scientific practice that we raise our voices. We trust our future to the strongly held principle of academic freedom, and to the fact that we both have tenure.

This book also leaves us vulnerable to the charge of "journal shopping," a process in which less competent authors of marginal products continue to submit a given piece of work until they find acceptance with a journal with sufficiently low standards. We emphasize another principle, however: the ethical responsibility to research subjects and to the progress of the discipline.

Although journal shopping is poor practice, on the other hand, it seems clearly unethical for authors to abandon attempts to publish the research that they firmly believe to be meritorious. Researchers owe it to their research subjects to affirm and preserve through publication the worth of their contributions. This ethical consideration is not very well understood.

If the product is good, tenacity becomes a virtue. Cummings and Frost (1985a) include tenacity as a necessary virtue for prospective authors. The acceptance of a submission that has been rejected by another journal does not necessarily imply lower standards, but could with equal justification indicate higher standards of reviewing by the publishing journal. There have in fact been cases in which even Nobel quality work was rejected at first (Yalow, 1982).

We do not believe that these evaluations reflect personal biases against either of us. Our point is quite the opposite: the system is biased against classes of authors, methodological approaches, and specific topics. These biases are systemic, not personal, and they result from the use of certain heuristics of evaluation, presumably because of time pressures (Harcum, 1992). In our view, this is an even more serious problem than a possible personal bias.

We contend that competent evaluators produce incompetent evaluations because they are not taking the time to read the submissions carefully and to reflect on them. Therefore, they are making guesses about the content and quality of the submissions based on expectations derived partly from articles on seemingly related topics. Probably, most often these guesses are correct. But when such guesses turn out to be incorrect, the evaluators support them by engaging in straw-man arguments, instead of digging into the substantive issues of the submission. Perhaps some other biases come into play at this point because some submissions are apparently deemed more worthy of a careful reading and reflection owing to their association with an author of prestigious name or institutional affiliation.

If authors retain faith in their rejected submissions, where can they gain a forum for scientific debate, especially if they are not well known? The complaint is likely to suffer the same fate as the original submission; nobody wants to hear about the rejections of an unknown author. Moreover, the full facts and argument require book-length exposition. At least the case against peer review has been made and is therefore available to those who will read it.

We have found that isolated objections to individual editors about specific issues in piecemeal fashion are generally a waste of time. Apparently, editors do not feel that they should, or can profitably, take the time to satisfy an unfamiliar author. Editors are not, after all, responsible for the professional development of authors. Such a view implies that the handling of appeals is simply a matter of explaining to the authors the errors of their ways. The concept of peer review literally implies, however, that any author has *equal* claim to authority. To refuse to evaluate appeals uniformly is to give the lie to the concept of peer review. Evaluators should be expected to give the same careful attention to appeals that they are expected to give to the original submissions. This should be understood as part of the implied contract when a professional agrees to serve as an evaluator. A legitimate appeal is a dispute over a scientific fact or interpretation, presumably between competent professionals. To ignore or summarily dismiss one side of an issue is not scientifically justifiable. Moreover, it is inconsistent with the concept of a self-correcting science.

The problem is important because, first, unpublished data are unavailable to other scientists. Second, if the data have actually been rejected from publication *for valid reasons* they should not be trusted by even the researcher who collected them. Therefore, the reviewing decision should be as definitive as possible, whatever the result. We offer some suggestions about methods to eliminate or compensate for the incompetent reviews that are bound to occur from time to time, given human fallibility. Our major suggestion is the institution of a viable appeal procedure for correcting factual errors and other false criticisms that can be refuted with a high degree of confidence among competent professionals. At the present time, evaluators apparently receive little or no feedback from authors and authors receive no feedback about the thoughtful views that they may have expressed on the adequacy of the evaluations.

If the fault lies with the journal evaluations, the specific evaluators can be confronted with their specific errors. If the fault lies, instead, with a tendency toward journal shopping by some authors, the same remedy through appeal should be appropriate. The journal-shopping author can be advised to suppress further attempts to publish. Not only will better decisions about acceptance or rejection of specific submissions be reached, but evaluators and authors will be able to learn from their successes and mistakes. Our intention is not to blanket all evaluators with the same criticisms. Certainly, some evaluators merit only praise, gratitude, and admiration. All evaluators should answer for themselves whether a given criticism applies to them. If this occurs, this book will have made a positive contribution both to individuals and to behavioral science. We hope that these points and counterpoints will further stimulate the burgeoning interest in the issues of peer review. These issues, it seems to us, are crucially important for a better science, which we hope will ultimately lead to a better plan for improving our culture.

We have tried to avoid being contentious. Nevertheless, we argue that incompetence from anyone who climbs into the arena of scientific publication should never be tolerated. The sheer grossness of some of the errors cited in this book are almost beyond belief. Moreover, the ad hominem nature of some comments should evoke strong emotions of dismay and regret in all scientists who are interested in professionalism and progress.

Because these reviewers were not preparing material for publication, we have tried to avoid irrelevant details associated with punctuation, spelling, and general presentation. Focusing attention on such details would be unfair to scientists who have volunteered their time and effort to perform a necessary function. At the same time, this function is too important for a person to attempt with less than full commitment. We submit that an evaluator, as one of the gatekeepers of science, has an even *greater* ethical responsibility in writing substantive evaluations that are *not* intended for publication under his or her own name than in writing identified commentary or in publishing personal research.

One final benefit of this book is that students can learn about conducting and evaluating research by examining these criticisms, defenses, and counter-arguments. The book represents an "in-the-trenches" view of the scientific activities of established researchers in psychology. It undoubtedly destroys the icon of a completely objective, error-free science, and enhances the conception of science as an endeavor of fallible human beings. Intelligent people can both disagree and make mistakes, of course. Perhaps some professional researchers and reviewers need to learn this lesson also. The full range of editorial responsibility is not served by merely rejecting many submissions, and passing only a very few others (Roediger, 1987).

The issue entails human costs as well. Toffler (1985), in summarizing the processing of her ultimately successful, but first-rejected submission, wrote as follows:

> Although this saga has an upbeat ending, the experience it relates was an extremely painful one. During the year from the March 17, 1980 letter, to the March 23, 1981 submission of the final revision, I did little that was productive in either research or writing. The possibility of a similar embarrassing and demeaning response to my work loomed as a black, constraining cloud. In time, of course, the cloud passed. However, before this experience, writing had been a labor that gave me considerable satisfaction and often a great deal of fun. Now, it is much more labor—and nowhere near the fun. (p. 649)

A more damaging commentary would be difficult to imagine. This situation is even more disturbing when one considers that the article in question would not even have been accepted in the particular journal if the chief editor had not intervened. Frost (1985), as a rejected author, similarly expressed the erosion of the joy of authorship, and the inhibition of the creative urges, which are the result of destructive reviews. Poor reviewing can stifle further research, particularly for the young, beginning researcher.

We thank those who have assisted in the production of the book, notably our psychology department secretary, Kathy Morgan, and our respective partners, Phoebe Harcum and Linda Petty, who listen with great patience to our tirades.

The Gatekeepers of Psychology

▲

1 ———————————————————

Practices and Complaints

The concept of peer review for journal submissions has such a welcome egalitarian sound and feeling about it that criticism seems almost petulant and unprofessional. The concept suggests the idea of colleagues in science engaging in a cooperative, systematic search for new knowledge about human behavior. When peer review functions properly, it "enhances rather than impedes the progress of science" (Peters & Ceci, 1982, p. 252). But some researchers have seriously questioned whether in psychology it functions as it should in terms of the actual prevailing practices (e.g., Harcum, 1992; Mahoney, 1985; Peters & Ceci, 1982).

Mahoney (1985) concluded that, in spite of the importance of publication in science, it has not been as effective as it could be in fulfilling its functions because of weaknesses in the peer-review aspect of the system. He argued that the evaluators, as gatekeepers of the scientific literature, tend to direct the literature down less productive paths:

A review of archival and experimental studies on the parameters of publication suggests that there are significant epistemic constraints on what is deemed worthy of publication. Rather than stimulating and facilitating "blind variation," trial and error, and conceptual novelty, our current policies, especially in the social sciences, tend to (a) effectively discourage some themes and styles of research, (b) selectively inflate the archival records of corroborative (significant) evidence, (c) generally discourage replicative inquiry and the submission (let alone publication) of disconfirmatory evidence, and (d) indirectly perpetuate the prevailing authority structure in science by constituting the primary epistemic selection process determining who should teach and study in the role of academic scientist. (p. 33)

Such conclusions are not rare, scattered, or isolated. For example, Le Shan (1990) gave an example in which some psychologists objected to publications in certain areas of research. At one time they thought it "obscene" to publish articles dealing with psychotherapy for cancer patients. He lamented:

Until this happened, it had not occurred to me that there were still taboo subjects in science. I knew well how there had been such subjects in the past; I knew stories such as that of the physician Ignaz Semmelweiss, who was thrown out of his hospital and teaching position when he tried to get physicians to wash their hands before they worked with a woman in childbirth. Although these and other similar stories are taught to every student in science, I believed that these problems existed only in the past, not in the present. I am wiser now. (p. 107)

The larger issue here concerns the very definition of the field of psychology. Editors and other evaluators, as gatekeepers of the science, have a major role in the definition of the science as operationally delimited by its literature. Kimble (1990) concluded that this definition may not adequately reflect the basic nature of psychology:

When psychology got back to business at the end of World War II, it took its methodology extremely seriously. Many of the major research-producing departments had resident philosophers of science, most of whom were logical positivists. Their influence during the next 20 years or so was profound but not entirely positive. During those years, psychology worked so hard to make itself a science that it forgot to make that science a psychology. At least to certain journal editors, this hard-nosed science ruled out, as operationally unclean, concepts such as volition, consciousness, and mind, as well as methods such as free recall and personal report. Such a psychology could not survive. (p. 559)

The psychological literature currently reflects a surge of appropriate interest in a comprehensive evaluation of the publication process. Complaints about the effects of biases in the peer-review aspect of the system have been frequent and forceful (e.g., Harnad, 1982). As Fiske and Fogg (1990) reported about these evaluative articles: "Largely critical, they often propose changes" (p. 591). Many kinds of biases have been attributed to numerous sources, such as hero worship, croneyism, incompetence, and theoretical preferences.

THE ROLE OF HEURISTICS

Harcum (1992) has concluded that evaluators tend to employ certain heuristics as decision rules in order to simplify the evaluation task and cope with their heavy burden of selecting a few positive cases for publication from a multitude of worthy submissions. He argued that the use of these heuristics is generally efficient and effective, but it is strongly biased against the unknown, the new, and the creative.

A heuristic is a general rule for approaching a problem that can aid in solving it by directing attention toward possible solutions. Unfortunately, its use does not guarantee the ultimate acquisition of a correct solution. The question is: Is there a better way than using heuristics to select articles for publication?

Most of the heuristics described by Harcum (1992) involved reliance on authority. His complete list is as follows:

1. Familiar authors produce better submissions.
2. Familiar theories are superior.
3. The better the reputation of the journal, the better the research in it.
4. The important topics are the currently popular ones.
5. The evaluator is more knowledgeable than the author.
6. Quantifiable data are better than nonquantifiable data.
7. Traditional methods are better than novel ones.
8. A study with any methodological flaw or weakness is not publishable.
9. Only results obtained by the consensual best procedures are publishable.
10. Laboratory research is more accurate but lacks external validity, while the reverse is true for field research.
11. The more recent study is more believable than earlier results.
12. A submission previously rejected by another journal is not worthy of publication.

The existence of some of these heuristics in the evaluative process is supported by empirical research, and some of them are supported only by anecdotal evidence. Definitive evidence is extremely difficult to obtain, because of both practical and ethical considerations (e.g., Peters & Ceci, 1982).

Blind reviewing might help combat the effects of some of these heuristics, if one could be assured in some way that an evaluator cannot guess the identity of an author from both subtle and obvious clues in the submission. This in itself would indicate that the author is too unknown to be identified from his or her work; that fact, in itself, is truly an identification of a significant kind.

We submit, however, that at best the guesses about authorship represent only blurred vision. For example, it would be virtually impossible for well-known authors to hide their identities. Psychologists tend to agree on this point. Bradley (1981) found that 76% of a group of psychologists, experienced in research, did not believe that blind review was highly effective. In fact, Sechrest (1987) asserted that blind review "may be about as 'blind' as a blindfolded stage magician" (p. 271).

Harcum (1992) agreed that the full use of the listed heuristics would probably produce excellent results for a great majority of journal submissions. But a mindless overreliance on their use as decision rules could block dissemination of rare, innovative ideas. When worthy ideas are casually rejected on the basis of certain heuristics that are in common use among evaluators, there is a false sense of validity through reliability—a kind of editorial groupthink (Janis, 1971). The outraged voices of "outsiders" are not likely to matter much to self-satisfied "insiders." Unpopular research ideas must therefore be continually recycled until an evaluator who does not blindly adhere to the "popular is important" heuristic is reached, or the frustrated potential author gives up the unrewarded struggle. In the latter case, of course, the open opportunity for rapid progress of the science is lost.

By the same logic, with more reflective evaluations, useless new ideas, regardless of their source, and the rehashed or renamed old ideas, would soon be discredited. Terminating such practices would save space, limit the reading responsibilities of scientists to "keep up," and otherwise reduce the current burden on evaluators.

THE SYSTEM

As we have charged, the evaluation process is often controlled by mechanisms that are similar to those of groupthink (Janis, 1971), thus limiting its effectiveness. The mechanisms of groupthink, that come about presumably through the felt need for unanimous agreement within an in-group, includes such barriers to effective thinking as feelings of invulnerability within the in-group, acceptance of stereotypes in thinking, and censorship of those ideas that conflict with a potentially emerging group consensus. These mechanisms would tend to produce biases particularly against innovative ideas and unknown scholars—essentially the out-group. As Garcia (1981) charges, editors tend to be "neophobic."

Some authors (e.g., Yalow, 1982; Ziman, 1982) simply fault the system for employing incompetent reviewers. We doubt that this is a major problem, although the issue may be purely semantic. We like to distinguish between the situation in which a competent evaluator, possibly because of extenuating circumstances, renders an incompetent evaluation, in contrast to the situation in which the evaluator is constitutionally incapable of anything other than an incompetent evaluation under any circumstances. An occasional dispositionally incompetent reviewer is surely possible, but admittedly not very probable, unless one also wishes to consider some editors incompetent for choosing competent evaluators. There must surely be a substantial positive correlation between an individual's success as an author of meritorious research, entailing an increased likelihood that the individual will be selected by an editor as an evaluator, and the individual's subsequent competence as a reviewer of research submissions. We believe, therefore, that in general evaluators are dispositionally competent. These individuals may, however, not be particularly competent to do the specific job that they are asked to do.

Our view is that the present system leads competent people too often to produce incompetent reviews. We submit that in some cases, the number of incompetent evaluations is alarmingly large. Further, the competent evaluators produce incompetent evaluations because the time pressures often cause them to use the heuristics, mentioned above, instead of grappling seriously with the scientific issues in a particular submission. There is an initial negative reaction to an unfamiliar, perhaps iconoclastic idea, followed by a search for an uncontestable basis to reject the submission. Thus, under deadline duress, they slip into habitual modes of stereotyped responding, lapses of functional literacy, and excessive reliance on the heuristics described above.

A description by an editor of his usual practice should be instructive at this point. Roediger (1987) describes his personal editorial practice:

> For what it's worth, I find that the best procedure is to skim the reviews to get a feel for the issues raised, then read the paper carefully, sometimes more than once. Then I read the reviews again, form a decision, and dictate an action letter, which is then worked over once or twice. Also helpful—given time—is final reading of the paper to ensure that the criticisms raised are actually warranted on careful reexamination and are not based on misunderstandings created by hasty reading or reviewer's misapprehensions. (pp. 232–233)

The above paragraph contains an important inconsistency: How can there be a misunderstanding based on a hasty reading if the editor always reads the submission "carefully" with attention to the reviewer's comments? Roediger seems to admit that the editor sometimes does *not* read a paper carefully, and also sometimes does *not* check his action letter for the appropriateness of the criticisms that he himself has directed at the manuscript or those of others that he has endorsed. According to this description, on a sheer probabilistic basis, there would be a finite number of manuscripts that were both hastily read and not checked after the action letter was written. That set of circumstances provides a neat blueprint for incompetent reviewing, whether or not it actually happens, or happens infrequently.

Although Roediger's journal is not involved in the case histories described in this book, his procedure could easily account for the incompetent reviews that we present. The problems of peer review go deeper than that, however, because the case histories to be described here indicate a consistency that indicts an array of different editors and evaluators, which speaks to systematic biases, rather than isolated lapses or failures of a viable system.

The Matthew Effect

As an example, let us consider one of the heuristics proposed by Harcum (1992): the evaluator is more knowledgeable about the subject than the author. This assumption can lead to extremely bad habits in the evaluator. As authors, often we have genuinely felt that an evaluator was not discriminating between us and his or her own students, and between our specific submission and an undergraduate term paper or laboratory report. Because of space limitations in journals, obviously certain basic information must be assumed by any reader—the evaluator included. For example, when an author concludes in a journal submission that an effect is significant after a statistical test, ordinarily there is no need for a full discussion of the possibilities for a Type-I error. For the beginning student, however, the instructor may, and should, want verification that the student does have the proper sophistication about the many pitfalls of the hypothesis-testing approach. But, such monitoring and admonition are truly insulting to an experienced doctoral-level researcher. The professional is not, and should not be, allowed to take up journal space with exercises merely for the purpose of demonstrating personal competence.

Clearly, famous scientists are not expected to perform such demonstrations. Merton (1968) called this phenomenon the "Matthew Effect," based on the biblical passage in St. Matthew that begins, "for unto every one that hath shall be given." He examined interviews of winners of the Nobel Prize in science in order to develop "a conception of ways in which certain psychosocial processes affect the allocation of rewards to scientists for their contributions—an allocation which in turn affects the flow of ideas and findings through the communication networks of science" (p. 56). He concluded that the more prestigious scientists are likely to be given disproportionately greater credit for collaborative effort and independently discovered findings. Moreover, the works of the prestigious researchers are more likely to be published, and their published work is more likely to be read and cited.

In one sense, these practices are quite reasonable, as we said above, because established researchers in a field are surely more likely to produce more works of higher quality. But there is a down side as well. Merton (1968) pointed out that meritorious work by unknown researchers can be rejected, to the detriment of scientific progress: "The history of science abounds in instances of basic papers' having been written by comparatively unknown scientists, only to have been neglected for years" (p. 62). He cited as an example the early discoveries of Mendel, the great geneticist. He also recounted an anecdote about the great physicist, Lord Rayleigh, for whom a paper was rejected because his name had been left off. The editorial decision was quickly reversed when the name of the author was discovered.

The Matthew Effect presents a problem for the evaluation of journal submissions. As Merton (1968) concluded over 20 years ago:

> When the Matthew Effect is thus transformed into an idol of authority, it violates the norm of universalism embodied in the institution of science and curbs the advancement of knowledge. But next to nothing is known about the frequency with which these practices are adopted by the editors and referees of scientific journals and by other gatekeepers of science. This aspect of the workings of the institution of science remains largely a matter of anecdote and heavily motivated gossip. (p. 62)

The evidence presented in this book suggests that the frequency in at least some areas of psychology reflects a serious problem still.

The Evaluator Delusion

When the mechanisms that produce the Matthew Effect enter into the judgment of a submission by an evaluator, it can become a factor in what we call the Evaluator Delusion. This is the uncritical use of Harcum's (1992) fifth heuristic—that the evaluator is more knowledgeable than the author in both the subject matter and the methodology of the submission. This would reflect a sort of reverse Matthew Effect: those who have nothing will be given nothing. They will not even be given the presumption that they know what they are doing. We submit that such thinking can lead to a false sense of superiority on the part of the evaluator, which in the extreme can result in a feeling of infallibility and invulnerability. This feeling is reinforced by the literal fact that there is—in some cases in our experience, at least—no accountability to anyone except perhaps their own journal editor. Literally, a submission is likely to be unpublishable if even a single evaluator contends that it is. According to the analysis by Roediger (1987), relatively minor factors often become operational in the editorial decision for the average article.

Some very disturbing data on the peer-review process were obtained by Bradley (1981) from two mail surveys in early 1980. One survey of a group of respondents that consisted mostly of psychologists, but also some statisticians, asked those individuals to describe the last article that they had been able to publish only after a substantive revision had been made. The respondents in this population reported that they had encountered: pressure to conform to the subjective preference of a reviewer (76%); false criticisms (73%—and of these 8% reported making erroneous changes in order to comply with the demands of a reviewer); inferior expertise of the reviewer (67%); concentration on trivia by the reviewer (60%); treatment as an inferior (43%); and careless reading by the reviewer (40%).

In a different survey of a selected group of psychologists (i.e., members of the Psychonomic Society), Bradley found that 53% of them had been asked to review an article that they themselves felt incompetent to review. Of these psychologists, 73% were not willing to concede that the evaluator knew better than the author when there was a point of disagreement. This high percentage could, of course, reflect the fact that admission to membership in the Psychonomic Society is dependent upon a satisfactory publication record. The problems in defining a "peer" are obvious.

Bradley (1981) concluded that, nevertheless, the respondents to both of his surveys generally endorsed the peer-review system, because they agreed that their articles were generally improved as a result of the suggestions of the evaluators. In the population of psychologists and statisticians, only 28% reported that the reviewing process did not improve the published article. In the population of exclusively experienced psychologists, only 13% did not agree that the editing process improved their manuscript enough to justify the review.

But, we interpret these results differently. In the context of other critical responses, these data clearly do not indicate a vindication or endorsement of peer reviewing. In a truly successful evaluation process, one should expect *virtually every* article to be improved by the comments of experts. The fact that 13% and 28%, respectively, of the evaluations in the two populations were viewed as *not* having a net beneficial result is an indictment of the system, it seems to us. Moreover, even when articles were improved, there were negative aspects of the evaluations.

One of the salient negative aspects of the evaluation process seems to be the almost universal requirement for a revision of the first submission. According to Fiske and Fogg (1990), only about 2% of the original submissions are published without requiring revisions from the author. Bradley (1981) discovered from his survey of the psychologists with established postdoctoral publication records that revisions of their submissions were routine. He reported as follows:

> 91% of the respondents answered "yes" to the question "Was a revision required on the last manuscript you published in a refereed professional journal?" and 30% answered "no" to the question "Have you *ever* had an article accepted as originally submitted (i.e., with no revision required) by a refereed professional journal?" It is difficult, therefore, to escape the conclusion that the peer-review system has been guilty of many bureaucratic excesses and that one of its consequences, virtually mandatory revision, is more of a conventionalized ritual than a scientific necessity. (p. 34)

Without a doubt, evaluators inject their own particular biases into what is published. Consequently, the literature is biased, of course, both in terms of what gets in and what is blocked out. According to Bradley's (1981) data, 77% of the psychologists in his survey had published an article in one journal that had previously been rejected by another. Although it may seem, therefore, that the biases ultimately even out across the various journals, this does not exonerate the system.

Because the number of possibilities for error in evaluation within even a single submission are great, a frequent evaluator is very likely to make at least one mistake over the course of a year—or over the course of a career. As psychologists, we know better than to expect perfection in anything other than the very simplest of tasks. The question is not whether isolated errors are made by individuals in implementing a system, but whether the system itself is flawed by consistently permitting related errors on related topics, or refusing to correct identifiable mistakes.

An author can forgive an error if he or she has the overall impression that the evaluator has been generally conscientious. But, we have in our own experience found that a so-called evaluator displayed the ultimate in arrogance by assuming that he or she understood the author's thesis without carefully reading the text, and then compounded the error by denouncing the resulting misunderstanding. A viable evaluation system should prevent such occurrences from being uncorrected for long.

Overgeneralization is an error of thinking to which evaluators are particularly susceptible, presumably because of sets produced by repeated similar experiences. Experience is known to produce sets to think about familiar problems in consistent ways. Such sets are a problem in evaluation only when they close the mind prematurely to alternative interpretations and solutions, however. But the competent evaluator keeps an open mind. When an evaluator fails to make a discrimination, and therefore fits an innovative approach into a stereotyped category, the result is both stultifying to science and frustrating for the author. Obviously, an author's theory and methods cannot make sense under such circumstances. A reasonable concern for context is appropriate, but nevertheless each submission should be evaluated on its own merits.

Spencer, Hartnett, and Mahoney (1985) offered a somewhat different objection to the system. They developed a method of linguistic analysis for evaluating journal reviews, which entailed simply counting the number of content-free comments in the review. In one sample of ten reviews of five rejected papers, for whom the authorship was known, a proportion of 25% or more of nonsubstantive comments in a review indicated that the authors of the submissions would judge that the review was not impartial. In an additional study by Spencer et al. of over 500 reviews provided by journal editors, about 40% of the reviews contained more than 25% such nonsubstantive comments, with an average of about 20% such comments for both accepted and rejected submissions.

These results imply an unwelcome general vacuity in the comments. There are obvious weaknesses in the method, however. For example, the method does not reflect the extent to which a general evaluative comment was later amplified by subsequent specific details and illustrations. Moreover, it did not assess the accuracy or importance of the summary criticisms or commendations.

Other interesting reports in Bradley's (1981) study, described above, was that the group of respondents judged the referees not to be consistent (56%); open-minded (40%); courteous (30%); competent (22%); or internally consistent (21%). In addition, 65% agreed that referees find things to object to just to prove they have been conscientious. In fact, 2% of the respondents admitted to leaving uncorrected errors that were easy to correct in the manuscript in order to appease the referees and prevent them from bringing up other objections that might be more difficult to handle.

Finke (1990) joined those who have charged that evaluators try to find flaws in submissions. He said:

> Many have come to believe that in order for their review to "count," they now have to find something "wrong" with the manuscript. As a result, reviewers today have often resorted to fastidious and capricious fault-finding, even to the extent of making their criticisms completely arbitrary. I have actually known of colleagues who purposely put minor flaws in their manuscripts, so that the reviewers would focus their criticisms on those easily correctable flaws and thus would be less likely to make the arbitrary, unaddressable types of criticisms. (p. 669)

There is surely something wrong with a system that would foster such unprofessional behavior.

Interevaluator Reliability

Mahoney (1985) pointed out that previous research on peer review has focused on the issue of reliability. But, he cautioned that the problem of validity of results may not be solved through achievement of enforced interrater reliability: "Enforced reliability is not a likely solution; indeed, it might well exacerbate the problem" (p. 32). This is not to say that the level of interrater reliability is high. But, the problem of trying to achieve validity through reliability is too familiar to require further discussion here.

Evaluator Overload

Although he does not present documentation, Finke (1990) expressed several serious charges against current peer-review practices. He pointed out that the most qualified reviewers tend to be overburdened and therefore do not have the time to complete thorough reviews on submissions that are not within their own areas of research knowledge or expertise. For other potential evaluators, the situation is different:

> In contrast, reviewers who do have the time to review manuscripts often do not have sufficient familiarity with the current research to provide a competent evaluation. This has the consequence that research that is readily published tends to be excessively conventional and platitudinous, whereas studies that are highly original and that constitute innovative advances in the field are often rejected because the reviewers are uninformed, quixotic, or simply irresponsible. (p. 669)

We believe that our book documents this last point through specific instances.

THE CASE-HISTORY APPROACH

The research problems in studying the publication process are enormously complex. Therefore, no single study is likely to provide an accurate global description of the true state of affairs. Horror stories are shocking and revealing, but the sheer horror of the stories may cause us to overestimate their frequency.

Statistical studies based on outcome decisions (e.g., Peters & Ceci, 1982) are helpful, but they still do not get at the validity of individual evaluations and decisions. For example, a positive correlation between the prestige of an author and the probability of publication would be entirely reasonable on the basis of consistent appreciation of meritorious work. Or, it could reflect favorable biases toward prestigious authors. A more detailed analysis is required to discover the mechanism. As Fiske and Fogg (1990) conclude, "Yet almost nothing has been reported on the free-response comments of reviewers" (p. 591). They report that, except for a few examples and general comments, "we have found no comparisons of the specific comments made by the reviewers of the same paper" (p. 591).

Such specific comparisons should be made, along with specific comparisons to the submission on which the comments are made. Only then can scientists achieve confidence in the validity of the evaluations, even if the evaluators were consistent in their overt comments. Because Fiske and Fogg (1990) show that evaluators are not consistent, the problems of evaluation are much more serious than Fiske and Fogg think. Their conclusion on the issue is as follows:

> Given the low degree of manifested consensus between reviewers, it is reasonable to ask whether the reviewers' criticisms were appropriate. Although we cannot give a definitive answer to that question, we believe that they generally were. We very rarely saw any criticism that we were inclined to question, on the basis of internal or other evidence, such as the reviewer's stating that a statistical test had a particular assumption. Also, in instances in which we consulted the original manuscript, we found no reviewer criticisms with which we disagreed. . . . Finally, it was very uncommon for an editor to indicate disagreement with a point made by a reviewer. (p. 597)

We have problems with the conclusion that the evaluations nevertheless are valid because each criticism is itself valid, although the evaluators cite different problems with given submissions. If *all* of the criticisms are valid, and not trivial, when the evaluations are not consistent, then *each* evaluator has obviously missed several real deficiencies in the submission.

Fiske and Fogg (1990) emphasize that, "Saying that two reviewers typically do not agree does not necessarily mean that they disagree" (p. 597). But this statement may not be true in the case of the present discussion. In the context of an evaluation, one would reasonably infer that a failure to comment on a point constitutes an approval or endorsement of that point, or at least a subthreshold level of disapproval. We do not understand how these authors can conclude that the evaluators do not agree among themselves, but also imply that the evaluators tend to be correct in pointing out deficiencies. Of course, evaluators for a given submission may be selected for their diverse approaches, but that should not introduce a large relativity factor into the process of determining what is good research and good writing.

Part of the issue here concerns the conception of a "deficiency." We submit that this is a relative term, dependent, for example, upon the population of journals examined. What may be a deficiency—or serious substantive flaw— from the standpoint of achieving publication in the prestigious journals of the Fiske and Fogg (1990) journal population, may not be a fatal flaw from the standpoint of the validity of the scientific conclusion. A minor deficiency could be seen by a prestigious journal as fatal to chances of publication in that journal, for example, if the author is employed at a human development institute rather than at a prestigious university (e.g., Peters & Ceci, 1982).

As Garcia (1981) pointed out, a minor deficiency in design may not always invalidate the conclusion of the study. In fact, one of the general categories of so-called deficiency in the Fiske and Fogg study was as follows: "Paper should be submitted to a less demanding journal" (p. 595). Whatever that means exactly, it surely implies that there is no fatal flaw that actually invalidates the scientific conclusions. Why else would publication elsewhere be proposed? We suspect that the deficiencies in these studies may be what Beaver (1982) has called "universal general deficiencies" (p. 200) that could be leveled at any article. As Fiske and Fogg admit, "Everyone who has submitted manuscripts for publication knows that reviewers always can and do find some weaknesses to report" (p. 597). We would prefer to call such practices, "gamesmanship," rather than evaluations.

The definitional problems indicate the difficulty in studies that rely on objective measurement and statistical evidence. It is extremely difficult to determine what conclusions are warranted by the data. For example, the tenor of the Fiske and Fogg conclusion is that authors do not eliminate mistakes in submissions before they are submitted for evaluation. We disagree. We propose that articles submitted to the prestigious APA journals in the Fiske and Fogg population were probably very carefully checked for serious flaws by the authors. Everyone is quite painfully aware of the high rejection rates for these particular journals. For example, a psychologist whom we respect highly once commented that he had given up as impossible trying to get something published in a particular APA journal. Therefore, submissions with even minor flaws are probably selectively omitted from submission to the journals in the Fiske and Fogg population.

We expect therefore that not many serious errors remain in submissions to the more prestigious APA journals. There have been, of course, some notable counterexamples, which need not be documented at this time. Because most of the submissions cannot be published, the evaluators point out so-called deficiencies that might even be unworthy of mention by evaluators for less prestigious journals. Therefore, different evaluators may not be missing flaws in specific studies, but merely using different bases of judgment about which of the minor deficiencies are worthy of mention.

Without more individualistic data, it is impossible to know whether the unreliability of these evaluations of journal submissions is caused by true mistakes in evaluation or tendencies to emphasize different minor deficiencies when there are no major flaws in the studies to be reported. We suggest that the unreliability of these evaluations is caused by the former. More data based on individual cases are needed to resolve the issue, however.

We believe that the best way to obtain a direct evaluation of the reviewing process is through the detailed case history, which until now has not been available. To be sure, there are notable brief "horror stories" in the literature (e.g., Garcia, 1981; Yalow, 1982), and sparse evidence in the form of complete case histories, with comparisons of the actual text of the submission to the verbatim text of the evaluations.

This book is based, therefore, on a case history of a research program that we initiated to test a hypothesis of important professional and social consequences. Our journal submissions that tested the hypothesis met with strong editorial resistance, to say the least. In fact, our various efforts were rejected by several different journals before eventual publication.

To be sure, rejection is not necessarily a false negative; it can be a correct assessment of a poor product. Obviously, we believe that our cases reflect the former, or we would not be writing this critique. Nevertheless, we wish to focus our discussion on the accuracy and propriety of the separate evaluations, rather than on the final editorial decision. We do firmly believe that the rejections represented false negatives, based on the poor evaluations, understanding that we are placing our judgment above more than a score of evaluators for prestigious psychological and cognate journals. We do intend to make our case in this book, so that readers can decide for themselves.

The situation to be described here represents a failure of the peer-review system, in any case, regardless of where the specific fault lies. For example, the submission that has produced the greatest problem for us (Harcum & Rosen, 1990a), shown in Appendix C, was originally submitted to a journal in March, 1987. After rejections from that journal, plus five other journals, substantively the same submission was finally accepted in February, 1990. If our argument is correct, the publication of results in a new and important research area was delayed for almost three years, and much effort of editors, evaluators, and authors was essentially wasted.

We attribute the general rejections of this work to the evaluator heuristics in the prevailing scientific model, although alternative interpretations are of course possible. For example, we may have been unlucky enough to have encountered a rare covey of overworked or incompetent evaluators. Although we do believe, of course, that the target materials were worthy of publication, and therefore ultimate editorial mistakes were made, as we said, such is not the main point of this book.

Editorial decisions are matters of individual judgment, and it is not news that intelligent people can disagree. Moreover, far better-known researchers than we have suffered from poor reviews (e.g., Garcia, 1981; Yalow, 1982). The important point is that the various routine individual evaluations on this one topic could include so many factual and logical errors. A preventive mechanism should be adopted, if one can be developed. If this aspect of science is truly self-corrective, then the process of correction should be greatly accelerated.

Several serious weaknesses of the peer-review system are revealed in this book in a way that can only be accomplished by the case-history method. While not denigrating the approach and effort of such researchers on peer review as Peters and Ceci (1982), we question the methodological and statistical legitimacy of their conclusions from the data. We do not question the validity of their conclusions, because those conclusions are consistent with our long-held opinions and also with the details of the present case history. The problems of controls and ethics in experimental research on such problems are barriers to the kind of clean research designs that are desired. Innovative approaches are necessary.

All of the quoted comments in this book have come from evaluations for journals that rejected our submissions. Our purpose is to improve the system, rather than to trounce and denounce. We hope that the scientific community will implement the suggestions that we make in the final chapter.

We have tried to present the evaluations as completely as is reasonable, and as fairly as we could. Other than correcting a few minor mistakes, such as spelling and punctuation errors, we have quoted exactly, where such exact quotations are indicated. It is not reasonable, of course, to expect an evaluation to be entirely free of typographical errors, or to reflect polished prose. We have tried to avoid such quibbles.

Incompetent evaluations lead to false positives, as well as false negatives, as has been amply discussed (Harnad, 1982). Errors are profitable only rarely and accidentally, and thus should be avoided. The errors of commission (false positives) may distract and confuse researchers, and take up space that could be used for more worthy research efforts. But the errors of omission produced by inaccurate rejections keep worthy research from public vantage, and keep scientists busy with multiple revisions and resubmissions, which in turn adds to the workload of subsequent reviewers. Researchers are often discouraged from pursuing further work on the topic.

We had expected—naively, it turned out—to do a small study to verify a phenomenon, and then go on to further, more analytic research on that phenomenon. The first response of the evaluators indicated that the initiating step was far from easy; consequently we were led to conduct more and more studies, using different methods, in an attempt to establish the phenomenon. We reasoned that the publication of more analytic and theoretically important results would be extremely unlikely if the scientific establishment would not accept our first basic premise and arguments. Subsequent events verified our concern.

SUMMARY

Occasionally evaluators of research submissions to journals rely more on certain heuristics (Harcum, 1992) than on focused scientific analyses of the submissions. Certain categories of research are apparently more vulnerable to this charge than others. The use of case histories of a series of studies on a particular research topic to document the existence of this phenomenon is a reasonable way to study this problem. The remainder of this book presents such a study and makes recommendations for an alteration of the peer-review process based on the evidence.

2

A Case in Point

The specific research program that provides the focus for this book involves Skinner's classic argument against the cultural value of the popular concepts of freedom and dignity. Skinner used this argument to explain why society failed to embrace his view of strict determinism and his proposed design for a productive behavioral science. His argument, repeated over a span of about 20 years, was the logical basis for his practical attack on freedom and dignity.

Skinner's most familiar statement of his argument was made in his classic book, *Beyond Freedom and Dignity* (1971):

> By questioning the control exercised by autonomous man and demonstrating the control exercised by the environment, a science of behavior also seems to question dignity or worth. A person is responsible for his behavior, not only in the sense that he may be justly blamed or punished when he behaves badly, but also in the sense that he is to be given credit and admired for his achievements. A scientific analysis shifts the credit as well as the blame to the environment, and traditional practices can then no longer be justified. These are sweeping changes, and those who are committed to traditional theories and practices naturally resist them. (p. 21)

> Any evidence that a person's behavior may be attributed to external circumstances seems to threaten his dignity or worth. We are not inclined to give a person credit for achievements which are in fact due to forces over which he has no control. . . . But as an analysis of behavior

adds further evidence, the achievements for which a person himself is to be given credit seem to approach zero, and both the evidence and the science which produces it are then challenged. (p. 44)

We recognize a person's dignity or worth when we give him credit for what he has done. The amount we give is inversely proportional to the conspicuousness of the causes of his behavior. . . . What we may call the literature of dignity is concerned with preserving due credit. It may oppose advances in technology, including a technology of behavior, because *they destroy chances to be admired* [emphasis added] and a basic analysis because it offers an alternative explanation of behavior for which the individual himself has previously been given credit. (pp. 58–59)

We have quoted extensively from Skinner because his intended meaning has so often been an issue between us and the evaluators of our submissions. As we read the above passages within the context of the book, Skinner's argument is perfectly clear: people have dignity or worth in the eyes of others *only* insofar as they manifest praiseworthy behaviors that society cannot explain in terms of hereditary and environmental factors. Therefore, society attributes these behaviors to voluntary choices. Skinner denied the *existence* of voluntary choice, of course, but he certainly did not deny the popular *belief* in the existence of voluntary choice.

The word "only" in the sentence above is central to a major controversy between us and several evaluators. Skinner admittedly did not use the word in this context. The reason for this omission, we argue, is that the word would be totally redundant within the framework of his argument. Clearly, the function relating the degree of credit to the amount of perceived voluntary behaviors must pass through the origin in Skinner's view because—as we emphasized above— advances in behavioral science according to Skinner "destroy chances to be admired." According to our dictionary, "destroy" is a transitive verb meaning "to bring to naught by putting out of existence." We emphasized this phrase in the above quotation in order to underscore the fact that the destruction will be complete if behavioral technology is successful in eliminating the concept of freedom. If the destruction of dignity is complete—that is, if dignity is put out of existence—when the concept of freedom is obviated, then no room is left for a residual concept of dignity. Therefore, the perception of dignity cannot be *based on some other event or characteristic of a person*. In a word, Skinner is in effect *denying a concept of intrinsic or unearned human dignity*, although admittedly he never said, "There is no such thing as unearned dignity."

Skinner never actually raised the possibility of a dignity based on some other source. He apparently never formally considered the possibility that dignity could be accorded on the basis of a person's sheer acknowledgment of existence as a human being. If dignity is accorded on such a basis, it will not be zero in the absence of voluntary behaviors, even if no dignity whatsoever can be earned on the basis of the voluntary performance of prosocial behaviors. Such inherent human dignity cannot be destroyed, although it may be masked, canceled, or overridden by voluntary performance of antisocial behaviors.

We do not believe that Skinner's intention was unclear on this point, although many evaluators have claimed that the formulation was not as we have described it above. As we will argue later, Skinner's formulation would not even make internal sense if one did not assume that the potential destruction of the concept of dignity by science can be complete. This is a far more powerful argument than the semantic analysis given above.

Skinner argued that the perception of dignity or worth in another person means that the person has been given credit for performing a response that cannot, as yet, be attributed to environmental influences. People perceive progress in behavioral science as inevitably finding environmental and genetic explanations for certain behaviors, and thus taking behaviors out of the unexplained (i.e., voluntary) category. Therefore, he argued, people fear that behavioral science will be able to continue the progress in the explanation of behavior to the point of being able to account for all of human behaviors, thus leaving none that cannot be explained by environmental and genetic factors. If dignity, or worth, is earned only by performing such unexplained behaviors, and there are then no unexplained behaviors, it follows logically that a person cannot have dignity because he or she cannot earn it. According to Skinner, people cherish their idea of dignity, and therefore they resist threats to it by, for example, opposing further progress in behavioral science.

Clearly, we are not the only readers who have interpreted Skinner's prose in this way. For example, Moser (1973) expressed the following interpretation of Skinner:

> He seems to equate dignity with the amount of credit a man receives from his fellows. . . . Thus, his dignity is ascribed to man by man, and is not at all intrinsic. Man, therefore, must earn his dignity. . . .
> To those of us who believe in the intrinsic value of life and the intrinsic worth of the individual, this view of dignity is despairingly shallow. But if we saw dignity that way, we would probably say with Skinner that man has no dignity. (p. 27)

Skinner's interpretation of dignity, then, is not universally accepted. In fact, Moser (1973) defined dignity as follows:

In the first place, the term *dignity* indicates man's intrinsic worth. One need not concede to a spiritual dimension to say that man has value because of nothing and in spite of everything. He has intrinsic value because he is human; because, for whatever reason, he is the supreme creature that possesses life and dwells on the earth. (p. 11)

This definition clearly supports the contention of Harcum, Rosen, and Burijon (1989) that persons in our society employ such a basis for definition.

Most of the argument by Skinner is a product of his own ingenuity, because he presented no data for it. Presumably, the entire formulation was based on Skinner's own casual observations of people going about their daily business, or his reading of antihumanistic literature, or his attempts to be consistent with his personal metaphysical position.

Part of what Skinner proposed is undoubtedly correct. As all of us have observed, society does in fact give more credit to the person who is perceived as performing creditable deeds without obvious inducements or coercion from the environment. This fact is definitely not an issue between us and Skinner. But other parts of Skinner's formulation apparently come only from the projection of his personal views, and reflect the danger of using only the data of personal observation.

THE DEFINITION OF DIGNITY

Skinner defined dignity in a single word: "worth." Therefore, the specific definition of the dignity or worth of a person is actually not a problem; a person has worth if another person behaves toward that person as if he or she were a thing of value, by honoring, helping, and preserving that person. We do *not* argue with Skinner's definition of dignity. Obviously, Skinner thought that the meaning was quite clear from any dictionary, and an elaboration of its meaning was not necessary. Perhaps a simple statement to that effect would have been helpful to those who were seriously concerned about his intended meaning.

The real problem with dignity or worth does not concern what it is, but the many possible bases on which one person decides that another has it. That is the crux and the sum of our argument with Skinner. He identified a single basis for according dignity or worth: performance of praiseworthy acts for reasons that were not apparent to others in terms of hereditary or environmental influences.

Skinner presumably knew the dictionary definition of dignity, or worth, and also presumably believed that the same definition was used by society. He also presumed to know the bases on which society accords that dignity, because he dismissed all of the evidence to the contrary, of other bases, as being merely casual and thus unscientific observations. As behavioral scientists, we are apparently asked to accept that those casual observations that fit with Skinner's view of the universe are legitimate, but the data from casual observation that do not conform to such biases are in no way worthy of consideration. We do not accept such an argument. If one would impeach the data from casual observation, surely one cannot base one's own personal formulations on the same or weaker kinds of evidence.

We do affirm a place for casual observation in science. We do not advocate its use as a substitute for the rigorous collection of more objective data under controlled conditions, where such is possible. Skinner should have collected the data that we collected and attempted to publish. Unfortunately, he based his formulation on the casual observations that fit his own biases.

We do agree with Skinner's observation that people typically accord dignity to others on the basis of the perceived voluntary performance of admired behavior. Thus, some dignity is the result of awarding credit for good deeds, performed voluntarily. We call this "earned dignity" or "credit contingent dignity."

Skinner proposed that society should discard all of the humanistic illusions and therefore award dignity as he would have accorded it. He would have awarded dignity to human beings on the basis of their possession of marvelously intricate bodily machinery. If society would accord dignity on the basis that he proposed, he believed that society would wholeheartedly embrace behavioral science as he conceived it, and the chances for survival of our culture would be greatly enhanced.

Skinner's conception of the proper basis of dignity could certainly be considered a kind of intrinsic dignity. The difference from a popular basis, which we have affirmed, is that in the popular view the human being is something more than a reactive machine. The popular view endows a person with dignity or worth even if the person cannot earn it by voluntary prosocial deeds. This dignity is not accorded because the person is a marvelous machine, but because the person is not *just* a marvelous machine. The person is given dignity because he or she is identified as a human being, and human beings have an intrinsic non-machinelike quality that is in itself a basis for according dignity.

Perhaps intrinsic or unearned dignity is not the best term for what we mean here. We wish to avoid the metaphysical or religious issue of whether a person has an intrinsic dignity independent of an observer, to focus on the issue of whether society *perceives* or *believes* that the person has such dignity or worth. According to the present formulation, a person in fact has dignity if it is perceived in him or her by another person. Probably the term "given" or "grace dignity" is more appropriate for capturing this sense of the concept. A person is given, as an act of grace, some dignity by virtue of sheer existence, gratuitously, and therefore the person does not have to earn dignity by voluntary performance of praiseworthy deeds. In sum, dignity is not contingent on good deeds performed voluntarily.

Whatever this extra basis of dignity is called, it means that even a complete understanding of the causes of human behavior can never eliminate the possibility for awarding some of this dignity to a person. Thus, people are free to award dignity on any basis they choose, without regard for Skinner's metaphysics, practical formulations, or pronouncements.

In addition, society does not agree that science can ever reduce the domain for freedom of response selection to zero, because society is firmly committed to the idea that behavior is not fully determined. Therefore, on such a basis, even the concept of credit dignity is safe because the concept of voluntary behavior is not questioned.

If we are correct on these points, Skinner would have had to look elsewhere for an explanation of society's reasons for rejecting his plan for improvement. There are, in fact, well-reasoned arguments against Skinner's plan by, for example, Chomsky (1973) and Nolan (1974). Chomsky (1973) attacked Skinner's metaphysics, emphasizing that Skinner included no provision for a process by which to persuade people to change their minds. Nolan (1974) emphasized Skinner's inability to specify the exact goals to be achieved by the operant technology, other than the implicit goals that presently exist. He pointed out that a functional analysis of behavior is neutral with respect to the desirability of the behavioral goals, but paradoxically may itself come to dictate the end state. That end state may include some undesirable side effects, such as the abolition of the concepts of freedom and dignity. Some people would surely consider such abolition undesirable. This seems to be the heart of the matter. We suspect that the actual reason for opposition to Skinner is his attempt to dehumanize science, which is contrary to current conceptions of science (Harcum, 1988), and consequently to dehumanize the members of society. In a word, Skinner's implied attack on intrinsic, or unearned dignity, is itself the very reason society should oppose that version of science.

THE PRACTICAL ISSUE

Several evaluators of our journal submissions faulted us for allegedly selecting more or less arbitrarily an off-hand comment by Skinner and magnifying it out of proportion. First, we assert that his argument as quoted above is the very thesis of his book, *Beyond Freedom and Dignity*. The purpose of his book obviously is to encourage society to give up the concept of personal freedom and the related concept of human dignity based on the assumption of that freedom. This was the starting point for his plan for an improved—or even surviving—culture through the effective use of science as he embodied it. He argued that the concepts of freedom and dignity, earned via freedom, stand in the way of such usage, and therefore must be abolished. This is simply a strategic or utilitarian argument. Without this argument, his book is simply a redundant recapitulation of his metaphysical position.

One might argue that so-called intrinsic dignity is nothing more than a recognition that everyone has the potential to perform marvelous deeds. That is true, of course, but in some cases we would have to say that the statistical evidence was against it. The odds would presumably be favorable for the child of a white professor at a prestigious university. On the basis of sheer educational, economic, and social disadvantages and other blockades to opportunities, the odds would be against a black child from a large, single-parent family in an inner-city tenement.

Second, the ideas expressed in Skinner's book were not the result of a momentary lapse of rigorous thinking and writing. They were in fact anticipated 15 years earlier (Skinner, 1955–1956). Skinner described his conception of society's views at that time as follows:

> So long as the findings and methods of science are applied to human affairs only in a sort of remedial patchwork, we may continue to hold any view of human nature we like. But as the use of science increases, we are forced to accept the theoretical structure with which science represents its facts. The difficulty is that this structure is clearly at odds with the traditional democratic conception of man. Every discovery of an event which has a part in shaping a man's behavior seems to leave so much the less to be credited to the man himself; and as such explanations become more and more comprehensive, the contribution which may be claimed by the individual himself appears to approach zero. (p. 52)

Moreover, the same ideas were reiterated almost 20 years after the above quotation (Skinner, 1975), and four years after the publication of his classic book, which formed the main assault against freedom and dignity:

> The difficulty is that if the credit due a person is infringed by evidences of the conditions of which his behavior is a function, then a scientific analysis appears to be an attack on human worth or dignity. Its task is to explain the hitherto inexplicable and hence to reduce any supposed inner contribution which has served in lieu of explanation. (p. 47)

We believe that the language of these quotations, plus the redundancy of the arguments and the time span involved, absolutely preclude any argument that Skinner was purveying an off-hand comment, not to be taken seriously. To argue to the contrary, as did several evaluators, would be to inject a truly astounding and dangerous idea into the scientific literature: one of the foremost psychologists in history consistently promulgated over a 20-year period a proposition that he himself did not seriously support.

We do not for a moment believe that such an argument reflects the truth about Skinner. We submit in fact that it was grossly irresponsible of the evaluators of our work to suggest such an idea.

How can one account for such truly mysterious and unacceptable behavior from evaluators? We suggest that this type of behavior is what some evaluators fall back on when faced with the prospect of otherwise having to agree with the contention that a great man has made a mistake. The heuristic is that a great man is less likely to have made a mistake than two unknown authors. The purpose of this book is to hold evaluators—and the system—accountable for this unacceptable proposition.

ABSENCE OF DISCUSSION

Many authors (e.g., Chomsky, 1973; Dennett, 1978; Rubenstein, 1971) have challenged Skinner's metaphysical view of strict determinism. Because no empirical disproof of his metaphysical position has been forthcoming— and probably can never be achieved—these formulations can remain viable in scientific thinking. But, to our knowledge, no author has taken scientific exception to his practical argument for the abolition of the concepts of freedom and dignity—namely, his argument that the culturally popular notions of freedom and dignity are incompatible with a science of behavior. Some, of course, have experienced and expressed moral outrage at the idea (e.g., Rubenstein, 1971).

If convinced of the *necessity* for a mutually exclusive choice of voluntarism versus environmental control of behavior, society will, we submit, choose in favor of voluntarism. And that would be disastrous for science, which must assume at least some degree of determinism of behavior. The demise of a modern science, as most would undoubtedly agree, would be bad for the progress of culture.

The absence of discussions about this issue in the current literature has two possible implications: (1) Skinner's argument is without merit and therefore has been allowed to die through inattention; or (2) Skinner's argument has persisted and possibly prevailed because it has remained unchallenged. We favor the second interpretation. Skinner's contention has not been challenged, but it has not been endorsed in print by anyone either. We submit that Skinner's argument remains, nevertheless, like an unacknowledged dead hand on the progress of the new science, and thus integration of the field of psychology (Harcum, 1988). Perhaps it contributes to an unconscious feeling that one's rejection of Skinner's views is not itself scientific. Therefore, we raised our challenge.

Because our assertion about the importance of the issue is also a matter of judgment, we could have reluctantly accepted an editorial conclusion that this issue itself was dead, and not worthy of research effort and publication. This reason was rarely given as a reason for rejecting our submissions, however. We were told, at least as often, that the issue we have raised is still important. Therefore, our belief in the importance of this research has been reinforced on a partial reinforcement schedule—making it difficult to extinguish, of course. We remain convinced therefore from such evaluations that the issue of an extra humanistic dimension in society's thinking is truly important. This issue currently divides the profession of psychology into two factions (Kimble, 1984), and it may even threaten the viability of psychology as an independent discipline (Spence, 1990).

THE COUNTERARGUMENT

We assert that, in the view of society, *voluntarily performing prosocial behaviors is not, as Skinner contended, the only way to possess dignity.* We have pointed out that Skinner offered no empirical evidence for his argument. We contend that even casual observation of human behavior, including that represented in the literature of freedom—an anathema to Skinner (1971)—will indicate a common belief in a different basis for according dignity. Society believes in an intrinsic human dignity, an unearned dignity that does not have to be achieved through voluntary creditable deeds. The existence of such unearned dignity is not, and cannot be, threatened by a science of human behavior, as Skinner asserts.

The first step of our program to refute Skinner's argument was simply to show that people see worth in a person *on some unspecified bases that are over and above the performance of voluntary meritorious behaviors.* Once the perception of an unearned dignity was established as common in our society, further research could be undertaken to determine what personal and situational factors modulate the judgment of this kind of intrinsic worth.

In the case of free will, other research psychologists have reached similar conclusions that are opposite from those of Skinner. Smith (1969) strongly supported the concept of free will as personal causation, and not as a manifestation of chance and indeterminism. He asserted that "Human freedom is not a postulate; it is a fact, which is present or absent in a degree" (p. 10).

Therefore, we can infer that the professed belief in free will can foster like belief in others, to their benefit. The perception of the opportunity for making choices increases the likelihood that choices will be made. Without testing the reality of freedom, the prisoner is unaware that the door to his cell is unlocked. Moreover, the believer in freedom is more likely to treat others differently. Smith (1969) describes the reason for this: "Social psychologists who believe in the potentiality, if not the actuality, of human freedom are likely to treat people, in and out of research, with the respect that causally enhances their actual freedom" (p. 10). This is both a personal commitment to beliefs in human freedom and in dignity, and also a practical argument for the value of such beliefs to the development of the behavioral sciences.

There is also empirical evidence that positive regard for a victim, independent of the victim's behaviors, is a determinant of whether the person will be helped. Betancourt (1990) showed an additivity and an interaction of induced empathic emotions and the attribution of less voluntary contribution by a victim. Empathic motivation caused the observer to perceive less control by the victim. Therefore, there is an emotional and cognitive mediation involved in helping behaviors.

In *Beyond Freedom and Dignity*, Skinner had chosen a pragmatic battleground of utility for survival of the culture, not a metaphysical arena, or even a scientific one. Although these other issues are in the background, they are tangential to the issues of whether the concepts of freedom and dignity are inimical to the progress of behavioral science, or essential to such progress. In a published article on this issue, Harcum, Rosen, and Burijon (1989), gave the following statement of the problem, which was consistently restated in the remaining studies:

> The purpose of this article is to refute by direct test Skinner's (1971) pragmatic argument against conventional concepts of human freedom and dignity. The present studies have no bearing on the validity of Skinner's (1953, 1971) formulations about the production of behavior through reward contingencies, but have been set up to test his interpretation of why society refuses to adopt his formulations as a basis for cultural evolution. (pp. 257–258)

THE PRESENT STRATEGY

Clearly, our initial goal was modest and straightforward. We had suspected that evaluators might respond that we were merely demonstrating what was obvious to all save possibly a few devout Skinnerians. Many of them did exactly that, although they did not agree that such evidence presented any problem for Skinner. Others vehemently did not agree with our evidence. Therefore, the initial methodological and conceptual objections pushed us into further studies, with different research designs. But, unfortunately for us, there was no change in the crucial bottom line of the evaluations—the decision to reject our submissions. Being as objective and as nondefensive as we were able, we could not accept the criticisms as reflecting fatal flaws in our studies. The only real consistencies in the evaluations were the recommendations for rejection of publication. Because some evaluators accepted the results, but denied their importance, and others accepted the sense and value of conducting the particular study, but denied the validity of our results, we found ourselves in a very frustrating limbo with apparently no scientific keys to unlock the doors.

PRESENT METHOD

Nothing in the evaluations convinced us that this research was unimportant or weak. This is a matter of opinion, of course, and therefore our judgment could be clouded by various defensive reactions. We have repeatedly considered this possibility over the past several years, as objectively as we could. We have discussed these issues with colleagues and with friends at other universities, as well as with students at this and other universities. We have decided that the fault lies in the evaluations and have committed ourselves to securing resolutions both for the freedom and dignity issues and also for the effectiveness and humanity of the peer-review system.

The only way that the scientific community can reach an informed decision about whether we have been blinded by self-interest and ego-defense mechanisms or our work has been unfairly rejected, is to examine and compare concurrently the actual evaluations and the actual submissions. Therefore, the present method is to compare the actual copies of the original submissions to the various journals and to quote the actual comments of the evaluators on these specific submissions. The eventual publications of the submissions are of course also available and cited when appropriate. This particular approach will prevent interpretational problems that can arise from combinations or groupings of dissimilar cases for some sort of statistical analyses. This approach will permit the members of the scientific community to make the necessary informed judgments for themselves about whether the evaluators were correct, appropriate, and proper.

A judgment about the reasonableness of the evaluations will also reflect upon the validity of our research results. Therefore, there is a larger implication of this problem for scientific progress in the application of psychological principles to human welfare. The fundamental issue is not our personal vindication, although we do readily admit to some emotional involvement in that outcome as well. The issue is whether the peer-review system itself in this case must be vindicated or indicted. Obviously, an indictment would have serious implications for the progress of science, because journal evaluators do determine by their endorsements which research projects move forward. Rejection from publication, of course, sets back a research program. We know that our own program has been seriously hampered by the scientific gatekeepers. Whether this barrier to publication was a serious setback to scientific progress in a larger sense is up to our readers to decide.

The final published version of each article is of course not exactly identical to the submissions that the first evaluators of the work had reviewed and rejected. Except in the case of the fourth submission (Chapter 6), however, there were no truly substantive changes for successive submissions in the report of a given study. Therefore, the published versions are not reproduced in this book, because they are available to the reader. The basic similarity of original submission and published version can be verified easily.

We have not reproduced all of the interim resubmissions between the first rejected submissions and the first published version because the changes were not substantive, except for the noted exception in the fourth submission. The comparison of evaluations of our later submissions with almost necessarily a somewhat different original submission, as we are doing, therefore has minimal disadvantages over exact comparisons with the exact wording and organization of the specific version to which those evaluators were responding. We believe that the multiple reproductions of very similar material from the various specific revisions would not be worthy of the extra space or the tedium occasioned by the redundancy.

To be sure, sometimes a criticism by the readers concerned the clarity of our writing in the given submission. Where such was critical to the point, therefore, we did reproduce the literal text of the specific version of the resubmission. Admittedly, the subsequent exposition in the final published articles was probably improved by corrections of misunderstandings that were uncovered in the reviews of the earlier submissions. We certainly did not give up the chances for publication by holding to a particular manner of presentation that may have been criticized previously. Thus, the subsequent version undoubtedly did benefit from the editors' queries and suggestions. But, because the specific details of presentation were not substantive to the publication decision, as will be apparent, the discussion will in the main ignore simple issues of presentation. As best we know, the reasons for rejection were always judged, presented, and handled as scientific and professional, rather than cosmetic, both by us and by the editors.

In no case did a negative evaluative comment cause us to make a substantive change in the interpretation of the data or in a theory. The subsequent changes were clarifications, explanations, additional quotations, or new analyses, all of which attempted to answer the questions and respond to the criticisms of the previous evaluators, and thus preempt later criticisms of the same sort. Therefore, we argue that each evaluator was responding to substantively the same article as the one ultimately published, although, as we said, there were undoubtedly improvements of presentation in the later drafts. Although the judgment is admittedly very subjective, we strongly believe that none of our later changes could be reasonably characterized as critical to the conversion of an unpublishable article into a publishable one.

In one instance we did depart from our usual practice of not quoting large portions of our original submissions. We did so in order to document the point specifically that an evaluator's comments were totally alien with respect to the specific narrative in our manuscript. In that case, we reproduced the verbatim language of our actual submission, in order to document exactly what the evaluator was responding to. Frankly, we feared that our readers would not believe that a serious and competent professional, prestigious enough to have been asked to make an evaluation for a reputable journal, would have produced such an unconnected, irrelevant evaluation. This evaluator could not reasonably have so misinterpreted our text if he or she had taken reasonable care in reading it. We trust, further, that this examination shows that our submission was intelligible enough to be understood by a serious reader. Thus, the exact reproduction of the text was the only sure way for us to substantiate our point.

We quote rather extensively from evaluators' comments in order to produce an exhaustive report of all substantive objections. This may be redundant at times, but it is necessary to permit informed judgment by our readers. To avoid confusion, the various journals will be designated by letters. The order in which the successive manuscripts were submitted is indicated by the alphabetical ordering of journals. Arabic numerals indicate the order of submission, if revisions were subsequently submitted to the same journal. We began the search for publication with what we considered to be the most appropriate journals, but later, as we became increasingly frustrated, we broadened our category of possibly appropriate journals to include a few cognate fields.

SUMMARY

This chapter describes and justifies the rationale of our research submissions. It contends that Skinner was serious in proposing beliefs in freedom and the possible loss of earned dignity as the reasons society opposed his design for a better society. The issue concerns this practical argument, rather than involving yet another critical discussion of Skinner's metaphysical arguments.

The inadequacies of the early reviews forced us into trying new approaches and methods. We ultimately concluded that the gatekeepers of the science in fact represented poor models of the scientific ideal.

3

Direct Test

The purpose of the study in the first submission was to demonstrate that college students, as representatives of society, have a belief in an intrinsic human dignity that does not have to be earned by voluntary performance of prosocial (positively valued) behaviors. In this study we simply asked college students to draw two curves relating perceived dignity and perceived voluntary choice of behaviors, one for praiseworthy and one for blameworthy behaviors. They drew the two curves on a predrawn graph frame in which the ordinate represented perceived dignity of a person and the abscissa the degree to which the particular category of behavior was perceived as having been performed voluntarily. We provided an operationalized dictionary definition of dignity: "A person has dignity to the extent that he or she has worth, excellence, value, usefulness, or is held in esteem, as indicated when other persons show such behaviors toward that person as overtly supporting, rewarding, admiring, saving, defending, and/or honoring." We also identified a new concept: "Negative dignity is the opposite of dignity. A person has negative dignity to the extent that he or she is unworthy, detrimental, injurious, harmful, and/or is a liability or failure, as indicated when other persons show such behaviors toward that person as overtly opposing, punishing, despising, expending, attacking, and/or discrediting."

Our complete theory is presented in Figure C.2 of Appendix C. We predicted that the subjects would draw both of the functions for praiseworthy and blameworthy behaviors with intersections on the y-axis (perceived dignity) above zero. This would indicate a perception of an intrinsic (unearned, given, received, noncontingent) dignity in persons who have not been perceived as exhibiting voluntary behaviors, contrary to Skinner's postulation.

The students were also asked to report their beliefs about the extent to which behaviors can be attributed to heredity and environment or to voluntary choice. They did this for: all people in general; people whose behavior was primarily influenced by environmental forces; and persons whose behavior was primarily influenced by deliberate personal intention. In addition, they were asked to write essays that indicated their beliefs about the origin of dignity in a person.

Students from introductory psychology courses who participated in this study indicated in their essays beliefs in personal freedom, as well as beliefs in environmental determinism. Their essays also indicated belief in a dignity that is intrinsic to humans and does not have to be earned. This first group of students was unable to draw the graphs relating various levels of perceived dignity to the various levels of perceived voluntary choice. The drawings were not interpretable in terms of a coherent belief system. We concluded that these results basically refuted Skinner's formulation, because the subjects could not articulate the beliefs that he asserted. If there were a basis of belief such as Skinner proposed for opposing scientific progress, it was inchoate and intuitive at best.

A second group of students, who were enrolled in an advanced psychology course, also reported their beliefs about personal freedom and dignity. After a classroom discussion of the issues, they were able to draw functional relationships between perceived dignity and voluntary behaviors, although there was great variability among the completed functions. The mean intercept on the y-axis (dignity) was significantly above zero, as predicted, indicating a belief in intrinsic dignity. Therefore, we concluded that Skinner's argument about society's views of dignity was not substantiated.

This submission was rejected by Journals A and B before being accepted for publication by a third journal (Harcum, Rosen, & Burijon, 1989). The original submission to Journal A is presented as Appendix A, except for the reference list. The published references are found in the general reference list. The version in Appendix A is naturally somewhat different from the other rejected submissions and the accepted submission. Subsequent resubmissions were amended to correct omissions and ambiguities of earlier submissions, and to amplify parts identified as needing clarification. The basic rationale and argument of the report, however, were not changed. The published version retains, therefore, all of the alleged basic flaws of the rejected versions, because we did not consider the objections to represent serious problems.

JOURNAL A

Evaluator I

The first evaluator for Journal A summarized the study as follows:

This minor study attempts to test Skinner's hypothesis that people in general do not attribute human dignity to their fellows, but do so only when there is good reason for it.

This characterization of our study is literally incorrect. This evaluator nevertheless continued with the evaluation as follows:

Skinner's notion is both vague and trivial and does not warrant serious consideration. The gist of the proposition in the present study was to ask fewer than 100 college sophomores to estimate on a percentage scale how much behavior of human beings is a result of environmental influence and how much derives from voluntary action.

First, Skinner's notion is neither vague nor trivial. As we showed with citations from Skinner previously, he was quite explicit and consistent in his argument.

The possibility of triviality is more difficult to handle. The issue of the role of conceptions of freedom and dignity in our society was seen by Skinner, at least, to be of major importance. Such humanistic versus behavioristic views constitute a fundamental schism among psychologists. The evaluator should explain why he or she thinks that it is trivial. The comment is equivalent to saying that Skinner's classic *Beyond Freedom and Dignity* was trivial.

Another issue concerns the particular question to which the evaluator was referring. Perhaps the evaluator was merely referring to our question about the relative influences on behavior of intentions versus environment. This would be another case of an evaluator failing to understand what our study was about. We did ask such a question in a supplementary part of the study. Somehow the reviewer missed the description of the experiment.

Evaluator I continued:

Skinner's proposition referred to the position that people take as reflecting a broad cultural view, and to suppose that college sophomores are representative of that kind of cultural wisdom is scarcely cogent. There is nothing wrong with investigating belief in voluntarism, but a single minor measure on a few college sophomores is of little value. I recommend terminal rejection of the manuscript.

Because Skinner made no restrictions on his generalization, even for college sophomores, this comment is literally vacuous. We never claimed that college students are representative of the larger culture. But they are undeniably a part of it. To disprove Skinner's generality, we only needed to show one counterexample from one reasonable sample of subjects. We were trying to demonstrate the existence of a phenomenon, not determine its frequency within the world's population.

Evaluator II

The second evaluator for Journal A began on a favorable note:

> Overall, the research attacks an interesting and important problem, both for the validity of various schools of psychology and for the culture at large.

Those were nice words. But unfortunately they were based on a false impression of the research problem, as revealed by further comments of this same evaluator:

> First, the authors attack Skinner's position as being unsubstantiated, but this is wrong on two counts: (a) many negative reviews of *Beyond freedom and dignity* lend strong qualitative support for Skinner's position; and (b) the social psychology literature (among others) offers varied empirical support. In these regards, the manuscript represents poor scholarship, as is further evidenced in the meager reference list. I know these are harsh words. I am not angry—only confused.
>
> Second, the authors' rendering of Skinner's views is idiosyncratic enough to qualify as misrepresentation. For instance, Skinner's view is that: "in . . . society's view, without personal freedom to make voluntary prosocial acts, there can be no dignity" (p. 3). Society would still speak of "dignity" even if free will did not exist, because, in Skinner's view, it is not free will that sets the occasion for speaking of dignity, rather it is a person's behavior in context. In other words, as a nonspatio-temporal entity, "free will" cannot affect an observer's behavior—only the behavior in context that leads us to talk of free will, and the behavior in context will not disappear should we see a passing of the concept of free will. This misunderstanding of Skinner's epistemology occurs throughout the manuscript (see marked queries), as, again, in the comment, " . . . Skinner contends that the only way a person can have dignity is to earn it by perform-

ing socially approved acts" (p. 10). This takes Skinner quite out of context—he would not disagree that some fair portion of society attributes intrinsic dignity to human beings, as is later asserted and supposedly refuted by the authors (see p. 13). These misunderstandings, and others, are deep and troublesome.

Third, the defining of "dignity" and the context offered for assessing its relationship to free will are so entangled with, again, seemingly idiosyncratic views of Skinner's position that the experimental manipulations and findings are not easily interpretable.

We were not addressing Skinner's epistemology. We were speaking to his assertions about societal beliefs as an attempt to explain why society did not accept his epistemology and his views on the nature of science. Further, we assert that it is this evaluator who misunderstands Skinner. The heart of the matter is, of course, whether Skinner would, or would not, disagree "that some fair portion of society attributes intrinsic dignity to human beings." We strongly contend that Skinner does deny the existence of intrinsic dignity in a humanistic sense, although we readily concede that he never expressly said, "People do not accord an intrinsic humanistic dignity." But, as we have quoted, he argued that advances in behavioral science would "destroy chances to be admired" (Skinner, 1971, p. 58). His conception, therefore, must be determined by his overall argument.

Because unearned dignity in Skinner's mind did not exist, where could the belief in dignity come from? Skinner proposed that it comes from perceived voluntary control of prosocial behaviors. He could have said that another kind or basis of dignity came from some source other than reward-contingencies in the environment, but he did not. Why not? Because if he had admitted that the members of society held such a humanistic belief in intrinsic dignity, there was no point to his book other than to recapitulate his metaphysical arguments.

The main point of this discussion is that Skinner's argument makes no sense if he assumed an intrinsic dignity, for the very reason that we claimed to refute his argument if we can document an existing societal belief in intrinsic dignity. Skinner's argument is that society's belief in dignity stands in the way of scientific progress, because a successful science would obviate the possibility for personal freedom, and the perception of dignity depends on the belief in freedom. Therefore, to protect the concept of dignity, society opposes progress in science. If the perception of dignity did *not* depend critically upon a belief in personal freedom, then it would *not* be threatened by progress in science, and therefore there would be no need for society to oppose science. Thus, existence of an intrinsic dignity, which is not dependent upon freedom and does not have to be earned, destroys the argument that belief in human dignity requires opposition to science. Therefore, Skinner must have denied the kind of dignity that is gratuitously given, or he must have given up his argument for why society opposed his brand of science.

Of course, everyone knows that Skinner's metaphysics have been extensively criticized. To argue that this opposition itself therefore proves Skinner's argument for *why* he has been criticized is illogical. Some people seem to be unable to conceive of an opposition to strict behaviorism other than as a defense against the unacceptable antihumanistic aspects. In this regard, they are as biased as followers of Freud who believe that any resistance to Freudian interpretation of behavior is simply proof of the principle of psychodynamic resistance. We do not assert that Skinner's metaphysics are wrong or claim to have proved that they are incorrect, merely that people can reasonably and sincerely oppose them.

We depart from our usual practice to mention a final personal criticism from this evaluator, although it is actually a matter of style rather than substance:

> Fourth, the tone of the manuscript was offensive and contentious. In many places, it amounts to little more than Skinner-bashing.

We disagree with this assessment, although we were rather critical and emphatic. Because this view was expressed by only this one of the five referees and by neither editor, we trust that our tone was only offensive in the eyes of this beholder.

We have mentioned this criticism, contrary to our proposed practice throughout this book, because the question may have occurred to the present reader. Other evaluators may have shared this sentiment, but declined to state it. Intemperate language is not appropriate; it should be edited from a submission, and therefore it should not in itself be the basis for rejection of a submission that otherwise has substantive scientific merit. In any case, the particularistic methodology of this book permits our readers to decide for themselves.

The final comment of this evaluator is more substantive:

> Still worse, the manuscript makes no positive contribution of its own. For instance, if Skinner is wrong, then what are the reasons for society to reject a natural science of behavior? This is a terribly important issue that is never addressed.

This comment is entirely out of order. As we clearly stated, our goal in the article was simply to test Skinner's grand assertion, by reporting some data instead of presumptions about societal beliefs. We view the refutation of an erroneous assertion of interpretation in the literature as a positive contribution to science. We are surprised that this evaluator seems to disagree with what appears to us to be a trite point. As advocates of the strong inference approach (Platt, 1964), we argue that disproof of a hypothesis may be of even more value than evidence consistent with a hypothesis. Moreover, attainment of further positive goals was contingent upon getting past this first basic step. If dignity is accorded only on the basis of perceived voluntary behaviors, then there is no need to look for other subject and situational characteristics as a basis for according dignity.

This evaluator apparently shows the same blind spot as Skinner about possible "reasons for society to reject a natural science of behavior." The evaluator is correct that we did not attempt to speak to the issue of Skinner's metaphysics and behavior theory, although many reviewers assumed that we had. We chose an empirical approach to the evaluation of Skinner's practical argument against the concepts of freedom and dignity, because the case against his metaphysics and theory has been debated many times (e.g., Chomsky, 1973) without a final settlement.

Part of the evaluator's problem is his or her uncritical equation of the Skinnerian formulation with a natural science of behavior. Skinner tried mightily to promulgate that equation. We submit that some social scientists reject Skinner's formulations on rational philosophical and psychological grounds. We submit that one possible reason lay society in general may reject a natural science of behavior is in fact the very equation of Skinnerian metaphysics with such a science. Someone who cannot make the discrimination is likely to reject both.

This evaluator goes on to complain about the writing style of our submission:

> Fifth and finally, the manuscript was awkwardly written in many places. I have offered some editorial suggestions on my marked copy, which I am returning with this review.

No doubt the writing could be improved; we cannot agree that it is not salvageable, however. Our readers can, of course, judge for themselves.

The final comment of this evaluator seems defensive and unnecessary:

> I realize that I have not exactly endeared myself to the authors with my comments. I have been the recipient of personally-perceived similar reviews, and I am not unappreciative of the unhappy effects. Nonetheless, I had to give what I thought was an honest appraisal of the

manuscript, which is not the same as saying I have given a truthful appraisal—the latter is always problematic.

Why does this evaluator presume that his or her comments will be "personally perceived"? There is too much protest here, which seems to be the point of the paragraph. If an appraisal is sincerely and appropriately professional, no final placating or patronizing disclaimers are necessary.

JOURNAL B

Evaluator I

The first evaluator of Journal B—the editor—reported as follows:

I was able to find three excellent reviewers, with expertise in social perception, attribution, and intrinsic/intentional behavior. As you will see from their reviews, they agree that although your paper raises an interesting attributional problem it is lacking in theoretical rationale and methodological precision, and even in data analysis and interpretation. . . . I can, however, provide some encouragement. Two of the three reviewers indicated that your other data, mentioned in the introduction, sound quite promising (see Reviewers B and C). This other research, which I gather you are reporting elsewhere, appears to have involved a more appropriate design for conceptualizing and conducting research in this area. A study assessing people's perceptions of dignity in a well-conducted 2×2 (Prosocial/Antisocial Behavior $\times$ Choice/Constraint) design might be of considerable interest. Nonetheless, the research reported in the present paper is simply not sufficiently well-controlled to enable us to draw unequivocal conclusions about perceptions of human dignity. On a more general level, let me mention that your work in this area would benefit tremendously by being couched in a stronger, better articulated theoretical context. All three of the reviewers agreed that Skinner's thinking on this matter simply does not provide an extensive enough theoretical framework within which to examine the concepts of intentionality and "dignity." Other literatures speak far more extensively to the hypotheses you seek to test (see Reviewers B and C), such as the large literatures on the attribution of freedom, intention, self-control, self-determination, blame, and dislike/stigmatization. This point in social and clinical psychology research cannot really contribute to knowledge about intentionality and perceived "dignity" without speaking more directly to these existing literatures. Along these same lines, one problem with the present paper is that it does not provide an explicit enough definition of the term dignity and/or a sufficient enough justification for the particular operational definition used to measure the dignity construct (Reviewers B and C). There are, in fact, many related concepts that subjects in the present research could have called to mind when judging the "dignity" of others, concepts that have been examined in other research (e.g., liking, responsibility).

We never claimed there was a theoretical issue. We were merely testing a practical issue of fact: whether society believes that all dignity must be earned, as Skinner asserted. The answer to this question does not depend upon a thorough understanding of the dignity concept. Certainly, Skinner did not think so, because his definition of the concept consisted of a single word: "worth." A researcher must rely on the dictionary definitions of the terms "dignity" and "worth," plus the context of Skinner's usage. We could understand an editorial comment that the resolution of the practical issues was not important enough for inclusion in his journal. We are deeply troubled by the fact that this editor assumed that we were making a theoretical argument. This meant that the remainder of this editor's comments were beside the mark.

We do not grasp what would be gained by investigating all concepts that may spring to mind in a sort of free-association process when one thinks of freedom and dignity. If any of these concepts have stimulated empirical research that would be relevant to the issue of whether society believes in unearned dignity, then that literature would be relevant, of course. Certainly, Skinner admitted to a large literature of freedom and dignity, but the point is that he would not accept it as scientific evidence, and therefore regarded it as irrelevant. We were attempting to provide a kind or quality of evidence against Skinner's assertion that he could not have impeached as "casual observation." If there is such prior evidence in the scientific literature, it should have been specifically cited by the evaluators. The crucial question concerns whether anyone had previously tested our hypothesis empirically, or had presented data directly relevant to it. For example, is there laboratory evidence that people "like" other people because they are human beings? Remember, for Skinner, anecdotal evidence or casual observation did not count as science.

The question of definition was later raised repeatedly. We do not see the relevance of this concern for definition at this early stage of our research. Skinner had formulated a hypothesis for why society rejects his approach to behavioral science. He alleged that there is such an entity as a perception of the worth of a person that is based on the creditable deeds that person performs voluntarily. We doubt that very many would dispute such a formulation. In fact, a later evaluator said flatly that the relationship is "painfully obvious."

The purpose of our research at this stage was mainly to document that worth is *also* accorded by members of society to persons who have *not* earned it by such praiseworthy behaviors. This is what the respondents in our studies report, indicating that they do identify a basis for worth in an individual that does not have to be earned. This evidence flatly refutes Skinner's argument. Having concluded that there is more behind the judgment of human dignity or worth than Skinner claimed, we can go on to discover the nature of the other specific bases of according dignity.

Evaluator II

The second reviewer commented as follows:

First, the authors do not make clear why we, as psychologists (and not philosophers), should be concerned with human dignity, the focus of their study. The only reason they provide for studying this variable is an assertion made by Skinner. The assertion is that the science of human behavior has been hindered by the false societal belief that when behavior of people is constrained, it robs them of their dignity.

One cannot be sure whether this evaluator actually misunderstood the rationale of the study, or was just careless in stating it. His or her version of Skinner's assertion can hardly be deduced from Skinner's text. It is impossible for us to place any credence in an evaluator who thinks that *Beyond Freedom and Dignity* is about what happens "when behavior of people is constrained."

As psychologists, we are not interested in arguing about whether people have dignity in some absolute sense. But we are vitally interested in whether people *believe* that they have dignity and on what basis they come to believe that others have it. Finally, we are interested, ultimately, in whether such belief is beneficial or harmful to the advancement of human culture. That, surely, must be of interest to psychologists, as members of society, if not as scientists.

This evaluator continued:

But, while the authors think this is "one of the most important propositions of our time" (p. 3) I believe that we need better reasons for doing the study than this bare assertion by Skinner. I also believe that this variable, human dignity, might be an important one for psychologists to study. It might greatly affect an individual's social relationships and it may, indeed, be influenced by the apparent freedom of someone's behavior. But I believe that it must be explained better than it is explained in this manuscript before we can gauge its value and the significance of studies such as the present one.

Apparently, this evaluator did not proofread for sense his or her own review. What sense can another author derive from a juxtaposition of two sentences by this evaluator? He or she contends, "The authors do not make clear why we, as psychologists (and not philosophers), should be concerned with human dignity, the focus of their study," and then asserts, "I also believe that this variable, human dignity, might be an important one for psychologists to study." Is belief in human dignity a worthy topic for psychologists to study, or is it not?

Apparently, the point is that we should get on to the problems that this evaluator considers important. This evaluator is focusing on the research potential of studying the concept of dignity. The potential of the project blinds this evaluator to the issue of the submitted research. The potential rewards should have been a reason to endorse our research, rather than to reject it.

This evaluator concluded with the following comments:

> The second problem is due to the way the studies were done and reported. The research seems only tangentially related to the proposition the authors are trying to test. What would appear to be a fairly clear test of the proposition would be to have subjects observe a target person engage in pro-social behavior (perhaps on tape) while varying information given to the subjects about how free vs. constrained the behavior was. Their preliminary research (reported in the introduction) seems better than the two studies reported in the manuscript. Moreover, the instructions given the subjects seem so obscure that at least some of them may not have understood them. The confusing results are consistent with this possibility.

Confusion about the results is inevitable, of course, if an evaluator does not understand the rationale of the study. The study proposed by this evaluator could provide supporting data for the present study. We would not concede that it would be a superior study, however. For example, how believable (real) could the target person and situation be crafted? A viewing of news footage of helping behavior would be ideal, if the ethical problems could be surmounted. But even that might have been too casual for Skinner, because the conditions might not have been rigidly controlled enough to satisfy his criteria for scientific evidence.

Evaluator III

The third evaluator began as follows:

I am somewhat at a loss for words. This paper is a good example of how to set up a straw man and knock him down, but it contributes nothing to our understanding of behaviorism, of lay conceptions of dignity, or of lay conceptions of freedom. It really doesn't even cleanly attack Skinner's personal philosophy though that apparently is the authors' intent. The problems are numerous. For instance, Skinner's philosophical position has little to do with his research. Also, his position as stated in *Beyond freedom and dignity* does not depend upon all laymen agreeing that the functional relation between freedom and dignity goes through the origin. Furthermore, the problems involved in operationalizing freedom and dignity are overwhelming. Finally, there is considerable evidence in social and developmental psychology that the basic relation between freedom related variables (such as choice of action, ability to perform an act, external constraints) and dignity related variables (such as liking, respect, attributions of responsibility) is similar to Skinner's position.

We cannot believe that our submission was so poorly written as to allow a careful reader to draw such false inferences about even the purposes of the study. We were using a new (practical) argument that represented—to the best of our knowledge and belief—an entirely new approach to the issue of the value of Skinner's approach to cultural design and change. It seemed to us as though many evaluators, like this one, simply classified us as anti-Skinnerians, and only looked for more of the familiar arguments against his metaphysics and theory. Their concerns were the projections of their own expectations and defensive dispositions. Therefore, this evaluator was simply flailing away at an imaginary target. We did *expressly* point out that we *did* agree with Skinner's argument concerning the relation between earned dignity and perceived voluntary choice. Our statement of hypothesis, given in the original submission in Appendix A and unchanged in the second submission (supposedly read by the evaluator) stated that the intrinsic level of dignity "is merely augmented by perceived voluntary performance of prosocial behaviors and diminished by perceived voluntary performance of antisocial behaviors."

What is the straw man that this evaluator sees us as knocking down? Skinner described his position rather clearly and consistently: he implied that dignity *only* comes about because of an assumption of voluntary choice. This was the position we attacked. Where does this reviewer get the idea that we were attacking Skinner's "personal philosophy"? We were using a different (practical) argument to evaluate Skinner's practical argument. It is small wonder that he or she did not see that our study was pertinent to Skinner's personal philosophy, because it was not, nor was it so intended.

We take strong exception to the flat assertion of this evaluator that Skinner's "position as stated in *Beyond freedom and dignity* does not depend upon all laymen agreeing that the functional relation between freedom and dignity goes through the origin." This evaluator simply stated that the premise of our research is incorrect, and moved on to other topics, while we slowly twist in the editorial wind.

We disagree that the "problems involved in operationalizing freedom and dignity are overwhelming," in the context of this stage of the research. We claim content validity for our measure of belief in dignity. The subjects reported that they believe in a level of given dignity that does not have to be earned through voluntary behaviors. The subjects also reported a common belief in earned dignity, as Skinner claimed. Should we accept one report as valid, and not the other? Surely, our subjects' direct reports of what they believe about dignity, despite potential problems with response biases, should be more scientifically justified than Skinner's simple assertion about what society believes, admittedly (assertively) not even based on casual observation.

That Skinner was not totally off the mark about society's beliefs is beside the point. This is blatant obfuscation, whether or not it is deliberate. The question is: Do the data alluded to, *or any other previous data*, support the contention that the function for dignity intercepts the y-axis at the origin? If it does, we will stand corrected. If it does not, this evaluator is just blowing pseudoscientific smoke.

Evaluator IV

The fourth evaluator had the following general reaction:

While the issues addressed in the manuscript are interesting, the two studies reported contain a number of serious deficiencies in design, method, and statistical analysis as well as a series of unwarranted interpretations and conclusions. The major flaw in the conceptualization of the study appears to me to be in the authors' criteria for refuting Skinner's hypothesis. In my reading of the manuscript, it appears that the only way the authors would accept Skinner's hypothesis is if 100% of the subjects drew functional curves with intercepts of 0 and *all* subjects neglected to mention intrinsic dignity in their narrative essays.

(Even if this were the case, I have questions about the adequacy of these methods for testing the hypotheses as delineated below.) Despite the way in which Skinner's theory is phrased, the paradigm and statistics we use in psychological research are probabilistic. Thus, the authors' criteria are inappropriate. Using the assumption that all subjects must behave according to Skinner's theory if it is to be confirmed, the authors either ignore or misinterpret their own data. For example, in Study 1, despite the fact that one-third of the subjects were given an experimental set (which, by the way, was not discussed in the paper) emphasizing intrinsic worth, only 13% mentioned it in their essays. However, the authors interpret these findings as in support of a belief in intrinsic dignity. Further, the most frequent graph drawn is Skinnerian. Again, because all subjects did not draw Skinnerian graphs, authors set up an unreasonable test of their hypothesis. An example of a more appropriate approach would be to compare the percentage of subjects who mentioned intrinsic worth to those who did not. A much different result would be obtained.

The number of gross errors in this one paragraph is truly astounding. Although his or her errors seem to us to be rather obvious, for the record we will point them out and discuss them. First, the subjects wrote their essays about the sources of dignity *before* they were given any manipulation of an experimental set; the sets were induced only later in a different part of the study. Therefore, what could be a devastating criticism of our study and interpretation is merely a result of shoddy reading of our manuscript. We venture to comment that it was totally inexcusable for an evaluator to write such a critical substantive comment without checking back against the manuscript to ensure that the criticism was indeed accurate. We suspect that such behavior is unethical as well. We doubt that an evaluator would be so slipshod if he or she were to be held in some way accountable for such grossly inaccurate comments.

Second, we deeply resent the implication that we would claim to have refuted Skinner if we found just a single person (plus ourselves?) who disagreed with him. Why would an evaluator think that *any* psychologist would make such a claim? Undoubtedly, a famous author from a prestigious research-oriented university would not have been so accused. This may be one of the causal mechanisms behind the Matthew Effect. For most universities, statistics is a required course for psychology at even the baccalaureate level. Therefore, it is strange that an evaluator would consider a lecture on probability in psychology to be either necessary or appropriate. The insult is even greater in view of the fact that one of us teaches graduate courses in statistics, and the other had taught experimental psychology for over 30 years.

As a matter of fact, Skinner did make a rather all-inclusive generalization, which permitted no exception. Several box-score statistical analyses favored our hypothesis, as did specific tests of significance. The language in the submission supposedly read by this evaluator was virtually identical to that of the first submission in Appendix A. We quote a two-sentence excerpt that was identical in both submissions:

> A simple t-test was performed to compare the mean intercept on the ordinate to the 0 intercept predicted by Skinner. The result was significant ($t(24) = 4.53$; $p = < .001$).

There probably is a problem with this statistic, inasmuch as no psychologist would literally predict a unanimous result, because of errors in measurement. Nevertheless, we did conform to a probabilistic approach for the determination of the nonchance nature of our results. Therefore, the criticism of our criterion for refuting Skinner is blatantly unfair. This would seem to be a most extreme manifestation of the reviewing mode (Roediger, 1987).

Third, a mention of an intrinsic dignity by 13% of the introductory-class subjects in the open-ended essays is sufficiently large to call into question the Skinnerian generalization that permits exactly no exceptions. In fact, the 13% figure is probably an underestimation of the true percentage of subjects holding the belief. Very likely, some held the belief but did not think at the time to mention it. There is no proof of this, of course, but it is not an unreasonable assumption, *as this same evaluator himself or herself suggests in a later comment.* Although we will discuss that issue in due course, at this point we merely comment that authors should receive evaluations that are at least internally consistent.

In contrast to the earlier contentions of this evaluator, we *did* perform statistical tests on the percentages of subjects in each experiment that mentioned intrinsic dignity as a basis of according dignity. This can be documented by a glance at the results sections in Appendix A. What would be the meaning of a comparison of the percentages of subjects mentioning intrinsic (given) worth versus those who did not mention it? As mentioned above, one cannot know how many subjects held the belief and did not, for one reason or another, mention it in the essay. Therefore, these data cannot be treated as yes/no answers, in which the percentages would have meaning. This methodological idiocy is impossible to tolerate from an evaluator who so recently explained to us the role of statistics in psychological research.

The issue of the subjects' beliefs when they do not make a spontaneous comment in an essay is raised, paradoxically, by this evaluator's next comment:

The open-ended narrative format is problematic in that it tells us what is salient to a subject but does not tell us whether the subject believes in the propositions being tested. One can't conclude that the respondent does not believe in intrinsic dignity if he/she does not mention it. A major confound in this measure concerns the fact that subjects generally believe in voluntary control. If the subject does mention intrinsic worth or dignity, it could be because the subject believes also in intrinsic choicefulness.

We agree with the first point, which however does not square at all with part of an earlier paragraph in the evaluation. But we fail to understand why it is seen as a criticism of our method. The evaluator is simply suggesting that the obtained percentage of comments is probably an underestimation of the true number of believers in intrinsic dignity. By most standards of research, a conservative test of a hypothesis is actually preferred if one is to accept the hypothesis as being supported by the data.

We do not understand the assertion of a confound with a belief in choice. Was the evaluator saying that the subject was not understanding the instructions? This is really reaching in a desperate attempt to find a basis for criticism. Apparently, this argument says that a person has worth because he or she can make choices. This statement is very close to a bare assertion that Skinner is correct. But the very issue we have raised, and the data we have presented, indicates that our subjects report that they will accord some dignity in the virtual *absence* of a choice. If dignity is accorded only because sometimes a person can choose his or her actions, although sometimes not, then proof of strict determinism would eliminate the concept of dignity, as Skinner claimed.

This evaluator also pointed out that

No information is provided about the reliability of narrative ratings. Was there any attempt to address reliability?

We did not address reliability because we were not concerned about the specific percentages, only that the percentages were significantly greater than zero and of a magnitude that seemed important in the context. Ordinarily, the reliability of a measure is considered to be a problem only when there is a conclusion that a null result has been obtained (Harcum, 1990). In any case, the measure was reliable enough to produce results that conformed to the hypothesis at a conservative level of statistical significance. An unreliable measure is not likely to produce coherent or significant results. This should be a trite point for all competent researchers.

The next comment of this fourth evaluator was as follows:

Because of the abstract nature of the function drawing task, it is difficult to believe that it would yield meaningful data. Further, the authors use this task without a reliable strategy for quantifying the kind of data that such a task produces. The task also forces the subjects to imagine an unrealistic zero-choice situation since subjects generally believe in intrinsic choicefulness. The authors state that they have in the past used a series of vignettes describing prosocial and antisocial acts and had subjects ascribe varying levels of dignity to actors given varying levels of choice. This sort of task seems much more meaningful. It isn't clear from the manuscript why the authors abandoned this method.

The methodological comment is literally incredible. In our view the data were meaningful. The responses were certainly quantifiable. In the curve-drawing task we could simply read the values on the coordinates off the graph that the subjects drew. A more quantifiable measure is difficult to imagine. Moreover, we were able to use the method to offer statistical support for our hypotheses.

There were two reasons for using a technique that was different from the vignettes: (1) we had been receiving so many evaluations of our work that complained of the specific methodology that we wanted to test the hypothesis through different approaches; and (2) one evaluator of the vignette study, to be quoted later, had complained that the method was in disrepute and never used anymore. It is difficult for us to take these inconsistent criticisms as serious scientific considerations.

This fourth evaluator for Journal B raised several other issues:

In Study 1 subjects apparently received one of three orientations toward conceptions of dignity. No rationale is provided for the use of an experimental manipulation and it would seem to bias the results.

The evaluator is correct in that we did expect—apparently foolishly—the reader to understand why we would tell different thirds of the subjects how Skinner or Rogers would respond, or that "each person must be correct in his or her own judgments." The technique is called systematic replication; it is used to determine whether variables that should not influence a result do not in fact have an effect. It actually represented an attempt to assess a possible effect in the task of bias due to an appeal to authority by attempting to induce different biases through reference to different authority figures.

This evaluator continued:

In Study 2, the N is very small. Because of this, it cannot address some of the shortcomings of Study 1.

Significant results were reported in Study 2; therefore, the N was obviously large enough. The N is small, true enough, but is it a problem?
This evaluator continued:

The results of Study 2 are suspect given that both the course instructor and experimenter discussed the issues in dignity and worth with subjects thereby biasing subjects in a way that the reader cannot evaluate.

The experimenter and course instructor attempted, as the submission stated, to make the discussion as unbiased as possible. The material was discussed as part of the regular class work in a course in personality theory. Moreover, any residual biases should have been largely counterbalanced, as we also noted in the submission, by the *anti-Skinnerian* bias of the experimenter and the *pro-Skinnerian* bias of the course instructor. One could argue, in fact, that an impressionable student would more likely be influenced by the course instructor than by a visiting researcher, if indeed there was a residual bias from the discussion.
The next concern of this evaluator was statistical:

Is the 56% statistic presented on page 12 with regard to belief in voluntary choice a mean? More information is needed about this statistic and a standard deviation should be included.

The evaluator had a point here; the values were means. Providing standard deviations would have been no problem.
This evaluator had still more objections:

What was the dictionary definition of dignity that the subjects were given? My own conception of dignity is that it is something one feels about oneself. How do ascriptions of worth to others relate to the concept of dignity?

Our subjects in Study 2 were instructed to use the given dictionary definition of dignity or worth with the admonition: "Objectively, a person has worth if someone perceives that he or she has it." This evaluator has missed the point of the study. Does this evaluator accord dignity to himself or herself because he or she feels good about his or her voluntary performance of praiseworthy deeds, or because he or she feels that dignity is some unearned entity that is possessed naturally as indigenous to being human? Presumably this evaluator, as several others to be mentioned later, would be prepared to answer questions about his or her own conception of dignity. Why should not our research subjects also be accorded the ability to form their own personal opinions about the basis on which they accord dignity?

Although the participants in our studies were probably not as sophisticated about such issues as the professional evaluators, still our disagreement with Skinner concerns the beliefs of society, without qualification. Skinner apparently did not intend his pronouncements to apply only to professional behavioral scientists. Nevertheless, as the comments of several evaluators indicate, the views of the professionals do not differ from those of the amateur psychologists in the undergraduate courses.

A further comment is in order about the assertion of this evaluator about his or her conception of the basis of dignity. The reaction is typical of the responses when we describe our research to various student and lay groups. We are often rather heatedly informed that we are dead wrong in even casting doubt on the existence of intrinsic dignity, by even deeming it necessary to perform a scientific study to demonstrate its existence. Most people are sure that it is a true belief, even though they cannot prove it. This evidence from casual observation convinces us that: (1) belief in intrinsic dignity is perceived as a socially desirable norm; and (2) there is a common conscious commitment to a personal belief in intrinsic dignity. The proponents undoubtedly do think that they believe in intrinsic dignity. If the critics contend that this thought process entails merely some sort of denial of nonhumanistic feelings, it would seem that the only acceptable research technique for them would be psychodynamic analysis of individual research subjects. Better than that would be probably impossible. We doubt that Skinner would have condoned such protestations of exotic psychodynamic mechanisms to account for deficiencies in overt responses and unconscious beliefs. In any case, there are certainly much more parsimonious interpretations of why society would oppose science than those proposed by Skinner.

Next, this evaluator, as have many others, wishes that we had tied the research more closely to other psychological literature:

> The issues addressed here are highly related to those addressed by attribution theorists in discussions of attributions of intentionality. The authors do not cite any of this previous work.

While the attribution literature will undoubtedly be helpful in later stages of this program, it does not, in our view, help in the interpretation of these first results. The question is not whether some of the attribution literature is related to the problem under investigation, but whether any of the attribution literature is particularly relevant or necessary for the interpretation of these data on this specific problem. The attribution literature assesses blame/worth for behaviors; we are concerned with accordance of dignity independent of voluntary behaviors. Would that literature substantively change the interpretation of these data? The voluminous literature on freedom is also related. What would be the value of discussing it in the context of the particular submission?

The attribution of intentions is not the issue here. As we said, we agreed with Skinner that some dignity is earned in the eye of the observer by the attribution of intention in performing praiseworthy deeds; dignity is lost by perceived intentionality in performing blameworthy deeds. In fact, as a later reviewer said, this is a "painfully obvious" result. Nothing, except further distraction from the main issue, would be gained by such a discussion. Moreover, a set of interesting problems, which we intend to pursue, involves the possible similarities and differences between the attribution of praise for a given good deed, or blame for an antisocial deed, and the accordance of worth as an attribute of the individual. Clearly, one can hate the sin, but love the sinner.

The final comment of this evaluator was as follows:

> My general feeling is that the interesting part of Skinner's hypothesis
> .   and of the studies reported here concern the relation between dignity
> and choicefulness rather than the zero-dignity, zero-choice issue. I
> assume, and I could be mistaken, that the data on these relations are the
> focus of another manuscript. If I were reporting on the results of these
> studies, I would combine all data into one paper. The result would, I
> believe, be a manuscript stronger than this one. As it is, these data cannot
> stand on their own and, if they were presented alone, would have to be
> reconceptualized, re-analyzed and re-interpreted.

The relationship between dignity and choicefulness was never an issue in these studies, or in any of our other studies. We did collect and report data on the relation, as part of our effort to establish the intercept on the ordinate.

The point about combining our various studies on this topic into one monograph is well taken. There were several reasons for not doing so. First, the various studies were separated by temporal intervals of varying lengths. We had thought that our first results would have adequately documented the existence of a belief in intrinsic dignity. Second, consistently negative reviews kept driving us to conduct additional studies, each one of which we thought should be enough to satisfy the critics.

We felt that we could successfully respond to all of the objections that had been raised. In fact, most of the objections seemed to be the result of careless reading of our submission by the evaluators. We succeeded in getting this report published, with minimal changes, on the third try (Harcum, Rosen, & Burijon, 1989).

SUMMARY

This chapter described and evaluated the several evaluations of a submission that was later published by Harcum, Rosen, and Burijon (1989). These journal evaluations were characterized by frequent misreadings, oversights, and illogical conclusions. In general, the evaluators for the journals were unwilling to come to grips with the rationale of the study and therefore they were unaware of the implications of the results.

4

Yes/No Questionnaire

The second submission on this topic used a different approach to test the same hypotheses as were tested in Submission I. The study employed three samples of college students, enrolled in two introductory courses and an advanced psychology course, and two samples of adult members of community service groups. The subjects were given short questionnaires consisting of direct questions about the conditions under which they would accord dignity to a person, or accord negative dignity, defined as before. The main question, to be answered "yes" or "no," was whether a baby can "be born somewhere today who will have such an unhappy combination of characteristics . . . that he or she will have no (zero) dignity?" The subjects were also asked whether, in their view, people could augment or reduce their dignity if they voluntarily displayed praiseworthy or blameworthy behavior, respectively.

All groups gave a substantial number of "no" responses to the main question about the possibility of a newborn baby having no dignity. Most of the subject groups actually gave more "no" than "yes" responses to this question. They also reported, as predicted, that dignity could be increased or decreased by voluntary performance of the appropriate prosocial or antisocial behaviors, respectively.

Spontaneous comments on the questionnaire, which had been encouraged, supported the conclusion that these subjects believed in a dignity that is always present in human beings. These narratives support the conclusion for a popular belief in a base amount of intrinsic dignity that is accorded to a person, in addition to the dignity that is earned by that person through the voluntary performance of praiseworthy behaviors.

Because of our difficulties in obtaining positive evaluations from the psychological journals to which we had been submitting our work on this issue, and because the issue was basically a practical one, in this submission we emphasized the practical aspects. Moreover, we submitted the proposed article to journals with a more applied orientation. Although not all were psychology journals, according to our judgment from the information provided, this work should be relevant to the goals of each journal.

The article was rejected by five journals before it was accepted by a sixth (Harcum & Rosen, 1990b). The first submission, to Journal C, is reproduced as Appendix B.

JOURNAL C

The only evaluation from Journal C was written by the editor:

I have read your paper and while I think it is clearly written, I am sorry to tell you that I think it is not right for [this journal]. I feel so sure that it would not survive the blind review that I have decided not to send it out.

For me, the problem is that we really do need research that is based not on hypotheticals but rather on so-called "natural" situations. I think the thrust of your argument and findings is certainly important, but I fear the significance of the work is lessened by the fact that the respondents are presented hypotheticals for response rather than your studying situations in which relationships between persons who have and do not have diminished voluntary competence are actually observed.

This editor's point is well taken. But, an equally valid one is that hypothetical situations give better control over the contextual variables.

JOURNAL D

The only evaluator for Journal D was the editor, who concluded that

The paper is really not suitable for publication in [this journal]. When I can make that determination early in the process, I prefer to reject the paper immediately. . . .

As things have developed [this journal] has a distinct bias . . . toward papers that explore the structure of social cognitions and the processing of social information. While not every paper we publish fits those categories, those that do not usually speak to content issues of some current importance. I have to admit that I wasn't quite sure what point you wanted to make with your paper. In a way you take on a straw person in Fred Skinner. I suppose there are those who still take his pronouncements seriously, but I haven't encountered any recently. That is not to say that his work (and that of other behaviorists such as Hull) has not had an impact on our field, some good and some bad, but that is not the same as saying that his particular (and somewhat peculiar) notions about dignity have any currency. Moreover I think you have read Skinner out of context. While I haven't read *Beyond freedom and dignity* in years, I would be very surprised if he meant that all forms of human dignity have to be earned. Skinner was (and remains), whatever you may think of his theory, an acute observer of human behavior, and would not likely have missed the obvious point that in this and other societies we accord the old, the young, and the helpless some forms of respect and dignity.

These comments are extremely helpful to us in making the arguments in this book. We did not aim our criticism at the man, Skinner, but at a plan for cultural change that was proposed by arguably the greatest and most influential psychologist of our time. We feel that Skinner's plan did not faithfully represent his own laboratory-based principles for beneficial behavioral change (Harcum, 1989). Therefore, this editor is the one who took aim at the straw target.

We are very interested to hear that some behavioral scientist friends believe that Skinner's plan for social improvement did not represent his personal approach to life. But, we must react to what he actually published. We also note with interest the characterization of Skinner as an "acute observer of human behavior." We find it difficult to understand what litmus test provides the operational criterion for distinguishing between acceptable acute observational evaluation and the unacceptable casual observational data that Skinner condemned. Surely, the theoretical bent of the observer should not be the critical factor. We proposed a specific test of a hypothesis without regard to the relative prestige, scientific standing, or observation skills of specific observers of different theoretical persuasion.

We do not believe that Skinner ever changed his views on freedom and dignity. Not a single other evaluator of any of our submissions has suggested that Skinner no longer believed in his quoted relationship between freedom and dignity—although some have argued that he was not really serious on the several occasions when he proposed it. We continue to believe that these issues are current, and they still provoke and prolong the major schism in psychology (Harcum, 1988; Kimble, 1984).

We resent the cavalier assumption that we must be incorrect in our reading of Skinner. Despite an admittedly poor recollection of the book, this editor concludes that we are most probably in error because Skinner was a great psychologist. Presumably, the editor is also rather prestigious, having a first-name relation with "Fred." But we too find it nearly incredible that Skinner would overlook, or discount, the massive evidence for a popular belief in unearned dignity. Actually, it is more accurate to say that he deliberately dismissed it as casual and thus unscientific (Blanshard & Skinner, 1966).

This editor, in his final lines, certainly agrees with our basic thesis, however. He apparently considers our thesis so "obvious" that we must be incorrect in asserting that Skinner missed the fact that "in this and other societies we accord the old, the young, and the helpless some forms of respect and dignity." After his early shaky start in discussing the concept of dignity, this editor eventually did get around to writing what could be a reasonable discussion section for our article:

> But beyond that it is quite clear that your working definition of dignity, whether or not it fits Skinner's, is fairly broad and ultimately unilluminating. When you define dignity for your subjects as you do as meaning held in esteem and as eliciting rewarding responses from others, it amounts to defining it as a generalized good person construct. Thus it is hardly surprising that your subjects report that few if any people lack dignity or that dignity can be increased by performing worthy acts. It does not strike me as interesting to discover that people who perform approved acts also are seen as having more "worth, excellence, value" etc. Nor is it interesting *per se* to find that hardly anyone reports that a baby could be so unfortunate as to not elicit supporting and defending behaviors; would you expect people to say that such unfortunate babies be immediately abandoned, which seems to be the only alternative given the broadness of your definition of dignity. I wouldn't know what to think of your subjects had they answered otherwise than they did.

Frankly, we were less surprised at this particular editorial response than we were at all of the evaluators who were actually not convinced by our empirical results of society's beliefs in human dignity. Although we were in fact sublimely confident that our subjects would respond as they did, good research procedure dictated that we verify this assumption empirically, especially when a prestigious acute observer of human behavior expressly denied that assumption. Our aim was to provide evidence for a belief in intrinsic dignity that could not be dismissed as casual observation by doctrinaire Skinnerians. Ironically, an editor considered our evidence to be vacuous because it was redundant with his own casual observations.

We like to remind ourselves of the above editorial comments when, later, we are accused of ignoring the possibility of a possible social desirability or other response bias in our self-report data. Certainly this editor's prose in stating a belief in intrinsic dignity is quite clear and emphatic. We see no reason not to take it at face value. Without initiating a tangential debate about whether the evidence from this editor represents only casual observation, or it meets some standard for a more formal method, we submit that this one citizen at least surely believes in intrinsic dignity. It would be difficult to imagine a context in which the pressures for producing genuine responses would be greater. This is only one observer, but the results are solid. To impeach this data is to impeach the journal peer-review evaluation process itself.

Concerning the concept of dignity, the only true issue at this point concerns whether we have used the same definition and concept as that of Skinner. If we focus on the less ambiguous, but synonymous, term "worth," it is clear that we have no definitional argument with Skinner. The dictionary tells all of us—Skinner, the researchers, the evaluators, the subjects, and the general society—what the word means. We are not discussing the meaning of worth, but the *basis* on which our society decides that a person has or incorporates this characteristic. This is an empirical question, not a semantic argument.

This editor, as apparently did most of the scientific community, uncritically accepted Skinner's assertion that dignity is just a "generalized good person construct." That means, we take it, that the person has value to the extent that he or she voluntarily performs prosocial acts, that he or she is a good person. Our point is that people are valued not just as "good persons," but also simply as "persons." This editor then attacks the "good person only" view as if it were ours, and points out that such a view would imply that certain unfortunate babies would be abandoned as worthless. This he believes to be patently false, and therefore asserts that the main purpose of our studies represents a goal that is obvious. What he asserts as obvious other editors refuse to acknowledge as even valid. This editor looks at the inconsistency within his own paragraph, and then projects it onto us.

We obtained, and attempted to publish, data that support the two ideas in the editor's paragraph above: in the eyes of society some dignity is earned, as Skinner says; and some dignity in the eyes of society is not earned, but given to all other human beings as an affirmation of their humanity. On this basis, we have argued that there is no practical reason to assert, as did Skinner, that the very concept of human worth must be abandoned because it is an impediment to progress in science, and consequently to human survival. Presumably, Skinner would have us save a "useless" infant for basically the same reason that he would have us preserve an antique automobile, a priceless work of art, or a natural wonder of the world. We argue that the members of our society would have a different, and better, reason to save the human life.

The following comments from this same editor now imply that he did not remember the first part of his own letter, concerning the importance of these issues:

> What might be more interesting is to discover whether people feel that mere humanness conveys intrinsic worth, something that natural law theorists have preached for centuries but that is under attack in a society that does seem to value mere utilitarian worth. *And it might be interesting to look at what features if any of human-ness convey this intrinsic value. For example, how far does one have to depart from normality before one is seen as less than fully human in this intrinsic sense* [emphasis added]. These kinds of issues are, of course, very much relevant to present day discussions of treatment for the terminally ill, for treatment and death issues of those born with severe birth defects, and even of abortion. What does it mean to be human? What rights do people assume that people have merely by being human? But those are not issues that can be got at with your questions and perhaps must be approached in an indirect way given the cultural and religious pressures to answer in certain ways. And these are really not the issues addressed by Skinner as I recall. In any event one gets credit for showing that someone's ideas are bad or are not credible in the larger society only if it is clear that the ideas do have some claim to be taken seriously. As I have said I don't believe that this particular set of Skinner pronouncements fits this category.

The first sentence in the above paragraph represents a direct affirmation of our main hypothesis. We are faulted for trying to demonstrate that some people believe what "natural law theorists have preached for centuries," but we are also faulted for criticizing Skinner for ignoring this same fact.

Perhaps, as this evaluator said, the formulations of Skinner with respect to freedom and dignity have already died a natural death. Because they were, in a sense, the last word on the topic, we thought that they should be dealt with before we moved on with our research in the area. Once the loose ends were tied up, we could move on to the aspects of the research that this evaluator proposes.

Ironically, it appears that our ultimate research goals would be within closer reach if we had simply presumed, or asserted, the truth of what we have expended so much effort in trying to prove by empirical techniques. As a practical matter, we should have ignored Skinner's pronouncements in favor of centuries of contrary casual literature, and moved on to the type of research that this editor advocated. We seem to be the victims of our own scientific training. On the other hand, some later evaluators would have us discount the centuries of literature that promulgates intrinsic human worth as merely the result of social desirability and response sets in literary license. Whether or not they are actually endorsing Skinner directly, they are agreeing with his denial of intrinsic dignity.

The only consistency that comes out of the thinking by this editor is the conclusion that Skinner surely must be correct, and we have been mistaken in criticizing his pronouncements. But, here again, we have an evaluator who thinks that some important questions are lurking about this area of research, if we would just get to them.

JOURNAL E

The editor did not add substantive comments to those of two evaluators. The following comment about the evaluation procedure of his journal was, however, interesting in the present context:

> Neither the reviewers nor the editor-in-chief learns the identity of the author at any point in the review. Consequently, they are unable to engage in correspondence about the basis for rejection or acceptance of a manuscript.

Attempts at blind reviewing are commendable, we suppose, but certainly not at the expense of scientific discussion and debate. As we will discuss in the final chapter, a major element of the idealized scientific process is missing if there is no chance for persons who are parties to a controversy to discuss it, and possibly correct errors.

Evaluator I

The first evaluator responded as follows:

> This ms., while interesting in some respects, does not present relevance [to this applied field]. There is no [human service] context and the final sentence of the Conclusion is antithetical to both the thesis of the paper

and the professional stance. A [service provider] can respect differences (accord dignity) without adopting the other's belief system.

We strongly assert that this research should be perceived as particularly relevant by and for those persons purporting to provide human services to others. As we will advocate in the final chapter, both concepts of free will and human worth are valuable to a viable society. In particular, if the worth of a person is based on willingness of another to help that person, a reflexive relationship should be assumed: the greater the perceived worth of a person, the more that person will be helped.

The final two sentences of the above quotation are also off the mark, because the final paragraph of our conclusion section stated that practitioners are more likely to be successful if their belief systems are consonant with those of the client (Harcum, 1989). Certainly, we provided a human service context in this final paragraph, if not before. We do not understand the assertion that the final sentence is "antithetical to both the thesis of the paper and the professional stance." This evaluator either does not understand our thesis or the meaning of the word "antithetical." The final sentence of our submission was inserted precisely to provide a human service context. It was subsequently omitted from our future submissions as unnecessary and distracting. We do not know whose "professional stance" is contrary to the thesis of our research. Our own professional stance is that, almost by definition, helping behaviors would be augmented by additional bases for according dignity to others.

This evaluator's last quoted sentence provides an excellent example of what this book is about. While we do not dispute the accuracy of his or her last sentence, we do not comprehend how it conflicts with our sentence. Actually, the evaluator does not speak to the question of whether respecting real differences between the beliefs of the client and the service provider is more effective for helping the client than maintaining the same belief systems. Are we to assume that the "professional stance" of this evaluator actually excludes a belief in the intrinsic worth of his or her client? Perhaps the reviewer did not understand the sentence to mean a shared belief in human dignity, but rather a more general shared belief system such as the sacredness of marriage or a belief in God. In any case, Harcum's (1989) argument was that the more common the beliefs of client and therapist, the better the odds for a successful therapy. Presumably, that commonality would be more important for issues relating to freedom and dignity.

Finally, this evaluator must not be familiar with the argument that we cited for our relevant human service context—the application to psychotherapy that we cited in the manuscript (Harcum, 1989). Again, we see the possible operation of the Matthew Effect: the evaluator criticizes the author because the evaluator is not in the possession of certain information in the literature, although a citation is provided. If the reference had been to the work of a prestigious author, the evaluator would likely have been already familiar with it, or would feel constrained to become familiar with it. The evaluator does not bother to consult the reference, preferring to blame the authors for the lack of documentation, and thus fails to see the relevance and value of the submission.

Evaluator I continued as follows:

> The author's first reason for objecting to Skinner's contention is that a deterministic bias stands in the way of effective psychotherapy (p. 4, line 3). Therefore, he assumes it is "detrimental to society" (p. 4, line 2). I believe that the author has been too quick to draw a conclusion—i.e., a deterministic philosophy can be detrimental to society simply because it has influenced the effectiveness of psychotherapy.

If we understand this evaluator, he or she means that a deterministic philosophy can be detrimental to psychotherapy, but it may have other benefits in other contexts and therefore it may not be an overall deficit to society. The point that our prose at this juncture needed improvement is well taken. In our efforts to provide a practical proposition for our research, we made a very broad generalization without adequate discussion. But one cited article (Harcum, 1988) emphasized the need for an integration of humanistic and deterministic attitudes in psychology and another (Harcum, 1989) described and advocated the use of such an integrated approach in psychotherapy. In both articles, the main point was that an overemphasis on deterministic thinking was detrimental to psychology and to society.

Moreover, in all fairness to us as authors, we must say that the demeaning set of the reviewing mode must have been at its zenith for one psychologist to assume that another did not see the absolute necessity for a concept of determinism in behavioral science. Instead of assuming that we were competent professionals (peers), who were a bit careless in exposition at this point, he or she assumed that we advocated abandoning deterministic thinking in psychology. Surely, a prestigious author would not be so accused. Hence, an additional basis for the Matthew Effect becomes functional.

JOURNAL F

The only evaluator for Journal F was the editor, who responded as follows:

> The reviewers felt that your paper represented a well constructed piece of social psychological research and that it would probably be suitable

for a journal in that field. [This journal], however, is more geared to a readership interested in the broad sociocultural dimensions of human behavior. While your research certainly has implications for such a perspective, it is, by [this discipline's] standards, a tightly controlled experimental inquiry. Moreover, as a journal of applied social science, [this journal] is most interested in articles whose policy recommendations are more explicit and concrete than those advanced in your paper.

In short, we believe that you have written a good and useful paper, and wish you the best of success in placing it in an appropriate journal.

We were of course surprised, on the basis of the information available, that this journal did not feel that this material was appropriate to its goals. We do not dispute the right of the editor to make such judgments, of course.

JOURNAL G

Evaluator I

The first evaluator of Journal G was the editor, who responded to our introduction as follows:

As noted by all of the reviewers, your introduction seems to be lacking in detailed explanations of theoretical positions and potentially relevant research. Based on the way the theoretical conflict is addressed, one would expect presentation of a "critical" experiment that contrasts the ability of two theories to explain the same phenomenon. As your introduction is currently presented, it reads more as though you are turning the idea over in your mind and developing a case for your own position. It would be very helpful if you were to give Skinner a fair shake and present hard quotes in their appropriate context that explicate his view.

The reviewers and myself were also somewhat distressed that you did not include any major theories dealing with person perception and attributions. After all, your self-report measures of perceived dignity are almost entirely based on attitudes and attributions. Research on the widespread biases and errors in attribution make your conclusions highly questionable. If this manuscript is going to be accepted as an example of scientific evidence in favor of humanism, it must carefully present both sides of the issue and the means for resolving the conflict.

The problem the evaluators seem to be having is understanding what our studies were about. We were not trying to contrast the relative abilities of two theories to account for the same phenomenon, and we were certainly not attempting to perform an experiment. We were using a survey of research subjects to establish what they believed. We argued that they believed in intrinsic dignity, whereas Skinner proposed a contrasting belief system that did not allow the possibility for a belief in intrinsic dignity.

We do not see the relevance of theories of person perception and attribution to the goals of this study. Of course, our subjects were perceiving and attributing, but the research issue of this submission concerned the products and not the processes. If the journal was interested in theoretical articles only, that could have been clearly stated. Instead, they suggest that we should have inserted a gratuitous discussion of such theoretical issues in our study of a factual question.

We are not sure what it means to be "turning the idea over in our minds." If this means that we have not thought through the issue, we definitely cannot agree. As we said in Chapter 1, our first submission to a journal on this subject was in March, 1987. After digesting the negative commentary on four articles from over a dozen journals and over two dozen evaluators, we thought that we had ample time and feedback to have gotten our thoughts together.

We plead guilty to developing a case for our own position. The charge that in doing so we have not given Skinner a "fair shake" is insulting. In the first place, Skinner presented his own case at great length and in the public forum. If this evaluator thinks that we have misinterpreted Skinner, then he should be explicit about how he thinks we have done so. If we were in error, we should have been corrected, and we would have appreciated the correction. Simply asserting that we are in error is irresponsible reviewing, serving no purpose. It stresses the authors, to be sure, but it does not serve the vital function of an evaluator to teach and assist the authors so that their submissions will not be deficient in some respect in the future. Without this corrective information, authors resubmit the same material to another journal. Therefore, the next journal must again deal with the same flawed material.

Our studies were designed with a very specific and limited objective. If our results had something important to say about theories of person perception, this editor should have mentioned their implications. We doubt such implications; although several evaluators articulated the view that such material was relevant, none of them justified the view, or gave examples.

The methodological issues, we have conceded, should have received more attention. We gave that attention in our latest publication (Harcum & Rosen, 1992). We dispute the contention that the meaning of our results is questionable. Perhaps the key to our communication problem is the editor's comment that our paper purports to be "scientific evidence in favor of humanism." But our evidence speaks to the issue of facts about specific behaviors, rather than to the nature of human beings or human perception and attributions. That is the only fair and reasonable basis on which it should be evaluated.

Evaluator I continued with the following specific comments about our methods and data analysis:

> To substantiate the conclusions presented in your manuscript, I suggest that you employ a methodology more rigorous than self-report. As noted in the reviews, attitudes and behaviors are two very different things. Also, if you were to stay with self-report, you would probably be much better off using attitude scales instead of yes-no response choices. Such an approach would allow you to perform more compelling statistical analyses and more easily assess between-group differences.

It seems to us that Skinner's argument is relevant to self-report of beliefs. "More compelling statistical analyses" were possible with the data that we reported; additional analyses were not necessary. We were not concerned with assessing group differences, but group uniformities. Moreover, another evaluator of another submission objected to the use of scales. In any case, given the success of our yes/no procedure, is an improved procedure necessary? The preference of the editor may be relevant to publication, but not to the validity of our results.

Next, this evaluator commented on our results and conclusions:

> Based on your results, the conclusions presented are too broad and unsubstantiated. You can infer nothing about the innateness of human dignity from this survey. As reviewer 3 states, the tendency to see others as having dignity may in itself be a learned response based on religious teachings, social norms, etc. Attributing dignity to others does not give them intrinsic dignity, and even if it did, attitudes do not always correspond to behavior.

Actually, we claimed "nothing about the innateness of human dignity from this survey." In an attempt to provide context, we stated our belief as such, and not as a conclusion from our data. In any case, this is not a critical issue for this study. If there is a belief in intrinsic dignity, whether learned or not, Skinner's argument fails.

We do not understand why the evaluators repeatedly remind us that "attitudes do not always correspond to behavior." The statement is trite.

Finally, this evaluator concluded as follows:

In sum, you seem to have taken on the extraordinarily difficult task of resolving a fundamental difference between two long-standing and equally valuable theories with a simple self-report study. If you plan to submit this manuscript again, I suggest that you "soften" it substantially by introducing qualifications for your findings, or strengthen it by providing theoretical background support and a more defensible method for proving the superiority of one theory over the other.

We do not agree at all with this characterization of our research. It implies a goal that is far more ambitious than we planned or claimed. We certainly did not claim to have provided critical evidence to prove the superiority of humanistic theory over behavioristic theory, even in practical terms. We did claim to have refuted the practical argument Skinner advanced in support of the *value*—not truth—of behavioristic thinking. Nowhere have we claimed that our data imply that Skinner's notion of strict determinism or any of his learning principles are false.

We do argue, on grounds other than our data, that certain components of humanistic thinking are valuable to our profession, to science, and to society. Therefore, we considered the negation of Skinner's argument against the concepts of freedom and dignity to be an important contribution to the profession and to society. But an affirmation of freedom and intrinsic dignity does not imply an opposition to basic principles of learning as incorporated into behavioristic theory.

Evaluator II

The second evaluator for Journal G was concerned about our scientific objectivity:

> I think I should start by saying that the writing is so blatantly biased and opinionated that it reads more like an editorial than a scientific paper. I have to admit that this bias tarnished my overall view and certainly made me more critical of the paper than I may have been otherwise.
>
> I suggest that if the authors want to publish this in a scientific journal they should present the paper as one that is *UNBIASEDLY* evaluating two theories with opposite predictions. If the data are as strong as the authors imply, they should speak for themselves.

First, our study did not attempt to evaluate competing theories, but competing allegations of fact about belief systems. We produced opposing predictions in a methodologically unbiased manner. Second, we dispute the implication that a researcher must be unbiased and lack opinions. The truth is quite the opposite: the author should reach conclusions and draw implications. Moreover, we have no criticism of a forceful style. It should not, however, be reserved as the prerogative of the prestigious author, or serve as a basis for rejecting a submission. If the author is charged with being opinionated—meaning to ignore or cavalierly discount opposing views— there must be specific *documented* instances of it in the treatment of the data and the discussion of the results.

The APA Publication Manual (American Psychological Association, 1983) is very clear on the need for reaching conclusions:

> After presenting the results, you are in a position to evaluate and interpret their implications, especially with respect to your original hypothesis. In the Discussion section, you are free to examine, interpret, and qualify the results, as well as to draw inferences from them. Emphasize any theoretical consequences of the results and the validity of your conclusions. (p. 27)

> In general, be guided by these questions: What have I contributed here? How has my study helped to resolve the original problem? What conclusions and theoretical implications can I draw from my study? The responses to these questions are the core of your contribution, and *readers have a right to clear, unambiguous, and direct answers* [emphasis added]. (p. 28)

Clearly, the APA Publications Manual does not advocate letting data "speak for themselves." Rather, the author is required to commit himself or herself to a conclusion. We cannot believe that a submission would ever be accepted without such a commitment by the author.

This evaluator apparently finds our style offensive. There is not much more that we can say in our defense, except to point to the last two sentences of our abstract, which state that the popular belief in intrinsic dignity "supports" a more humanistic approach toward understanding and positive regard for both oneself and others, and that we "submit" that this belief is important for cultural improvement. To say that our data "support" a conclusion does not seem to exceed the necessary requirement for an author to reach a conclusion as a result of the research. The verb "submit," meaning "to propose or urge respectfully," hardly reflects an opinionated style.

In marked contrast, however, this evaluator's comment, "if the authors want to publish this in a scientific journal," is clearly sarcastic, because we did submit the article to a scientific journal, and there can be no doubt about our intention. This is a display of the gatekeeper's badge of authority. The occurrence of such comments is a strong argument for signed reviews. This evaluator seems to be suggesting that we do not know what constitutes good science. The evaluator's writing lacks sensitivity, and again demonstrates the lack of an egalitarian conception of "peer review," of equals trying to help each other.

This evaluator continued:

> The authors spent several pages describing Skinner's theoretical position. However, I don't really know what the *authors'* theoretical position is, except that it is "humanistic." That's fine, but vague. Indeed, Freud has been described as a humanistic philosopher. Is this where the authors are coming from? I'd like to see a stronger outline of the authors' theoretical perspective.
>
> I'm sure that I sound contradictory by saying that the paper is biased and yet I don't know what the theoretical position is. The bias appears in what the authors are against: "We hate Skinner!" The absence of theory leaves me wondering what the authors are for, or at least what the alternative is.

The details of our personal *theoretical* position are basically irrelevant to the evaluation of this research. Again, the important issue is simply a question of fact about what people believe about the relation between freedom and dignity. This study is not about whether people can exhibit voluntary behaviors. It is also not about whether people believe that they have freedom to choose, because we agree with Skinner that people do have such a belief.

The study touched on arguments for or against humanistic theory or behavioristic theory only insofar as it would provide evidence for a practical advantage for either. The Skinnerian argument with respect to dignity was summarized in our introduction and presumably read by the evaluator.

The purpose of our studies was to refute his contention, as we explained in the introduction to Study 1:

> The first study attempts to provide additional evidence from college students to disconfirm Skinner's contention about public beliefs relating freedom and dignity. Such evidence would destroy his *practical argument* [emphasis added] against the value of freedom and dignity in social action.

Thus, as the APA publication manual mandates, in our introduction we expressly stated the point of our study, the specific hypotheses to be tested, and the implications of the study. In the conclusion section of our submission, we stated what we thought we had accomplished with respect to these points:

> Both of these studies refute Skinner's (1955–6, 1971, 1975) contention that dignity can only be attributed to a person if it is earned by voluntary performance of prosocial behaviors. Thus, his *practical* [emphasis added] argument against the concepts of freedom and dignity, as contrary to a science of behavior, is refuted by laboratory evidence as well as by casual observation (Blanshard & Skinner, 1966).

Therefore, we assert that a reasonably careful reading of our manuscript would have revealed where we were "coming from." We vehemently dispute the characterization that "we hate Skinner." This is another example of how our research has been discounted by simply labeling us as Skinner-haters, and our research as "Skinner-bashing."

The evaluator should have been aware of Skinner's position from the quotations we reproduced, from the introduction to the submission, from the prior publication on the same problem (Harcum, Rosen, & Burijon, 1989), or from a reading of Skinner himself. Our position, again, stated in the introduction to our submission, was as follows:

> The present article challenges these contentions of Skinner about society's metaphysical beliefs. . . . The hypotheses are that persons are accorded intrinsic, unearned dignity, and also that dignity is augmented by voluntary prosocial behaviors and reduced by voluntary antisocial behaviors.

These quotations—all available to the evaluator in the submission—seem to us to represent a very clear statement of what we are "for." Because Skinner does not mention the possibility of an intrinsic dignity, our first hypothesis above represents a positive step or alternative to Skinner, not merely an assertion that we are "against" Skinner.

The next comment by Evaluator II of Journal G concerns our attempt to present our views:

> Their first argument here eludes me. They state that " . . . a deterministic bias stands in the way of humanistic social attitudes. . . . " That might be correct, but as a reader I'm never told why humanistic social attitudes are important. In fact, I'm aware of some people who would want to avoid these. (I'm reminded of the story of Gloria Steinem going to speak somewhere and being greeted by people holding placards saying

that she was a humanist. Although she at first thought these were friends, she later learned that they were foes, for whom being a humanist was a terrible thing.) Again, the authors need to state their theory more clearly. Their second argument here is fine. Skinner may never have presented his own data, but this is followed by the authors' argument in favor of *casual* observations. Apparently, that's what Skinner was doing if he didn't present data. So is it a problem or isn't it?

This evaluator will never understand an argument if he or she simply reads selectively and locks onto some phrases and then skips other phrases. For example, the end of the sentence that he or she quoted in the above paragraph gave a reason why humanistic social attitudes are important. We said: "a deterministic bias stands in the way of humanistic social attitudes, *especially effective psychotherapy (Yalom, 1980)* [emphasis added]." We did give a reason and we cited an authority. Such tactics surely reflect inept reviewing, to a degree that borders on the unethical. Of course, some people, including Skinner, have thought that humanism is bad for behavioral science. Nevertheless, experts in psychotherapy think that it is important to the success of some psychotherapies. We saw no point in pursuing a detailed argument for this point in this particular article. The evaluator could have asked for some amplification, but was clearly and inexcusably incorrect in complaining that he or she was *"never* [emphasis added] told why humanistic social attitudes are important."

Further, we had listed various social advantages of a humanistic attitude in our first publication on this subject (Harcum, Rosen, & Burijon, 1989). The publication was cited in our submission and was readily available to the evaluator. It would have been entirely inappropriate to repeat all of this material in each of the later submissions. Readers of a journal may not be familiar with all of the cited literature, and, therefore, some brief recapitulation is helpful to them. An evaluator can properly suggest that more of the background should be stated in the article. But, it is not appropriate for an evaluator to keep himself or herself ignorant of the background information that has been cited, and then complain that the relevant background information has not been provided, particularly with the implication that it does not exist.

Concerning his or her comments on casual observations, this evaluator lapses into nonproductive sarcasm. The evaluator is the victim of his or her own definitional confusions, apparently trying to discover confusing ways to read our text. We said of Skinner that his

views are presented as the *scientifically* necessary conclusion, and alternative conclusions are not based on science. Ironically, however, Skinner

(1971) does not present empirical evidence to support his opinion about the impracticality of the concepts of freedom and dignity, while disregarding the so-called "literature of freedom" (Skinner, 1971, p. 31) as unscientific. But data from casual observation should not be ignored by scientists, even if such observations are based on the writings of artists or other humanistic scholars.

Skinner said that casual observations were not scientifically acceptable and therefore he did not present any. We said that casual observations provided scientifically acceptable, empirical *data*. In charging Skinner with presenting no data, not even casual data, we were not inconsistent. If Skinner had based his conclusions on even observational data, he would have avoided his mistake, and reached the same conclusions that we did. This evaluator simply does not know what he or she is talking about when he or she makes the pronouncement that "apparently" Skinner was basing his argument on casual observation.

Again, we do not wish to entertain semantic arguments about categories of scientific or nonscientific observation. Although some observations are obviously made under rigorously controlled conditions, this is not to say that other observations made under everyday conditions are unscientific. The issue concerns the validity of the data that are obtained, and not some abstract principle proposed by some category of psychological theorists. So-called casual observation outside of the laboratory may be more useful than rigorous observation under artificial laboratory conditions.

Next, this evaluator expresses concern about our data:

> Here the authors review self-report studies that they interpret as inconsistent with Skinner's argument. That's fine again. But to give Skinner his fair share, I'd like to argue that he would not be too distressed by these data (or those of the present study for that matter) because of the self-report nature. I feel confident (though, of course, not certain) that Skinner would argue that dignity is afforded to a target by an actor through the actor's BEHAVIOR. To observe dignity, we must study overt behaviors. Thus, the students who did not understand the task (p. 6), may indeed behave towards others without voluntary control over their behaviors in such a way as to not afford them dignity. Finally, the data presented in the introduction and in the present study itself are attitudes. We are quite aware of the relatively large body of literature on attitude-behavior inconsistencies.

The concern, we take it, is that the subjects may not be reporting their true attitudes on the questionnaire. This issue, which has been raised before, can always be brought up as a potential problem, for the obvious reason pointed out by this evaluator. But we do not think that the point is specifically relevant in the context of the present research. The question of such relevance will be dealt with extensively in Chapter 7 of this book.

With self-report there is always the problem with honesty, of course. Even if the researcher were to conduct an in-depth interview of each subject, there is always the possibility of deception or self-deception. A converging operation would be very helpful. It would be nice to set up an experimental situation in which the dependent variable was actual helping behavior, instead of reports of attributions and attitudes about the target person. Even in such a case, a critical evaluator could still maintain that the subject was responding on the basis of social desirability, demand characteristics, and such, even if the study employed a true-life simulation. To pursue this point to the extreme: what can one conclude from direct observation of *real* helping behaviors in the world about us? Undeniably, our society *does* help victims of hurricanes and earthquakes. We *do* send foods and medicines to save the lives of newborn babies who could not have earned our admiration by just being born and dying. How "scientific" does this observation have to be to avoid easy dismissal as "casual"?

But, to be theoretically pure, the dependent variable must represent truly altruistic behavior. The psychological community does not even agree that truly altruistic behavior actually exists. Probably the cynic will never be convinced.

We accept the fundamental validity of these verbal reports for two basic reasons: (1) the reports were anonymous, given without obvious ego-threatening instructions or conditions; and (2) the absolute size of the effect under these conditions does not suggest that the effect is due entirely to a general response bias. The spontaneous comments of these subjects, as well as spontaneous comments by several evaluators, indicate that society does identify a *category* of intrinsic dignity. Therefore, on the basis of a tight logical system, society can still consistently support the progress of science, because logically there is the possibility of dignity in a person whose behavior is completely determined by environmental and genetic factors.

This evaluator betrays, by his or her next comment, that he or she does not even understand the purpose of our study:

> I would also add at this point that for quite a lot of behaviors, Skinner's model predicts quite well. A critical test of his position on dignity would be to explain his model (i.e., operant learning principles) to subjects and then ask them to what extent they would afford dignity to others.

This is an incredible—not to say distressing—comment! We have no idea how this evaluator could import the issue of the validity of Skinner's operant learning principles. We never said a word about the validity or value of operant conditioning principles. In a previously published article that had been cited (Harcum, Rosen, & Burijon, 1989) as a reference in the submission, however, we had said, as follows:

> The present studies have no bearing on the validity of Skinner's (1953, 1971) formulations about the production of behavior through reward contingencies, but have been set up to test his interpretation of why society refuses to adopt his formulations as a basis for cultural evolution. (pp. 257–258)

> The present study supports a more modern attitude toward science and a more humanistic attitude toward helping behaviors. *While endorsing the full use of learning principles to modify behavior in a manner beneficial to society* [emphasis added], it also endorses the humanistic concept of intentionality as necessary for practical applications, particularly in complex social relations and psychotherapies. (pp. 266–267)

This reviewer should, therefore, have been aware from our cited prior publication that we endorsed Skinner's use of operant learning in behavior modification. We presume that the evaluator had not consulted that article, the relevance of which could hardly be doubted. From the above documentation, we conclude with great confidence that evaluators do *not* make themselves familiar with the references cited in a submission before completing their evaluations. We suspect that this is a major mechanism underlying the Matthew Effect.

The "critical test" proposed by this evaluator makes absolutely no sense to us, because of the irrelevant issue of learning principles. In fact, however, we did incidentally perform virtually the exact study that he or she proposed, as cited in the previously published article (Harcum, Rosen, & Burijon, 1989):

> The study was conducted during a regular meeting of the class when the instructor was discussing Skinner. The experimenter discussed the issues involved in the conceptions of how presumed choice and dignity might be related, describing how various psychologists would presumably respond, and interpreting the implications of different possible subject responses. He answered questions to clarify the task, but emphasized that the only "correct" answer was a true reflection of the individual student's own beliefs. The course instructor, because of a behavioristic

theoretical persuasion, was an effective monitor to assure that the issues were fairly discussed. (p. 263)

The students were therefore familiar with Skinner's learning principles and approach to theory. We had, actually, mentioned this fact in the very submission that this evaluator was commissioned to read and to evaluate, as follows: "When Harcum et al. employed a group of more advanced students, *for whom the issues were discussed before the task was attempted* [emphasis added], the results clearly contradicted Skinner's contention. Spontaneous comments by both unsophisticated and sophisticated subjects indicated a belief in intrinsic dignity." The most annoying part of this "crucial test," however, was the evaluator's proposal to use *uncritically* a self-report measure. He or she seems to have forgotten the serious reservations that he or she purportedly had about the validity of self-report. This inconsistency reinforces our belief that evaluators tried to drag out trite problems when searching for weakness in a study. The alleged problems seem to disappear when *they* are designing the studies and therefore find it convenient to avoid the problem.

There is further evidence that this evaluator is not unequivocally opposed to self-report:

As for the experiments themselves, I was wondering throughout why the authors never asked the subjects what they thought (or to what degree they thought) that the targets had voluntary control over their own actions. I think this is rather crucial for the interpretations.

The evaluator has a point here, but a small one. We assumed that the subjects would agree that a newborn baby would not have the opportunity to have earned dignity by voluntarily performing praiseworthy deeds. Evaluators tend to assume that the particular research subjects are either intellectually gifted or mentally retarded, at different points within the same study. Nevertheless, we agree that researchers should back up their assumptions with empirical data, even self-report data, if they can do so without negative consequences. Of course, unnecessary effort might be a negative consequence. We think, frankly, that to ask college students to rate the degree of control of a newborn baby over its own behavior would be more appropriate as a thought experiment than as a basis for empirical research. As our undergraduate students would say to the author of such a suggestion: "Get a life!"

Next the evaluator expressed concern about the nature of our data:

As regards the data, I'll focus primarily on Question 1. The authors feel their position supported because 100% of the respondents did not say "yes." This does appear to be inconsistent with Skinner's view, but it is unclear to me (at least from the authors' review) that by saying "society" Skinner meant "every single person." Indeed, one-fifth of the students responded as Skinner would predict (and more among the older sample) . . . that's about how many people show up to vote every four years (and it's these people's opinions that we say are "society's").

We have dealt with this criticism before. Certainly no well-trained and experienced research psychologist would ever predict that a large sample of subjects would ever respond unanimously to any question. Perhaps with a large enough sample one could even find an American subject who professed a disbelief in the law of gravity. Would the researcher then claim that American society did not believe in the law of gravity? We wonder why any evaluator would even guess that we would make such an argument.

The voting analogy is only useful in illustrating what the definition of society might be. To define society in terms of the percentage of the population that votes really is not sensible. One person, if at the right time and location, can determine the course of history. Does that mean one person is a good definition of society? Presumably, majority has some weight here. Most issues in psychology are not clear-cut anyway. In psychology we are usually satisfied with the modal position or use some other measure of central tendency. What we have discovered is that the most frequent position is a belief in intrinsic dignity—not in an absence of basic human worth.

Presumably the results at the polls are some indication of the views of the total population of eligible voters, just as the results of our sample represent a more or less similar proportion in the total society. Of course, nonvoting citizens may reveal different preferences, just as nonparticipating potential subjects could have different beliefs. But we were attempting to demonstrate a phenomenon, not document the frequency of the phenomenon in American society.

The above criticism by the reviewer is not good experimental psychology. Because we must assume that the evaluator himself or herself is a competent psychologist, we must attribute the incompetent response to some aspect of the "reviewing mode" (Roediger, 1987), which goes far beyond the hypercritical. This alleged evaluation betrays not only a cavalier, "groupthink" (Janis, 1971) attitude of infallibility, but also a tendency to write without thinking. The evaluator is not engaging the issues, but seems to be writing the first ideas to spring off the top of his or her head.

The next comment of this evaluator was specific:

On page 12, I think there's a typo. The authors write, "For all six questions, there was a progressive increase in "Yes" responses for the Serve. O [Service Organization] and G. Club [Garden Club] subjects, respectively, relative to the college students." But that's not the case for Question 4 on Table 1, Study 2.

The evaluator is correct in that our statement is not absolutely true, but only generally true. For one question—Question 3, not Question 4—there was a decrease for the Garden Club members relative to the Service Organization members, although both groups gave higher percentages of "no" responses than the college students.

The next comment of this evaluator betrays careless reading of the submission:

Finally, I would have to say that the second paragraph of the discussion is completely out of place. The data have no bearing on what the authors say here. The data say *ABSOLUTELY NOTHING* about the "innateness" of our beliefs. The authors should stop and think about what they've just done. They presented subjects with a self-report inventory and inferred innateness from the responses. What would the authors think if I gave blacks and whites self-report intelligence tests and found racial differences and inferred that they were innate? This is clearly not consistent with the humanistic values that I'm aware of.

We never said that our data had anything to say about the innateness of beliefs. Our actual statement was as follows: "Our belief, in agreement with many humanistic psychologists (e.g., Rogers, 1959), is that the members of society have an innate predisposition to believe in internal intentional control of their own behavior." We certainly did not present this belief as a conclusion based on our data. A careful reader would not have made such an inference. This belief was not mentioned in either our results or discussion sections, but rather it was mentioned at the end of the article under the heading of "Conclusion." In the first paragraph of this section, we reiterated the conclusion that we had refuted Skinner's contention by providing contrary laboratory evidence. The sentence in question began the final paragraph of the article, which spoke to the point that a program for cultural improvement should be responsive to the beliefs of the society in order to be successful. Perhaps it was not appropriate to share this opinion, which was relevant to the importance of the research. But it is clearly labeled as our belief and should not have been confused with the conclusions that were based on our research data.

The evaluator was critical of some other parts of the discussion concerned with implications of the research:

I don't know from any evidence that the authors presented that "internal intentional control" is a "cherished belief."

We did not present evidence in our submission that the belief in intentional behavior is cherished, nor did we claim to have done so. The adjective "cherished" was used by Skinner (1971) in this context. That people strongly believe in personal freedom *has* been documented, however.

Evaluator II continued to object to our conclusion:

The data have no bearing on the effectiveness of particular helping methods.

The submission did not purport to offer evidence for the value of particular methods in helping. We did cite another article (Harcum, 1989) that did discuss such evidence.

Again, it is clear that this evaluator did not understand the purpose of our study:

The authors seem to feel that they've dealt an important blow to Skinner. To my knowledge, the Skinner–Rogers debate ended 20 to 25 years ago. We're all aware of the problems with Skinner's ideas; Chomsky did quite a good job in discrediting operant learning theory as the mechanism for language development. I suppose I would want to know why is this research important NOW.

As we said before, we were not trying to continue or reopen the debate on Skinner's metaphysical position, but with his *pragmatic* argument against the beliefs in freedom and dignity. Nevertheless, it is still fair to ask why we raised the question now. We raise the question now because it had not been raised before, nor had Skinner changed his position. As we have said, we believe that the issue is important for the future of our society. It certainly continues to divide our profession (Kimble, 1984); therefore, a resolution would seem most desirable.

We gave some of our reasons for raising the question in the discussion to which the evaluator raised so many objections. In doing so, we went beyond the data, to discuss our view of the importance of the outcome of the study. That view is summarized by the following excerpt from our discussion:

Presumably, the attitudes with respect to newborn infants would apply to citizens of any age who might be victims of incapacitating conditions, such as aging, mental retardation, or physical or mental disabilities. We submit that a viable society would not deny the worth of any person merely because that person was now unproductive in some limited sense.

We subsequently deleted these statements from the final published article because they do represent opinions, instead of facts. We are not sure that the article is improved because of this deletion.

Evaluator II continued:

> Given all of the criticisms above, I will say that the data are *generally* in line with what the authors expected, and may find an interested audience. I would suggest that if the authors want this published, they should re-write the paper substantially (as I suggested above) and frame their ideas in a more social context. After all, they did submit this paper to a social psychological journal. The question might be framed: Is dignity something that is socially defined? Is it meaningful at all to speak of dignity outside of a social context?

Whenever we attempted to frame a general social context we were told that our statements were not justified by the data, as we have just discussed. This evaluator is nothing, if not inconsistent. To us, the notion of innate dignity implies a relative independence of specific social context, particularly and paradoxically in the case where the environment (context) controls the behavior entirely. We agree that the answers to his or her questions above are important; they are part of our proposed research program. We view these earlier attempts to demonstrate a belief in intrinsic dignity as a first step toward answering these questions.

The final comment of this evaluator contains good news and bad news:

> The authors should consider some of the methods issues I discussed above and conduct another study.

The good news is that this line of research shows promise. The bad news is that our previous research efforts have been summarily dismissed, with no better ideas on how to do the research.

Evaluator III

The third evaluator for Journal G was also rather confused about the rationale for the study:

This study attempts to refute the contention of Skinner (1971) that dignity, or worth, must, in the view of society, be earned by voluntarily performing prosocial acts. More specifically, it was first hypothesized that persons accord intrinsic dignity to others, which does not have to be earned through voluntary praiseworthy behaviors. A second hypothesis was that dignity is either augmented or decreased by voluntary praiseworthy or blameworthy behaviors. The authors assumed that lack of subjects' endorsement for these ideas are supportive of the humanistic orientation. Unfortunately, the authors failed to support their argument because of poor conceptualization and inadequate explanation of the findings reported.

It is not clear that this evaluator understands that the two hypotheses were ours, not Skinner's, and that we predicted they *would* be supported. Such support, we argued, would favor the use of a humanistic orientation. The evaluator is the one with the problem in conceptualization. Obviously, the rest of the evaluation cannot be expected to make much sense.

This evaluator's specific comments are not very specific. He or she comments on our introduction:

Overall, the introduction is not focused. The idea is not new, nor does it seem a significant contribution to the field. The presentation of Skinner's idea on dignity and control is too simplistic and is amenable to misinterpretation. The review of the literature does not seem integrated, and includes only the authors' own previous research.

This evaluator seems to be just stringing together stock criticisms. There is not much but opinion to react to here, except the comment that "the idea is not new." If true, this would be an absolutely lethal criticism; therefore, it should not be made so casually by a gatekeeper of science. We do firmly believe, however, that the idea of challenging Skinner on these grounds is new, and we challenge this criticism. This evaluator should have given some citation or hint of a reference that would indicate priority of the research idea or a closely related one. We cannot be absolutely certain of a negative—that no priority exists—but a simple assertion by our evaluator, without a citation, does not shake our confidence. Moreover, the evaluators who understood our thesis generally did not contend that the idea had been published previously.

We do not understand what is simplistic about our presentation of Skinner's idea on dignity, and how it is amenable to misinterpretation. Is this evaluator saying that we have not presented Skinner's position accurately or fairly? It is irresponsible of an evaluator to drop such a comment like a devastating bomb, and then move on without some explanation. Like Skinner, this evaluator is asserting opinion without empirical evidence. This evaluator's comments are like getting the newspaper headlines with no text, no article. If this evaluator thinks that we had distorted Skinner's argument, he or she should have specifically described the nature of the distortion.

The further comments of Evaluator III concerning our method were picayune:

> *Study 1.* There are many ambiguities in the procedure. Although it was stated that C.S. 1 and C.S. 2 subjects were tested outside of class (p. 7), it is not clear if the subjects took the questionnaire home or simply answered the questionnaire during a recess. There was no manipulation check on the subjects' comprehension of the concept "dignity" and their perception of its relevance to the scenario including a newborn baby. Also, it is not clear what dimensions of cultural experiences (p. 8) were assessed. *Study 2.* The characteristics of the subjects in each group (Serv. O, G. Club) are needed. What "other differences"? (p. 11)

"Tested outside of class" meant that the subjects appeared for testing at a prearranged time. There was no manipulation in either study, so how could there be a manipulation check? Because the subjects "were asked to describe any cultural differences," the question concerning specific "dimensions" does not make sense to us. How much further would this evaluator expect us to have gone in describing the characteristics of the subjects in the Service Organization and Garden Club groups? The Service Organization group were tested at a noon luncheon meeting in a hotel dining room, whereas the Garden Club subjects were tested in the morning after coffee and Danish in the basement recreation room of a club member.

When the evaluator asks, "what other differences" among the groups, he or she is responding as if we *claimed* there were other differences. We said: "undoubtedly, there were other differences" in addition to age. Most readers, we think, would take this to mean what we intended: we cannot document that there are other differences, but we strongly suspect that there are some. Truthfully, we did not even document that they were American citizens. Is that a legitimate criticism? In any case, the major issue here does not concern possible differences among groups. As this evaluator says later, "obviously not!" We were not specifically interested in the attitudes of the members of service organizations, but used each group because it was available and represented a different population from college students. The goal of Study 2 was stated as follows: "To establish the generality of the Harcum-Rosen hypothesis." We were looking for uniformities—not differences among groups. We supported this by use of two obviously (we think) different populations, with basically the same result. Because the results were the same, the importance of possible differences among groups is lessened. Larger, documented differences among groups would only strengthen our case.

The following are specific comments on our results and discussion sections by this evaluator:

> Findings are not accurately presented, nor are they elucidated clearly in these sections. In fact, the Results and Discussion sections are mixed, which tends to be very confusing and inappropriate. Overall, the data analysis was too simple and did not provide adequate tests of the predictions. It was not clear whether they were interested in differences between groups (obviously not!) or the magnitude of their response endorsement in each question.
>
> *Study 1.* The percentages of the responses to the six questions vis-a-vis the predicted responses are presented in Table 1; however, it is not clear how these predicted responses are derived, and how the subjects' responses are supportive of the author's prediction. Although the author simply claims that some of the predictions are strongly supported, they did not present significance tests to attest their arguments. Also, on page 10, it was stated that "efforts to relate subject characteristics to the various responses" were made. It is not clear how they were done and why it did not produce "general conclusions" (page 11). The discussion is too simplistic and needs more elaboration.
>
> *Study 2.* Most of the comments above on Study 1 apply here as well. In addition, as the author states (page 11), although there are undoubtedly differences between the two groups included, the author failed to test the difference in terms of the first dignity question, which seems possibly due to gender differences. Again, the discussion section did not adequately address the outcome of this study.

We have admitted that there was a minor inversion at one data point that we ignored as inconsequential. While mistakes are never justified, this one hardly warrants the conclusion that our "findings are not accurately presented." Such a statement implies that our conclusions are not justified by our data. We had made no differential predictions for the two older groups.

Predictions are derived from the hypotheses that a researcher purports to test. An evaluator who does not understand how the predictions are derived cannot possibly evaluate the results and conclusions. It should be recalled that this evaluator thought rejection of our hypotheses would support the humanistic orientation to freedom and dignity. The hypotheses, as quoted above, are: (a) "persons are accorded intrinsic, unearned dignity"; and (b) "dignity is augmented by voluntary prosocial behaviors and reduced by voluntary antisocial behaviors." The predictions from these hypotheses are generally quite straightforward:

Question 1: Can a baby be born today without dignity?
Prediction: No, from Hypothesis (a).

Question 2: Can a person increase his or her dignity?
Prediction: Yes, from Hypothesis (b).

Question 3: Can a person decrease his or her dignity?
Prediction: Yes, from Hypothesis (b).

Question 4: Can a person lose all dignity?
Prediction: Yes, from Hypothesis (b).

Question 5: Can a baby be born today with "negative dignity"?
Prediction: No, from Hypothesis (a).

Question 6: Can a person develop "negative dignity"?
Prediction: Yes, from Hypothesis (b).

We do concede that this evaluator has a tiny point in the case of Questions 4 and 6. We did not expressly state in Hypothesis (b) that the dignity could be decreased by voluntary antisocial acts all the way to the point of zero dignity or negative dignity. Nevertheless, we had stated in our introduction that we endorsed the concept of negative dignity, and therefore predicted it, as follows: "Voluntary blameworthy behaviors would decrease dignity, possibly enough to produce the alleged negative dignity, in which the society would perceive itself to be better off without that person." This precise statement, along with Hypothesis (b), justifies the predictions of zero or negative dignity.

We looked at all reasonable ways to relate subject characteristics to the various responses. It did not seem necessary to describe all of the failures specifically.

Finally, with respect to our conclusion, this evaluator maintained:

> The findings reported did not support the author's conclusion that the humanistic orientation is more accurate and/or correct. Also, it is not warranted and premature to argue that the findings be applied to human service providers to the extent that they adopt the humanistic approach.

We did not conclude "that the humanistic orientation is more accurate and/or correct." We were not arguing for the truth of the approach, but its greater practical value. In the discussion section of Study 1 we reached the following conclusion: "With the one exception, the results were as predicted from the Harcum and Rosen [Appendix C] formulation. Therefore, Skinner's (1971) contention, that society accords dignity only to those who voluntarily perform prosocial acts, is contradicted by these data." In the discussion section of Study 2 we interpreted our results as follows: "This study clearly supports the notion that older adults also believe in voluntary control of behavior, and, moreover, that they employ this concept in differentially assigning dignity to individuals. These subjects also believe in intrinsic dignity at birth, which is therefore not contingent upon a person's ability to behave voluntarily." The conclusion, that our results indicate a common belief in intrinsic dignity, is entirely consistent with the stated purpose of these two studies: "The purpose of the present studies is to provide additional laboratory evidence on this controversy. We contend that society accords an intrinsic, unearned dignity to each human being." The value of these results to human service providers is, of course, a matter of opinion. We do not know what credentials the evaluator offers to support his or her contention that our results do not entail a current practical application. He or she presents no argument to validate this claim. In contrast, we cited personal references (Harcum, 1988, 1989) to bolster our claim for the value of beliefs in freedom and dignity. We also cited Rogers (1959) as one who supports the concept of personal freedom as important—if not essential—to the success of psychotherapy. Rogers includes in his description of a person who has matured as a result of psychotherapy or life experience, the following: "Self-direction is positively valued. The client discovers an increasing pride and confidence in making his own choices, guiding his own life" (p. 166). We are undoubtedly on solid ground on this point.

Evaluator IV

The fourth evaluator begins on a negative note:

This manuscript is riddled with undefined terms, slack presentation of relevant literature, and sweeping generalizations. In addition, I feel author fails to demonstrate the significance of the research.

These are rather damaging summary criticisms. One would expect to see specific examples in a detailed commentary to follow. This is certainly not the case with alleged "undefined terms." The only definitional problem to be mentioned by this evaluator concerned the adjective "viable" in reference to a "viable society." The meaning of the word can be found in any dictionary. We were not introducing some new concept, and did not give the impression that we were. We were merely picking up on Skinner's contention that chances of survival of our society—therefore, to become a viable society, one would presume—would be enhanced if society abolished the scientific concept of freedom and the prevailing conception of the basis of human dignity.

A full discussion of the issue of relevant literature will be deferred. For now, we will only reject the claim; we did cite all of the necessary literature in the context of a journal article. If the evaluator identified an important, specific omission, he or she should have cited it.

This evaluator seems to be actively looking for a way to become offended and offensive:

> Author categorizes newborn, aged, and mentally and physically handicapped individuals as people "who are unable to earn dignity." This terminology sounds extremely condescending and is very offensive when applied to the aged and handicapped. Such individuals are not "unable" to earn dignity, it is simply society's prejudice that makes it more difficult for them to do so. Change it.

This evaluator is taking a main implication that we had drawn from our study and pretending that we are guilty of the very sin that we are protesting. It appears that he or she cannot quite put together the relation between our results and this important implication. Frankly, it seems rather obvious to us that a handicapped person who cannot perform in a manner to please society—to earn dignity—is not, and should not be denied dignity. Remember, we are the ones who support intrinsic dignity for all, available to everyone, which does not have to be earned.

The evaluator's emotional tone belies the literal wording. The advocacy of this evaluator indicates that he or she nevertheless accords dignity to handicapped persons. Again, we have an evaluator who heatedly asserts (direct report) the truth of our hypothesis, but later will deny the value of our direct-report evidence.

At this point, we cite a passage that was subsequently deleted on the basis that it was merely an expression of opinion:

> Presumably, the attitudes with respect to newborn infants would apply to citizens of any age who might be victims of incapacitating conditions, such as aging, mental retardation, or physical or mental disabilities. We submit that a viable society would not deny the worth of any person merely because that person was now unproductive in some limited sense.

We submit that this paragraph does not represent, to a benign and open-minded reader, a condescending and offensive style. The very topic of the present book concerns the mystery of how any evaluator can sincerely say that it does.

This strong and inappropriate criticism by this evaluator is a prototypical example of the apparent mind set of so many evaluators. They seem to be striving to find a loose end to criticize, or a detrimental way to read a sentence. There is no way that an author can write so clearly and unambiguously and not be misunderstood (distorted) by a clever reader who is searching for an alternative, damaging way to read the words. Roediger (1987) believes that the evaluator tends to adopt a way of thinking that he calls the "reviewing mode," which is a mind set or state of mind that is inordinately critical of any manuscript that he or she is asked to review. We agree. We find it otherwise incredible that an evaluator in good faith can misread us in such a way that is harmful to our chances of publication. The point of our series of studies is that dignity is in the eye of the beholder and that everyone is accorded an intrinsic dignity, and therefore possesses dignity unless he or she performs sufficient antisocial behaviors to lose it. How can someone conscientiously and sincerely read this to sound condescending and offensive to any group of disadvantaged persons?

Concerning our introduction, Evaluator IV alleges the following flaws:

> The introduction fails to tie the current research to relevant bodies of literature. Almost exclusively, author references either Skinner or Harcum and colleagues—and doesn't always do a satisfying job at that. For example, author states (p. 3) "In Skinner's view of society's beliefs, as more prosocial behaviors are ascribed to greater voluntary control, there is an increase in perceived dignity." This paper's underlying purpose is to provide evidence against this statement; such a key concept should be backed with an appropriate quotation from Skinner, so that the reader cannot assume that the author has misrepresented Skinner's "view."

First, we dispute that, in the context of a journal article, relevant literature was omitted. A journal article cannot mention all concepts or data for which one could find some logical connection. As far as we know, we are the only researchers who are working on this particular problem. Second, this evaluator also has entirely missed the point of our study. We do, in fact, *agree* with Skinner that society ascribes greater dignity for greater voluntary control of prosocial behaviors. We cannot imagine how a serious reader would think that we were trying to provide evidence *against* this point of Skinner's formulation. We even cited data of Harcum and Rosen (1990a) that was interpreted as supporting the following conclusion: "Dignity was augmented by voluntary prosocial behaviors and decreased by antisocial ones." We cited other data of Harcum and Rosen (1992) as follows: "Results again supported the concept of intrinsic dignity, and also the increase and decrease of dignity with voluntary prosocial and antisocial behaviors, respectively."

The major purpose of our study was, of course, to show that subjects *also* accorded intrinsic, unearned dignity. This evaluator had not read our submission carefully, nor had he or she become familiar with our prior publication on the topic. This factor of familiarity with prior publications probably provides some of the advantage in acceptance rates for prestigious authors relative to unknown authors; some of the evaluators obviously do not bother to read the prior works of unknown authors, and the Matthew Effect is born.

In our first published article (Harcum, Rosen, & Burijon, 1989) we quoted Skinner extensively. If this evaluator was concerned about our reporting of Skinner, he or she should have consulted that article, or read Skinner in the original. This comment implies that a reader of a published article cannot rely on the evaluation process to verify the correctness of a statement by the author, even when the statement can be easily checked against an original source.

This evaluator next criticized the content of a quotation from our submission:

> Pg. 4: "There are two reasons that Skinner's erroneous contentions are detrimental to society." Author's use of "erroneous" represents a rather judgmental statement which he/she fails to justify. Are they erroneous? Where are the references to back up this statement? And why are these contentions necessarily detrimental to society? Similar arguments have been leveled at social exchange theories (cf. Batson, 1990; Wallach & Wallach, 1983; but Kelley & Thibaut, 1983), with a debatable degree of success. In defense of their theory, Kelley and Thibaut point out that such analysis (similar to the current paper's) ignores "multiple" causes of moral behavior (i.e., learning). Author does not convince me that Skinner's analyses are "detrimental" to society. Author does make a good point in faulting Skinner for believing his views to be the "scientifically" necessary conclusion, denigrating all others as unscientific.

We have previously answered the criticism of our charge that Skinner's contentions against freedom and dignity were erroneous. That was the whole point of the initial phase of our research program. Our data contradicted Skinner. The evaluator unfairly implies that we have merely rendered an opinion without data when he or she called our conclusion "judgmental."

We did not do more than introduce an argument in favor of a belief in freedom, citing Yalom (1980) as an authority on the need for humanistic thinking in psychotherapy. There are, of course, some psychologists who would deny the effectiveness of such psychotherapy, but most would not, even some of those who are not satisfied with the evidence in support of such effectiveness. Even our legal system is based upon the assumption of freedom of choice. The argument over the issue of "diminished capacity" hinges upon the possibility of other factors limiting freedom of choice. But, the evaluator is correct in that the assumption that psychotherapy is beneficial to society is a judgmental statement. Obviously, we do believe in the effectiveness of psychotherapy, but even that has been questioned, of course. The belief is not ours alone, nor is it without empirical documentation. The conclusion that a belief in a personal will is beneficial to psychotherapy has been documented (e.g., Erickson, 1973; Harcum, 1989; Reisman, 1971; Rogers, 1964).

We find the yoking of Skinner's metaphysics and social exchange theory quite interesting. We have no problem with the basic premise of exchange theory, any more than we do with Skinner's stated principles of learning. Our concern is with certain cognitive factors that are not easily understood in terms of conventional learning paradigms. For example, principles of learning have not satisfactorily dealt with the phenomena of incentives and creativity. Cognitive appraisals of rewards and punishments are rather crucial in the application of social exchange theories, but surely not in Skinner's thinking.

In any case, we would not like to think that the publication of any of our research articles on this topic was contingent upon convincing any given group of evaluators that Skinner's views, on balance, are detrimental to society. The goal of our article was to refute *Skinner's* argument for *why* the concepts of freedom and dignity are detrimental to science. In fact, just as everyone does not agree that psychotherapy is beneficial to society, not everyone agrees that science itself is unequivocally beneficial to society.

Next, this evaluator criticizes another of our statements:

Pg. 5: "We contend that society accords an intrinsic, unearned dignity to each human being." Author should draw parallels to Sears's discussion of person positivity bias. In addition, what about the norms of social justice and social responsibility? How do these differ from author's conceptualization of innate dignity?

The evaluator is probably correct that we would have strengthened our case by showing similarities to concepts and evidence already in the literature.

Conforming to a norm of justice, responsibility, or social desirability would presumably produce the same prosocial behaviors as the perception of innate dignity. We would tentatively suggest that the difference is whether the act is performed on the basis of personal conviction, rather than a conditioned conforming response. The personal conviction may be at least partially the result of learning, of course, but it would seem to be more stable as a basis of responding. It might provide the enduring basis for a person to resist conformity to a leader or group that advocated elimination of a group of persons who could not make voluntary contributions to the society. Perhaps the difference is a stronger affective component associated with a belief in innate dignity. As Rogers (1964) says, a person's "feelings and his intuitions may be wiser than his mind" (p. 164).

Putting this issue into perspective, we ask if fine distinctions among these concepts—if they are different—are relevant to the question of why the members of society do not offer stronger support, or less opposition, to science. To follow along with Skinner's argument a bit, what would be the consequences of a completely successful science that obviates the concept of human freedom? If there are still bases to affirm the worth, value, and positivity of human life, then Skinner's argument against the value of the concept of human freedom, and therefore human dignity, collapses.

We reported in our introduction that Harcum and Rosen (1990a, 1992) found evidence for "the concept of intrinsic dignity, and also the increase and decrease of dignity with voluntary prosocial and antisocial behaviors, respectively." With respect to the change with voluntary behaviors the evaluator asks:

How does the halo effect and negativity bias relate to author's findings? Can't these be alternative explanations?

Fundamentally, we would say that these are very similar phenomena. The halo effect presumably involves generalization of a positivity bias. The explanations for these similar terms are probably quite similar. Nevertheless, the purpose of our research at the initial stage is to demonstrate the existence of a particular belief, rather than to explain the belief.

Next, this evaluator is concerned with our description of the college student subjects:

In the final paragraph author uses "unsophisticated beginning students"—must be more specific.

Apparently, we made a mistake in emphasizing that the beginning students were "unsophisticated." The term is actually redundant, considering that the students were in an introductory course. In fact, there was nothing otherwise unusual about the group, as far as we knew. Specifically, we did not select them for lack of sophistication relative to some other sample within the class. The subjects in the introductory classes were self-selected in the sense of volunteering for this particular study from among those studies that were advertised as eligible for fulfilling the research participation requirement for the course.

This evaluator then asks about the method of Study 1:

Was there random assignment? If not, acknowledge that this is a quasiexperiment and address possible difficulties and benefits with such a design in the discussion.

We do not understand the question, or the instructions. Subjects self-selected by signing up for the individual studies; they were not assigned by the researchers. Of course, a researcher may at any time have different populations appear for different studies. But, in our case, it did not matter. Our study was simply a survey of several different groups. We can view the use of different groups as an example of systematic replication using diverse samples so as to have a database more representative of the population at large. We were working to avoid the criticism that this study was based solely on "college sophomores," a criticism commonly leveled against psychological research. We did not intend the differences among groups to represent either a manipulation or a quasi-manipulation of some independent variable. Our predictions were the same for each group, and we really did not expect to find differences among them, despite the obvious formal differences between the college students and the older club members.

Evaluator IV criticized the procedure of Study 1:

The study uses a questionnaire that could easily be open to self-perception bias. Author does not address this fact anywhere.

Self-perception bias is a legitimate concern, as always in studies of this type. Admittedly, we should have given more attention to this as a potential problem, even though we did not view it as critical. There is of course no way to eliminate such a potential artifact completely. Several methodological and statistical procedures have been developed for this purpose. But there is no possibility of justifying with absolute certainty that the subjects are not as clever at analyzing and understanding the method as the researcher was in developing it. The legitimacy of statistical corrections can always be questioned, because of the possibility of interactions with changing sets. For example, we cannot assume that a so-called constant error produced by a response set was in fact the same and truly constant across all of the substantive questions.

In discussing the results of Study 1, this evaluator contends that

> Author states that the predictions were supported, but it appears author simply eye-balled the data, failing to give a statistical test comparing the percentages.

There are actually two criticisms here that should be distinguished. Considering the issue of whether our data supported our predictions, the results were undeniably confirming. That we failed to give a statistical test is correct, and may be a legitimate criticism. The reasons for omitting the statistical test were threefold: (1) the sheer size of the effect (in most cases the majority of the subjects responded contrary to Skinner's contention; (2) replicating a result with three different groups of subjects—or five groups, depending on how you count—tends to reduce the importance of the statistical test; and (3) for the main questions (1 and 5) the exact value to use for a Skinnerian prediction was not known. As discussed previously, a predicted value of exactly 0% or 100% is not reasonable. Therefore, the precise value of t could not be determined. In the published version of the paper we solved this problem by showing that the obtained values were significantly less than 50%, meaning that a majority of the subjects responded in a manner contrary to Skinner's prediction for individual subjects. This more conservative test should be satisfactory for the purpose.

Next, this evaluator complained about our attempts to correlate subject characteristics to the responses about dignity:

> "Efforts" to relate subject characteristics to "various" responses about dignity need to be elaborated upon. What kind of efforts? What does author mean by "various"?

We simply could not find significant relationships between the reports of subject characteristics (i.e., age, gender, probable major, possibly different cultural experience) and the answers to the six questions on dignity. As far as we know, we looked at all possibilities; this is what we meant when we said that we could find no relationships for the demographic information that we had collected. "Various" referred to all of the responses to the questions on the questionnaire. What else could we reasonably have done?

The next criticism by Evaluator IV was legitimate, but rather trivial. Concerning the introduction to Study 2, he or she said:

Author uses "the Harcum–Rosen hypothesis." It would be nice to specify what this is in the introduction.

We did specify Harcum–Rosen results from several studies, and we did describe the hypotheses to be tested in Study 2. But, we did not name the hypotheses of the earlier studies, and we did not identify a hypothesis for Study 2 as the "Harcum–Rosen hypothesis." This was admittedly a poor job of writing, and we accept the criticism as technically valid.

Next this evaluator asks with respect to Study 2:

What kind of "service" organization?

We thought that our description implied a civic service organization, similar in orientation to a garden club. We submit that a more detailed description is irrelevant, particularly because we were not investigating group differences.

Evaluator IV had the same problems with the presentation of our results from Study 2 as with Study 1, plus some different ones. He or she began with quoting our submission:

" . . . than the 100% claimed by Skinner . . . " seems *way out of line*! Author implies that Skinner believes 100% of people can ignore biases and make objective decisions. I think Skinner would acknowledge learned response patterns that would support author's "dignity" belief (e.g., religious teachings). Responses based upon all the biases mentioned previously are not inconsistent with learning theory and are identical to what author's predictions would be.

First, there is no convention in psychology, as far as we know, for dealing with a specific prediction of empirical results when the theoretical prediction is essentially 100% or 0%, as is true in Skinner's case. Surely, Skinner would never have predicted literally complete unanimity—nor probably would any other psychologist. The simple presence of variable error would suggest that the empirical prediction for a mean result should actually be less than 100%. Apparently, this evaluator would accept any value that Skinner would predict, so long as it was not too close to 100%.

In commenting on our discussion of Study 2, this evaluator says:

"This study clearly supports. . . . " I disagree. Author needs to re-port/conduct appropriate analyses; author must provide sufficient jus-tification for his/her hypothesis over alternative hypotheses (e.g., socially learned response patterns); and he/she must integrate the results into the current theoretical structure of the paper. Author does none of these. "We submit that a viable society. . . . " Define "viable"; and where is the justification for this sweeping conclusion?

These hypotheses tested in these studies did not involve the issue of whether the belief in intrinsic dignity was learned or innate. Our counterargument holds even if the belief is learned. If such a belief merely exists, regardless of its origin, we have refuted Skinner's argument. Therefore, the question of the source of the belief is not relevant in this context; it is simply a distraction.

We are not exactly sure what the evaluator means by saying that we have not integrated "the results into the current theoretical structure of the paper." We assume that he or she means by this comment that we have not related our results to our hypotheses. This we dispute, and document by quotations from our submission. Once more, our hypotheses were as follows: "that older persons are accorded intrinsic, unearned dignity, and also that dignity is augmented by voluntary prosocial behaviors and reduced by voluntary antisocial behaviors."

The first paragraph of the discussion includes the following conclusions: "that older adults also believe in voluntary control of behavior, and, moreover, that they employ this concept in differentially assigning dignity to individuals. These subjects also believe in intrinsic dignity at birth, which is therefore not contingent upon a person's ability to behave voluntarily."

We have discussed the potential definitional problem earlier in the book. Here, the evaluator is using what Harcum (1992) has called the "CQ (Carp & Quibble) Tactic." Authors do not bear responsibility for defining all of the words in their manuscripts when the meaning of the words can be readily determined by consulting a dictionary. There was nothing in our prose to indicate that we intended our use of the adjective "viable" to imply a technical term. We referred to a viable society because Skinner argued that the abolition of the concepts of freedom and dignity were important for *survival* of our society. Presumably, a surviving society is a viable one. We merely have stated the reverse philosophy. This point of view is not presented as a conclusion from our data. The justification for our belief was based on psychotherapy and social service. A thorough attempt at such justification would require a book-length discussion. Moreover, it would be a digression from the main point of the article.

We note that this same evaluator was more than a little distressed when he or she thought that our manuscript was "extremely condescending and is very offensive when applied to the aged and handicapped." Are we to believe that society is just as viable if we do *not* accord dignity to such people; and that this evaluator is supporting the dignity of such people only because it is the socially desirable response, or because of some other situational or conditional bias, and not because of some personal conviction?

Finally, Evaluator IV quotes and evaluates our conclusion for Study 2:

> Pg. 14: "Our belief, in agreement with many humanistic psychologists, is that the members of society have an innate predisposition to believe in internal intentional control of their own behavior." Just because individuals "believe" something does not make it so—compare litera-ture on illusory correlations and attributional biases (e.g., the funda-mental attribution error). And what about Lerner's just world hypothesis? It sounds like the same thing as author is proposing.
>
> "Moreover, we forecast, contrary to Skinner's prediction, that the belief in intrinsic human worth will be important, if not necessary, for the *survival of our species*" [emphasis added]. Wow! Back off this state-ment—it's a real s t r e t c h [*sic*]. If it must stay—justify it.

Of course, we know that beliefs can be true or false. We also understand the difference between true beliefs and knowledge. We are not claiming knowledge of an innate belief in intentional control of behavior. The factual issue of the article concerns whether society maintains certain beliefs, not whether these beliefs are true.

Our advocation of the concepts of freedom and dignity, as important for human survival, is not much of a stretch at all. Of course, we are not stretching to reach this opinion as a result of the data from these studies. Our belief is based on multifarious evidence provided by personal observation, by the written comments of persons such as this very evaluator in defending the handicapped, in the work of humanistic authors (e.g., Lewis, 1954), by the work of psychotherapists (e.g., May, 1965; Rogers, 1964), and by general literature search in psychology (e.g., Harcum, 1988, 1989). We cannot know the future, of course, but we certainly can forecast what will work for us on the basis of what seems to be working now. This idea of predicting what would be aids to survival of the culture on the basis of what seems to be working now was in fact advocated by Skinner (1971), although his conclusions were different, of course.

SUMMARY

We had submitted this paper to journals with a more applied focus, hoping that the practical nature of our study would be more valued. Obviously, that was not the way to eventual publication. Instead of evaluation, we received some sort of free-association protocol from these reviews based, first, on misunderstanding and, second, on the presumption that we did not know what we were doing.

5

Vignettes

The third submission had the same research goal, but yet again a different methodological approach. In two variations of the study, a hypothetical vignette described a prosocial or antisocial behavior performed under different environmental circumstances, representing different levels of voluntary control of the relevant behavior. The subjects scaled the degree of perceived voluntary control and rated the dignity of the actor. We presented a graph (Appendix C, Figure C.2) that described our hypotheses, indicating an increase in dignity with increasing voluntary control of prosocial behavior and a decrease in dignity with increasing voluntary control of antisocial behavior. The intercept of both functions was the same, and intentionally at an appreciable level above zero. We stated that both we and Skinner would agree on the hypotheses that proposed changes in perceived dignity with perceived voluntary control of both the prosocial and antisocial behavior. Our prediction of an intercept above zero, however, differed from Skinner's formulation.

The data from both studies indicated a positive level of dignity accorded to an actor who had no voluntary control over personal behavior, as well as the predicted increases for greater voluntary control of prosocial behavior and corresponding decreases for voluntary antisocial behavior. There was, therefore, a very gratifying overall correspondence between the data and theory.

This manuscript was rejected by six journals before eventual publication in a seventh journal (Harcum & Rosen, 1990a). The first submission is reproduced as Appendix C.

JOURNAL H

Evaluator I

This first evaluator for Journal H (the editor), while complimenting us for the value of our efforts, complained that we had not entirely completed our intended research program:

> I think that you are beginning to address a concept and issue that could become a very important one in the literature. An understanding of dignity, its antecedents, its implications, the conditions under which it is ascribed to people, and its place in implicit personality theory would certainly represent a worthwhile program of work. However, it seems to me that you have made only a small beginning. The work is really not advanced enough or conclusive enough for it to warrant publication in a major social psychology journal. . . .
>
> The biggest problem involves an understanding of the concept that you are trying to measure. It is not at all clear what you mean in a conceptual way by the term "dignity." In addition, your measure of this concept (whatever the concept is) raises questions about what subjects are actually inferring about the actor. Are you sure that you are measuring something different from morality, positivity of action, or even simple liking for the actor? If you really want to develop research aimed at clarifying perceptions of dignity, you will have to do a lot of groundwork designed to define and measure the construct. Construct validity is very necessary here—and you have not really attempted to establish it.
>
> The paper does not make much in the way of a theoretical contribution. It is not clear why the predictions are made or what the relevance is for understanding psychological processes or issues of social cognition. It is a simple demonstration study that at times appears more suited to philosophical rather than psychological issues. More theoretical ambition will be needed if this line of work is to be published in a major social psychology journal.

Basically, we were trying to establish a phenomenon. We could not consider ourselves as even having made a "small beginning" until we could say from data that society believes in unearned, given dignity. If society does not, the advantage may shift to Skinner and to a strict behavioristic approach for cultural design. Surely, issues of a more sophisticated construct validity are premature at this stage of our proposed research program. We assert that our measure of perceived dignity has a degree of content validity; it represented a written response indicating a belief in dignity. This is the level of the issue with Skinner. But the question of what society really believes is important; we intended to move our research toward answering that question. If a journal were interested only in publishing *theoretical* contributions in social cognition, our submission should have been returned immediately with that notation. Also, the editorial boards should explain such constraints in their information to prospective authors.

This evaluator shows other indications of not coming thoroughly to grips with our data:

> I don't much like within-subject designs of the kind that were used. Subjects can easily see the variables of interest and they respond in ways that may not reflect more natural processes of ascribing dignity.

The within-subject aspect of the design in Experiment 1 could have influenced the functional relationship, which was not at issue, but it would not have influenced the major issue—the intercept—except perhaps to foster the Skinnerian result. The same holds true for the demand characteristics, although of course one can *never* fully discount the possibility of such effects. Apparently, this evaluator missed the point that Experiment 2 did not use a within-subject design for the variables of interest; different subjects read prosocial and antisocial stories. Therefore, the comment reflected insufficient care in reading the submission and a failure to check comments for accuracy or relevance.

This evaluator's next point did hit upon the greatest weakness of the study:

> In a related way, inferring dignity about a person on the basis of a single behavior seems silly. Dignity is established by many acts over time, and your method oversimplifies what people do in ascribing a quality such as dignity in the real world.

We did recognize this as a problem, and tried to reduce its effects in the second experiment. Surely, it is a fascinating question to ask to what extent subjects are willing to make distinctions, for example, between judgments of credit or blame as caused by situational forces or dispositional characteristics of the actor (Shaver, 1987).

It hardly becomes an evaluator who purports not to understand the concept of dignity, or what fosters the perception of it, to assert that "Dignity is established by many acts over time." That conception is, to be sure, a personal view of dignity, "whatever the concept is." If an evaluator does not know what dignity is, how does he or she know how it is established?

At a commonsense level, everyone seems to know what dignity or worth is. This was apparently the level of the concept in Skinner's formulation, as was entirely appropriate.

We expected that our subjects, like this evaluator, had personal concepts of dignity and the factors that produced it, and that they could answer questions based on that concept, whatever it was to them. The purpose of our study was to disprove, with data, the unsupported opinion of this evaluator that "dignity is established by many acts over time," as Skinner claimed. The simple assertion of a personal faith to the contrary hardly seems a valid basis for impeaching our laboratory data.

Our subjects might not have had a scientifically acceptable concept of dignity or worth, but they were still quite willing to make judgments and pronouncements about their own personal conceptions of it, just as was the case with several evaluators. Subjects, and several evaluators, including this one, were quite willing to report on what basis they accorded dignity, which was precisely what we had asked them to do. In fact, the subjects reported beliefs that were contrary to those Skinner imputed to them as members of society.

Evaluator I for Journal H continued as follows:

> I was confused about several of your statements. You claim to be evaluating Skinner's second assertion. However, I don't see that your study addresses the issue of whether freedom is a barrier to progress for a science of human behavior. At least the study does not do this in a very direct way.

We were not trying to show that freedom is or is not a barrier to the progress of science. We were merely trying to refute Skinner's argument for why a *belief* in freedom is a barrier to scientific progress. These issues are definitely not the same.

Next this evaluator complains:

> I also did not understand your comment on page 15 that demand characteristics probably were not a factor because they would have been equally effective in the two studies. Why? The changes in procedure might well have increased issues of social desirability or demands.

Our contention was that we could not reasonably identify bases on which the demand characteristics would differ in the two studies. Of course, some of the changes could have increased facilitating effects of demand characteristics. To produce a valid criticism, evaluators must offer more than just a suggestion of a possibility; they must show how the procedural changes could produce such an effect on demand characteristics. In fact, Experiment 1 used a completely within-subject design, which this evaluator did not like for reasons of demand characteristics. Experiment 2, using basically a between-subject design, produced a stronger predicted effect. Therefore, some evidence indicates that a reduction of demand-characteristics effects produces a greater effect. In other words, *demand characteristics tend to support Skinner's predictions—not ours.*

The next concern of this evaluator involved the exposition and presentation of the studies:

The method and results sections were rather thin. Details were left out, and only minimal statistical analyses were done.

If true, these were apparently not fatal flaws. Presumably, such problems could be handled in a revision.

This evaluator then pointed out that other literature could have been cited:

All three reviewers note your failure to relate this work to previous research on attributions and moral evaluation. They cite several lines of work that would be important for you to consider. Because it is not clear what your measure is really measuring, there is some question about what your findings add to this previous work.

We would accept this criticism if any evaluator had been able to cite some study that provided survey data for a belief in intrinsic dignity. In the many evaluations of our several submissions, none ever did. We were not adding to previous findings at all—merely doing the basic work that the other studies, if they were in fact relevant, simply overlooked or assumed.

This evaluator summarized his reactions as follows:

In short, this line of work has a way to go before it makes the kind of contribution that we usually look for in a [this journal] piece. The additional work that has been suggested will not be easy, but I hope that you will be encouraged to take it on.

This type of comment is what Harcum (1992) called the "Pink Ribbon Tactic": The work is not publishable until all the answers have been tied together in the figurative neat package with a pink ribbon. Our contention is that we did resolve an issue of some practical importance for psychology. Other important issues in the area have admittedly not been addressed in our studies. This editorial criticism may not be so much a valid indictment of these studies as it is of the neophobic editorial policies of some journals.

Evaluator II

Evaluator II for Journal H began, as have many others, on a short-lived positive note:

> The correspondence between the figure that provided predictions and the figures containing results had a certain elegance to it.

This evaluator nevertheless seems not to like this research, but does not know why. He or she indicates a failure to understand its purpose:

> The basis for the theoretical predictions is unclear, and I suspect that if what's in the paper were clarified I wouldn't buy it. In particular, I don't think the research or findings have very much to do with the material from Skinner (except for the "y-intercept" issue). The use of material from Berger might be more relevant. However the authors didn't really provide an analysis here, relying instead on quotations and paraphrases of Berger. Moreover, a close look at the main Berger quote on p. 6 raises questions of whether the issues Berger is addressing in that quote are really the same ones as those of the present paper.

We are given the impression that this evaluator will defend Skinner, come what may, regardless of our data or arguments. He or she is not sure what we are saying, but, in any case, is predisposed against "buying" it. This reviewer does not understand that the intercept issue *is* the issue of the paper. Proof of an intercept above zero dignity is all that we asked him or her to "buy." Therefore, what some evaluators thought was trivially obvious, this evaluator does not want to accept, even if he or she was truly certain of what we proposed.

The quote from Berger (1970) merely illustrated a belief in intrinsic dignity from the literature of dignity. It is just one of the many that could just as easily have been quoted.

The review continued:

> I wonder whether there isn't an inherent contradiction in the authors' analysis. On the one hand, people are held to have a bias toward a belief in the basic dignity or worth of the individual. On the other hand, if a person does a harmful act for which he or she is culpable, perceived

dignity may go into the negative region. The question is whether something as deep as the perceived dignity of another person really can be modified so dramatically by observation of a morally undesirable act. Even the most hardened criminal has rights in our society (e.g., no cruel or unusual punishment is allowed) which derive from something like a conception of *unconditional* human dignity.

Again, the data that we presented to answer the question we posed are disregarded, in favor of a criticism that we did not answer a different question. Then, our empirical answer is overridden by a simple assertion that the evaluator has known the facts all along, apparently from his or her own casual observation. We assert that any difference between unconditional dignity and unearned dignity would be trivial in the context of this research. Apparently, the intuition of this evaluator is to be believed, but our data, which achieves the same conclusion, are not to be believed because of some alleged statistical or methodological weaknesses. "Unconditional human dignity" is just about the exact concept that we had in mind. And, as the evaluator said, this gratuitous accordance of worth to a perpetrator of heinous crimes is probably precisely what prevents society from exacting an eye for an eye. The point is: Skinner did not consider this factor in his formulation.

It is easy to become confused about whether this evaluator is for us or against us, theoretically and scientifically. Clearly, however, he or she is apparently against us concerning possible publication of our submission, as the next comment indicates:

This logical quandary involving situational variability of dignity may be part of the reason why social psychological researchers typically consider "evaluation" or "moral evaluation" instead of "dignity." It's part of the reason why I think the present study probably is about evaluation or moral evaluation, not dignity.

Because the construct of "perceived dignity" is an unfamiliar one to social psychology, it would require more theoretical and empirical analysis before a study of this kind would belong in [this journal]. Whatever "perceived dignity" may be—and it never was defined by the authors—I doubt that the measures get at it. Upon examining the "dignity measure" (see last para. on p. 8), a more appropriate label for the conceptual variable captured by the measure seems to be "moral evaluation of the actor."

There is a literature and theory concerned with moral evaluation in relation to degree of voluntary control. Primarily I have in mind Bernard Weiner's research (Weiner & Peter ?) covered in the theory and review papers he has written (and, I assume, in his recent book on attribution). There is some relation of the present work also to work by Shaver (1970 or so) and Walster (1966), but it is probably not as central as Weiner's work. To some degree I am agreeing with the author's statement on p. 14 that "attribution research assesses culpability or credit for a given instance of behavior" when I question whether Shaver and Walster are directly relevant here. But I don't think the work by Weiner or similar to Weiner's can be dismissed in this way.

My opening comments notwithstanding, the handling of the data was superficial. Where the authors said "clearly" there is a relationship between variables (p. 10), I wanted to see some kind of a statistic (e.g., to know whether the variances around the means plotted in the figures were enormous, etc.) Where the authors said "the averaging process . . . virtually precludes a value at zero" it wasn't clear to me why something like a t-test of the significance of the mean difference from zero wasn't possible in Study 1. In Study 2 we're not told the test used on p. 13 (though I believe that a 70–30 split with the sample size of the cells of Study 2 involved in the comparison reaches .01). In several places where the authors refer to the shape of the curves it wasn't clear to me why fit-to-curve parameters couldn't be presented.

Our understanding of statistics is that they are a tool for helping scientists make decisions when the data are not clear, that is, when there is a lot of overlap between the data points. This data seemed clear enough to us and even the reviewer suggests apparent statistical significance. Furthermore, this argument recalls the argument from the previous chapter about doing statistical tests using zero as the Skinnerian position. The earlier reviewer had commented on how it was unfair to Skinner to demand that zero be his predicted value when clearly there was a lot of variation among people.

We said we did not want to make an issue about the shape of the curves. Curve shape was certainly not an issue between us and Skinner. Skinner implied only that the function began at the origin and was monotonic. Perhaps, later, curve shapes will become crucially important for something, but to raise such a question at this point is simply a distraction from the purpose of the study.

Next this evaluator complains:

I didn't find the arguments at the opening of the "General Discussion" to be persuasive. The difference between the way the questions were posed in Studies 1 and 2 struck me as quite subtle and not crucial as the authors believe. Of course, the authors could prove me wrong on this if they had some data on the point; lacking the data, it's my hunch against theirs.

If the authors want to pursue work on the topic of "perceived dignity," my suggestion would be to focus on two issues: the nature of perceived dignity and determinants of perceived dignity such as situational events, causal attributions, and individual differences (having to do with one's overall orientation of the worth of others, as given by one's religious, moral, or philosophical bent—not merely social desirability as the authors considered briefly). The lack of construct validation of the measure of perceived dignity is much more acute here than is the case in the typical [this journal]-type study, because of the kinds of theoretical issues the authors want to address (where is the y-intercept, etc.). For example, the authors haven't adequately supported their primary conclusion that people "accord some intrinsic positive dignity to persons who have not earned it through voluntary praiseworthy deeds," (p. 15) because I don't know if "intrinsic positive dignity" has been measured. Moreover, I don't yet see advantages of working on a dependent variable called "dignity" when "moral evaluation," or, more simply, "evaluation" (including liking) are available—unless the theorizing about the nature of perceived dignity progresses a good deal further.

We never intended to measure "intrinsic positive dignity." Once again, we have an evaluator who will not accept our research conclusions—that people believe in intrinsic dignity—and then blithely asserts his or her own personal belief in intrinsic dignity, although he or she prefers a different name for it.

Again, we had an evaluator who told us that he or she did not understand what the word "dignity" meant, and then asserted that, in any case, it was the same as some other concept. We ask the reader to imagine with us what reviewers of a manuscript would have said if we had asked our subjects to rate "moral evaluation," and then contended that we had refuted Skinner's ideas about the relation between freedom and dignity. Although we actually had used the same word as Skinner, some evaluators had asserted that we had data pertaining to something different. It had to be different, according to the evaluators, or otherwise our data would have contradicted Skinner's classic formulation.

This evaluator, as previous ones, worried about the definition of the concept of dignity, and then finally defined it as simply a positive regard *that is earned*. Hence, he or she sees obvious relevance to certain other previous work. If the relevant concept were some kind of "evaluation" response, it would most certainly have to be based primarily, or perhaps exclusively, on voluntary performance of prosocial and antisocial behaviors. The very nature of the alleged unearned dignity is that it is *not* the result of an evaluation of a person's behavior, but that it is bestowed as an act of grace by one person or another. It is not an evaluation, but a *valuation*.

This evaluator's criticism supports that of several others concerning literature that we did not cite. Our judgment was that these substantial bodies of literature in social psychology were not sufficiently relevant for citation in our reports of the empirical research. This criticism of our presentation is ironic, because Skinner's assertions about the relations between freedom and dignity had, to the best of our knowledge, remained unchallenged on the basis of empirical evidence by social psychologists for almost 20 years. We must acknowledge, of course, that previous attempts at the challenge could have been made, but never were passed into the archives of public knowledge by the gatekeepers of the science. Other less persevering authors might have given up the attempt to publish similar arguments and findings. Perhaps some earlier pioneers will come forward after this book is published. Oddly enough, this alleged wealth of prior evidence in social psychology is now cited for the purpose of attacking the empirical research that refutes Skinner's speculative formulation. The alleged problems in defining dignity are at least as applicable to Skinner's initial argument as they are to our current counterargument. An additional irony is the fact that Skinner's argument, despite the obvious lack of empirical support, survived for so long without a published empirical challenge. Nevertheless, when we did raise an empirical challenge, we encountered a most rigorous scrutiny of our methodology and contrary evidence.

Evaluator III

That the third evaluator also did not understand the point of the study was obvious from the following comments:

How (and whether) people attribute dignity to others is certainly an appropriate topic for investigation, but the authors' treatment of this topic can hardly be considered a breakthrough. What the authors essentially have shown is that a truck driver who smashes into a school bus, killing 33 children on board, is not admired very much, especially if he is judged to have had voluntary control over this behavior. On the other hand, if the truck driver voluntarily averts this disaster by driving over a cliff, thereby killing himself but saving the children, he is seen as a praiseworthy person.

Aside from representing perhaps the most painfully obvious "findings" I have ever encountered, these data seem only tangentially relevant to the more profound issues of "freedom and dignity" with which the authors are ostensibly concerned. Establishing agreed-upon, precise definitions of such concepts, not to mention clarifying the relationships among them, has proven elusive in philosophical as well as psychological circles. To equate "dignity" operationally with a list of trait adjectives in this research does little to clarify matters.

We could not imagine, in our most pessimistic moments, receiving a larger array of such nonrelevant comments. Authors deserve at least to be given the feeling that an evaluator took the time to read their manuscript with reasonable care. If our writing were incomprehensible, presumably the figures presenting the hypotheses were not.

The "painfully obvious 'findings' " were, as we have said, not an issue between us and Skinner or presumably anyone else in the scientific or lay community. The empirical data were needed to verify through laboratory research these assumptions before the research program could move forward. Painfully obvious though these results may be, nevertheless the coherence of these results redounds to the credit of our methodology, which has been so thoroughly disdained. These results were in fact "tangentially relevant" to the main purpose of the study. The evaluator should have understood this.

The shape and slope of these functions are clearly secondary to the location of their intercepts. We can cite about two dozen evaluators who would deny that the exact location of the intercept should be painfully obvious to anyone. The comments of this evaluator actually provide neat anecdotal evidence for the validity of our method. Obviously, this presumedly sophisticated researcher did not pick up on the point—although it was even explained—that the main purpose of the study was to determine the location of the intercept in the dignity-voluntary choice relationships. Therefore, the social desirability of indicating the intercept on the function would not have been a factor in responding. Surely, therefore, not all of our unsophisticated subjects would have been able to interpret the study well enough to have incorporated a social desirability basis for responding. We believe that the importance of the social-desirability issue has been overestimated.

This evaluator, as did many others, regrets that our research program is not further along:

If anything, the authors seem to be tackling issues of choice and responsibility, and with respect to a very special set of circumstances at that. With this in mind, the authors would be well-advised to become familiar with the fairly substantial literatures devoted to attributions of choice, freedom, and responsibility (e.g., Harvey, 1976; Shaver, 1975; Steiner, 1972; Walster, 1976; etc.). As work in these areas commonly addresses issues of outcome valence, it would seem to readily subsume the data presented in this ms. In the oft-cited study by Walster (1966), for example, subjects' attribution of responsibility was strongly influenced by the amount of damage done, independent of the mitigating circumstances surrounding the act.

The authors might also check the work on impression formation, trait attribution, and the like, since they are basically concerned with evaluations of the truck driver. They would find, for example, that it is not unusual for people to "accord some intrinsic positive dignity to persons who have not earned it through voluntary praiseworthy deeds" (p. 15). Stated differently, most models relevant to impression formation assume a baseline (i.e., no information) evaluation that is slightly positive rather than neutral. (I must confess I was surprised by the above-neutral ratings for the truck driver in Experiment II who was described (p. 9 middle paragraph) as routinely killing busloads of children.)

The strong point of the study is precisely the *prediction* that members of society would accord positive dignity, even to the perpetrator of blameworthy acts, if the acts were beyond the voluntary control of the actor. That is exactly what our theoretical figure *predicted*, and our *data* revealed. We, too, think that this is *not* an obvious point, and thus is worthy of something more than an off-hand expression of surprise by an evaluator, along with a recommendation for suppression of publication. If the literature that this evaluator considered relevant to our study spoke decisively to the issue of the intercept, he or she would have thought that this result was painfully obvious also. This evaluator is cavalier in suggesting that some corpus of literature "would seem to readily subsume" our data. If this evaluator knew of such data, he or she should by all means have cited it. We find it strange that there is so much relevant data in the social psychology literature on the issue we have raised, some of which allegedly subsumes our results, yet so many evaluators of our research would not accept our results and conclusions. We cannot help but feel that something less than ideal science is happening here.

This reviewer seems to be stringing together comments off the top of his or her head. We presume that most of the literature to which the evaluator refers is based on "outcome valence," or evaluations, of specific behaviors in various contexts, and is therefore not relevant to the hypothesis that we wanted most to test.

Evaluator IV

The fourth evaluator for Journal H was concerned about our methods and statistics:

> Although the results of the study are potentially interesting, I have serious reservations about the manuscript which keep me from recommending it for publication. To begin with, the method section and results section are too cryptically presented. I simply found that there was insufficient detail in the method section to allow me to evaluate the experiments carefully. For example, what was the range of circumstances manipulated in the stories? We are only given one example of the six manipulated levels. A similar problem emerged in the results section. Few statistical tests were performed, and when they were performed, it is difficult for the reader to determine which specific tests were used. For example, although the authors assure us that the results from Study I provide some support for the hypothesis, only informal summaries of the statistical tests are reported in the manuscript. Similarly, in Study II only two tests are reported. In the first of these the authors report that significantly more of the dignity ratings (70%) are above zero rather than below zero. This seems an indirect test of the hypothesis at best. Second, they report that "If one collapses the data for the three Circumstances closest to zero voluntary control for the blame stories, the difference from zero is again significant ($p < .01$), and even more convincing." But here I have problems determining what the meaning of this analysis is, given that the studies apparently failed to create situations in which the protagonist was seen as having no voluntary control. According to my reading of Figures 3 and 4, all protagonists were perceived as having some degree of control over their fate. Therefore, to accept the interpretation that the authors put forward, I must assume that the prosocial and antisocial curves will not cross and that the curves will flatten out as choice approaches zero. I am unwilling to make these assumptions simply because the authors tell me that "It would not be reasonable to expect the two functions to cross, or for the blame curve to decrease with less voluntary control" (pg. 12–13).

Although we did not see the necessity of presenting our six circumstances of the vignette, we could have added this. The fact that the subjects themselves rated the degree of voluntary choice should be of greater relevance than how this evaluator himself or herself would have rated them. The specific context is not crucial to the interpretation, because the intercept, rather than the curve shape, was the important issue.

Of course, the authors did not expect the readers to accept an assumption simply on their word. We expected—naively, it seems now—each reader to consider for himself or herself whether such an assumption made sense. It does not seem even reasonable to argue that a perpetrator of an apparently voluntary blameworthy act would be accorded *more* dignity than a person who performed the *same* antisocial act apparently *involuntarily*. Skinner's (1971) text clearly implies a monotonic function. How could one reasonably interpret an empirical reversal of the trend in either function?

That the curve for blameworthy behaviors *ever* achieves a positive value for dignity is strong evidence against Skinner's formulation. That result cannot be dismissed by an evaluator who wantonly suggests that the curve might show an inversion to pass down through the origin. If such a worse-case scenario were to occur, we would still have a person who voluntarily performed antisocial behaviors, but yet is still accorded a positive level of dignity.

That the subjects virtually refuse to perceive a level of zero personal choice is also strong evidence against Skinner's practical argument against freedom and dignity. Apparently very few people are seriously concerned about the emergence of a completely successful science in a deterministic world that could obviate the concept of human freedom.

The next objection by this evaluator is another quibble:

> Even if I were willing to make such assumptions, however, I would still have reservations about the adequacy of the measurement techniques involved in the author's procedures. In most studies relying upon bipolar scales, the investigators are interested in either directional differences or relative differences between conditions. Rarely do we assume that the observed value has meaning independent of the experimental context. But this is exactly what we must assume if we are to believe that the finding of a positive intercept on the y-axis is evidence of the presence of perceived dignity.

The issue between us and Skinner concerns whether society manifests a belief in intrinsic dignity. The strength of the belief may be important to some issue raised later in our research program, but it certainly is not relevant at this point. This evaluator is simply importing a false issue. The statistical significance of our results strongly validates the adequacy of our measurement.

This evaluator continues an obvious search for some basis of criticism:

I think that the manuscript would profit from a closer link to the attribution literature. The research on the fundamental attribution error would seem to be highly relevant to the authors' thesis. In both the authors' own work and the FAE we see that people appear to make inferences (in the author's case the inferences are about dignity whereas in the FAE case the inferences are about causality) even in conditions in which the behavior of the actor is highly constrained.

We did not formulate Skinner's hypothesis; we were merely trying to test it. Several areas of research, such as attribution of blame, are certainly related to this line of research. But such research is not helpful in discussing the specific goals of this study. The attribution of credit or blame involves a perception or assessment of performance in terms of situational or dispositional factors. These factors are surely important in the functional relationships between voluntary choice and dignity under various circumstances, but not in an obvious way related to the issue of the y-intercept as a measure of the intrinsic dignity. These other literatures will probably reveal some common relations to perceived dignity with further study. But, as this evaluator says, they are not the same.

There is a critical difference between the concept of intrinsic dignity and the concept of fundamental attribution error. The proposed equivalence between them had been suggested to us long before we submitted our first manuscript on this issue for publication. The fundamental attribution error is, as the evaluator says, about a dispositional cause of behavior. The intrinsic dignity, however, is not contingent on the proper behavior, whether the cause is perceived as dispositional or environmental. Therefore, this evaluator would actually have to make a case for the relevance of the fundamental attribution error.

JOURNAL I

Evaluator I

The first evaluator for Journal I (the editor) responded as follows:

I have enclosed the reviewer's comments concerning your manuscript. You may find the evaluations helpful if you decide to submit it to another journal. Based on my own reading of the manuscript and the reviews, the main problem with the manuscript in its current form is that it does not address the most relevant literatures on the general topic (including the large literature on attribution theory and research, as noted by

Reviewer A) and does not present clearly the logic and design of the study (see Reviewer A, paragraph 2, and Reviewer B, points 1–3). The actor-observer distinction is critical to your research problem as is the literature on the use of vignettes. In sum, the topic is interesting but the article has serious weaknesses. One reviewer suggests that a research note for [another named journal] might be forged from this manuscript if a revision could clarify the issues raised in these reviews.

Because these comments are basically endorsements of the reviewers' comments, they will be discussed in the reports from the reviewers. The suggestion to submit elsewhere is noteworthy; if we were journal shopping, such behavior was encouraged.

Evaluator II

The second evaluator of this submission for Journal I agrees about the interest of our study:

The authors have addressed an interesting question regarding the effects of the voluntary control of praiseworthy and blameworthy behaviors on judgements of esteem and dignity. As the authors note, this is a central point in B. F. Skinner's speculations in *Beyond freedom and dignity*. For Skinner dignity derives from situations in which people are seen as controlling their own behavior.

Although the two experiments conducted are too casually described (the variables and their measures should be more formally and clearly stated, the conditions the various groups of subjects received should be listed), they do shed light in different ways on the central issue. Clearly, at least in the response to vignettes, perceived degree of voluntary control does explain a very considerable amount of the variation in estimates of esteem, usefulness, and worth (Experiment 1) and dignity (Experiment 2).

It would seem from the above that this is a study supporting Skinner's contentions, but the authors would have it otherwise. For reasons that escape me, they interpret Skinner's somewhat casual remarks to mean that *absolutely all* a person's dignity derives from personal control. The key remarks by Skinner are the following: "Any evidence that a person's behavior may be attributed to external circumstances seems to threaten his dignity or worth. We are not inclined to give a person credit for achievements which are in fact due to forces over which he has no control."

For me, at least, words like "seems to threaten" and "are not inclined" imply a large or substantial effect, but hardly an absolute one. If this interpretation is the most reasonable, then the difference between Skinner and the authors disappears and the polemic upon which the paper is structured also vanishes. This paper might be rewritten as a research note in support of Skinner's prediction, but in that form it would probably be more suitable for a journal such as [a subsidized journal].

The most interesting point of this commentary is that the evaluator seems to agree with us about the importance of the issue that we have raised, but apparently he or she mistakes what the actual issue is. The evaluator seems to think that the "effects of the voluntary control of praiseworthy and blame-worthy behavior on judgements of esteem and dignity" is the issue, whereas the "casual remarks" of Skinner about the proposed relation between freedom and dignity merely give rise to chimerical problems on our part.

We have tried to avoid semantic arguments, but feel that we are on solid ground with this one and should not let it stand. As we quoted above, Skinner said that progress in science threatens to "destroy" the concept of dignity. Given that synonyms for destroy are "put an end to," "seal the doom of," "blot out," "erase," "delete," "exterminate," "annihilate," "eradicate," and so forth, Skinner's meaning does not seem to be semantically ambiguous. But, semantics aside, our point is simply this: Skinner had no argument at all if progress in science is not seen as capable of destroying completely and absolutely the concept of dignity. Otherwise, society would have no need to oppose the progress of science to save the concept of dignity. The context of his book supports the unambiguous meaning of the words.

The issue with this evaluator concerns who is constructing the straw man. Again, we are presented with the idea that Skinner built his classic book on a casual remark, and used it simply as another opportunity to present his familiar metaphysical thesis. We vehemently deny this. Once again, if society still perceives some positive dignity when voluntary control is zero, then a science that threatens to eliminate freedom (voluntary control of behavior) does not threaten to eliminate dignity, and there was no point to Skinner's classic book.

Nott (1977) agreed with our reading of Skinner. As she pointed out, Skinner showed his concern for the importance of society's beliefs in freedom and dignity by writing his book to urge the *abolition* of the concepts from our thinking. The fact that the perceived dignity changes as the perceived personal choice changes is not an argument against the usefulness of the concept of perceived dignity unless the function intercepts the ordinate at zero, representing such abolition. The assertion that the intercept on the ordinate does not have to be "absolutely" zero does not help Skinner; therefore it is a pseudoscientific red herring. The existence of *some* dignity, which is significantly different from zero in the absence of credit dignity, means that the concept would still be viable even if all genetic and environmental causes of behavior were known, and strict determinism were true.

Evaluator III

This evaluator begins:

I believe that it is interesting and can be profitable for social scientists to re-consider Skinner's ideas from *Beyond freedom and dignity*. The present work goes a bit of a way in that direction. But it falters, I think, in its neglect of substantial literatures germane to perceived freedom and responsibility. It also falters in its exclusive focus on observer perceptions (Skinner's account has more to say about actor perceptions than about observers, or at least as much). Overall, not only do I believe that these matters need to be rectified before publication in a major forum such as [this journal], but also I think that a lot of refinement is necessary in terms of design and analysis of data.

How is the work remiss in its address of pertinent literature in building its case? No word is noted about highly relevant literatures on perceived responsibility, perceived blame, and perceived freedom. The blame concept is directly discussed (with apparent hypothesis), but attention should be given to works such as Kelly Shaver's recent *Attribution of Blame* (Springer-Verlag, 1985). There is extensive literature on the attribution of responsibility, much of it using the well-criticized hypothetical situation method used here. That work started in the late 60s with Walster's well-known study arguing that severe accidents led to greater attributions of responsibility to the participants. There are now many qualifiers—as well as a body of work on determinants, appropriate dependent variables. . . . Further, there is literature on the determinates of perceived freedom starting with a chapter by Steiner in the Berkowitz *Advances in Experimental Social Psychology* series; the au. is referred to a couple of 75 JPSP articles by Harvey and colleagues discussing determinates of perceived freedom and in 31, 22–28, 1975, directly testing an idea from Skinner's BF&D book. While noting omissions in reference in literature, I should note too that the au. might read on the literature on attribution theory and research that has now gone well beyond a concern only with singular acts, or behaviors (p. 14 discussion point).

See for example, 1984 *Annual Review of Psychology* review of attribution work over last 5–7 years.

Importantly, this literature that isn't cited at all also has evolved into interesting considerations of actor-observer differences in various perceptions. We now have quite a bit of information about the conditions under which As and Os differ. Such considerations are quite relevant to the present work because if one reads Skinner's thesis carefully, he is clearly focusing on the illusory nature of the *actor's* perceptions. I believe that the present work needs to incorporate that fact into a defensible design if we are *to begin* to find something relevant to Skinner's ideas.

I have other more fundamental concerns with this work, as the report reads now:

1. It isn't clear what the independent or dependent variables are in the two studies. One has to guess from the figures. It isn't even clear that a direct probe of perceived dignity was carried out (it appears that related traits and freedom were more clearly tapped).

2. No statistical test evidence is presented. What are we to assume about the curves presented in the figure? That they differ simply because they are drawn to reflect different trajectories?

No concern is advanced about the representativeness of the vignettes used. As noted above, that area has been the scene of much discussion in related literatures. Do the authors believe that their procedure is generalizable to all types of instances of observed acts pertinent to attributions of dignity and so on?

The difference between the Skinnerian view and our own view, illustrated in our figure that described the hypothesis, was only in the intercept at the zero level of perceived voluntary control. Therefore, the stated goal of the study was to refute Skinner's unqualified generalization about the intercept. The scope of an entire book certainly provided space for Skinner to have stated exceptions to his formulations, if indeed he believed there were any.

This evaluator is completely wrong in saying that Skinner's formulation is about an actor's perceptions. It is about an observer's perceptions. An observer makes assumptions about whether an actor's behaviors are voluntary or forced, and whether the behavior is prosocial or antisocial. Partly on the basis of these interpretations, and partly on the basis of some nonbehavioral attributes, the observer accords some level of positive or negative dignity to the actor.

It seems rather strange to question the representativeness of our data when Skinner's unqualified generalization was based on *no* data. Skinner bragged that his sweeping generalization was not even based on casual observation.

Our research situation did not have to be representative of some norm of situations to be encountered in life and to which attitudes about the basis of dignity could be assessed. To be valid, would our vignette have to represent a situation that was likely to occur anywhere on a daily basis? It certainly could happen, and be reported in a newspaper any day. Would this evaluator disbelieve the story if it were reported in a newspaper? Because the story is realistic, the response to it reasonably reflects the beliefs of a segment of our population. Because Skinner's formulation permitted no exception, any reasonable counterexample should suffice.

Our comments about missing literature remain the same. Although we had subjects rate perceived degree of voluntary control of behavior, these ratings did not relate to a controversial issue in our studies. The relevant point is that the subjects indicated positive levels of dignity even when they, as subjects, judged the actor in the vignettes to have some freedom when he committed a blameworthy act.

The other literatures are not relevant to the issues in question because we were not studying the determinants of perceived freedom. We did show that, when the subjects judged a person to have freedom, and presumably responsibility, the person's dignity was augmented or decreased if the behavior was prosocial or antisocial, respectively. Beyond that, even when there was minimal perceived freedom, some positive dignity was accorded. The crucial question remains: Is there prior data to document such belief in intrinsic dignity? We do not believe that the attribution literature cited as important by this or other evaluators speaks to either of the above points. For example, the purpose of the Harvey, Harris, and Barnes (1975) study, mentioned by this evaluator, was described in the authors' abstract:

> An experiment was conducted to investigate actor-observer differences in the perceptions of responsibility and freedom. . . . As predicted, observers attributed more responsibility and freedom to actors the more severe the consequence of their behavior, but actors attributed less responsibility and freedom to themselves the more severe the consequence of their behavior. (p. 22)

We fail to see how these processes of defensive attribution shed any light on the issues under discussion. The evaluators simply assert that these data are relevant, without a suggestion about some basis for connection.

This evaluator contended that the article by Harvey and Harris (1975) was another relevant example. The evaluator believed that the case for relevance was strong because it was a study "directly testing an idea from Skinner's BF&D book." This would presumably make a rather strong negative impression against our work if the action editor were not familiar with the details of the specific study. The relation to Skinner is not noted in the abstract of the article, but the following excerpt from the introduction of the article describes the relation to Skinner:

> When an individual is making a decision about which of a set of actions he will take, the degree to which he thinks he will feel control over his behavior in the future situation (i.e., in the situation which results from his decision) should be directly related to his perception of choice in making the decision. In this connection, it should be noted that in his book *Beyond Freedom and Dignity* (1971), Skinner suggests that people often fail to recognize the environmental controls over their behavior when it is not under aversive reinforcement contingencies (which implies that they feel personal control) and, significantly, that this lack of recognition is associated with a sense of freedom. In the present study, it was hypothesized that expectancy about feelings of internal control over own behavior in a future situation will be greater when the selection is to be made from positively valenced actions than when it is to be made from negatively valenced actions. (p. 102)

Other than the citation of Skinner, we see no relationship between this project and our research. Further, the relevance of their results to Skinner is not mentioned in their abstract:

> The results supported the hypothesis that both perceived choice and expectancy about feelings of internal control are greater when a decision involves positive options than when it involves negative options. The results also provided evidence for the predicted effect of difference in attractiveness upon perceived choice when the decision involved positive options but not when it involved negative options. (p. 101)

The task of relating this article to ours in a single report of empirical research would probably require far more creativity than we could muster. Even if this were possible, such importations of unnecessary material would be contrary to good practices of scientific writing.

With respect to the relevance in general of attribution theory to our research, we confess to continuing bewilderment. We are at a loss to understand, for example, how an examination of the Harvey and Weary (1984) review of the literature could, or should, have been reasonably or profitably incorporated into our research report. Therefore, we dispute the claim of this evaluator that such literature is "highly relevant," and that its omission is a serious flaw in our article.

JOURNAL J

Evaluator I

The only evaluator for Journal J was the editor, who deemed the submission not to be appropriate for his journal:

> Without making a judgment on the merits of the article, its contents are outside the area normally covered by [this journal]. To be specific, the [journal's] scope is limited to the fields of general experimental psychology.

We must, of course, defer to the editor in interpreting the scope of his own publication.

JOURNAL K

Evaluator I

The first evaluator for Journal K (the editor) responded as follows:

> As you can see both reviewers were quite critical of the paper and recommended rejection. Their prime concerns were for the need to place the investigation in a broader theoretical context. . . . You are working in a very interesting area and I wish you good fortune with your research.

We quote this evaluator primarily for the expression of interest in the area of research. The specific comment about the relation to a broader theoretical context will be discussed with respect to the reports of the individual reviewers.

Evaluator II

The second evaluator for Journal K stated:

> The problem with this study is that it is tied to a theoretical position (Skinner's) that it really does not test. Skinner says that the average person is misguided in assuming that people have control over their own behavior. It doesn't really make sense to try to quantify this by *varying* voluntary control in a story. The authors should start from their data and ask, "what have we found?" I think the answer to this question is that people give more credit to prosocial acts, and more blame to

antisocial acts that they believe are under voluntary control.

This is not surprising. Heider discussed it in 1958, as have many studies in the literature in social cognition (attribution of responsibility) and neoPiagetian intention vs. consequences.

Once more, an evaluator has missed the whole point of our research, and then tried to discuss the relevance to certain published research. We did of course state our agreement with Skinner that perceived dignity is augmented by perceived voluntary prosocial behaviors and diminished by perceived voluntary antisocial behaviors. We used Figure C.2 in Appendix C to present our complete hypotheses. Although our prose may not have been sufficiently clear, this cannot be said of our theoretical figure. We also presented our understanding of Skinner's argument, which is reproduced as Figure C.1 in Appendix C, in order to provide a graphic comparison of our two hypotheses. A competent professional would not have misinterpreted these graphs if he or she was paying even minimal attention to them.

The predicted changes of perceived dignity with changes in perceived intentionality were not an issue in our research, as the theoretical figures show. As one evaluator of this submission, mentioned above, characterized the findings of changes in dignity with changes in voluntary control, they are "painfully obvious." Apparently, these results tended to distract the evaluators from the true purpose of our research. A further discussion, and a provision of a fuller historical perspective, would probably be more distracting. Obviously, this evaluator was simply cavalier, relying only on a cursory scanning of our text and apparently completely ignoring our theoretical figure. Such negligence should be confronted by someone—preferably someone with authority and power. The editor did not choose to do so, and the authors could not.

This evaluator was concerned about our inability to obtain ratings of low voluntary control:

Unfortunately, the key data, for the author's predictions at low levels of estimated voluntary control, are missing.

We cannot know whether this is an alleged criticism of the study, or just a gratuitous comment. We think that it is not trivial to discuss the meaning of the phrase "key data are missing." The phrase implies that there are data that could have been obtained, but, for some reason, the appropriate conditions were not presented to the subjects, or the authors simply did not report the data. Missing data represent a serious flaw in a study. In our case, however, the subjects would not give ratings of zero voluntary control by an actor;

therefore no data for zero control could be reported. The key data represent the least level of perceived voluntary control. Because the rated dignity was significantly greater than zero at those key points, this criticism is invalid.

Evaluator III

The third evaluator for Journal K concluded:

> While the question, as the authors formulate it, is of some interest in light of things B.F. Skinner had to say about dignity, there is little here that contributes to our understanding of the data on impression formation and attribution. This is an important shortcoming because the manuscript reports two studies that are essentially social perception experiments, notwithstanding the author(s)' failure to cite any work in the area.

We can hardly dispute that "there is little here that contributes to our understanding of the data on impression formation and attribution." In fact, there were many other areas of social psychology for which our data had virtually no relevance. But obviously this would only be important in the reviewing process if we had claimed that there was such relevance. We were trying to open up social psychology to some new areas of research, but the evaluators persisted in trying to force our studies into the same old categories. This is worse than neophobic—it is a failure to even identify our research as new and different. We can in fact question that these are social perception experiments for the very reasons later expressed by this same evaluator: we deliberately provided no context for social perception.

On the basis of his or her particular labeling process, however, this evaluator now criticizes the study for the lack of social context:

> In part, the problem stems from posing too general a question. To find that subjects are willing to give another person the benefit of the doubt and ascribe some measure of "dignity" in the particular denatured circumstances the author(s) created, tells us very little because introduction of just a little more context (e.g., physical appearance) would create a multitude of exceptions to the postulated effect. Put another way, the research pursues a postulate that is so general and removed from context that the only possible support one could find for it is in the kind of impoverished situation that was created for subjects. Thus, the usual "other things being equal" disclaimer includes so much in this case as to make the examined premise uninteresting. In addition, under such

minimal circumstances, the fact that subjects tended to view the target positively, may be nothing more than responding to the social desirability constraints of the lab context (wanting to appear generous in one's evaluations of others). The authors say nothing about such an experimental artifact constituting an alternative for the main findings.

It appears that the evaluator is strongly agreeing with the fundamental point of our study, and wants us to get on with the program. This was one of the most tantalizing and frustrating aspects of the entire peer-review process with this program of research. Paradoxically, many evaluators wanted us to make further progress with this research, but they balked at affirming the necessary first basic step. We were thus encouraged to think that the ultimate goals of our proposed research program would become worthy additions to the literature, and would cut across several areas of interest. At the same time, we were being told in effect that our starting point was in disfavor. This mixed message was in fact typical, and responsible for literally freezing our program at a very preliminary level. We were forced into repeated rewriting and multiple submissions.

The issue of impoverished context is intriguing. We wonder if the social situation in Skinner's formulation was indeed impoverished. He clearly intended his formulation to apply to all social situations and contexts. Does this imply a complete richness of context, or no context at all? It seems that a more germane point—made by other evaluators (see comments of the editor of Journal H)—is that we provided too much context. By providing the specific context of a vignette, we were asking the subjects to rate the dignity of a person on the basis of a single episode in the life of that person.

The possibility for effects of social desirability is always real. Because in this study we did not collect data from the subjects to establish their tendencies to make socially desirable responses, admittedly we could not document that our effects were not produced entirely by such social desirability tendencies. Nevertheless, our procedures did entail considerations that would reduce such tendencies (i.e., anonymity and questions focusing on the participants' opinions rather than on a personal evaluation).

Evaluator III continued with more criticisms in the same vein:

Aside from the general conceptual framework for the study, there are other basic problems as well. The failure of the author(s) to cite the impression formation and attribution literature is particularly unfortunate. Had this been done, it might have seemed unnecessary to examine the implications of volition for inferring attributes associated with positive or negative acts. Furthermore, to find that people do not always adjust their perceptions of choice in accordance with situational pressures is also not surprising given the extensive literature on the fundamental attribution error.

Once again, this evaluator is faulting us for not taking the second step in our research program, while failing to understand the importance of the first step. If this step is successful, the second step is to determine what personal characteristics of both actors and observers influence the degree of perceived dignity.

Our understanding of the fundamental attribution error is that it represents a tendency toward attribution of internal control of an actor. The crucial point in our study concerns the attribution of dignity in the perceived *absence* of voluntary (internal) control.

The next comment of this evaluator is a familiar one:

> Just as problematic is the failure to adequately explicate the concept of dignity. As operationalized in the research, it is not clear how "dignity" is distinguishable from general positivity or likableness.

Our answer to this familiar objection, is that, for the purpose of this study, it really did not matter what the subjects were using as a definition of dignity or worth in a person, as long as they were arguably using the same definition as Skinner. At this point it does not matter whether we are discussing different bases of according a monolithic dignity (or different ways of operationalizing the concept), or we are referring to two different *kinds* of dignity. Given our dictionary definition, and Skinner's laconic one, there is no solid basis for suggesting that they are different. In short, for our purposes, it really does not matter whether there is one kind of dignity, with two bases of according it, or two different kinds of dignity (earned and unearned). The existence of the second basis—or kind—of dignity is in opposition to Skinner's assertion that there is no dignity over and above the earned category. Without some basis for raising this concern, other than the trite one that research subjects can interpret the words any way they please, this evaluator is simply pointing to a "universal critical deficiency" (Beaver, 1982, p. 200). This comment represents what Harcum (1992) has called the Carp and Quibble Tactic.

JOURNAL L, CYCLE A

There was an original submission to Journal L and two resubmissions. The three cycles of evaluation will be identified by the letters a, b, and c.

Evaluator Ia

The first evaluator from Journal L was the editor, who responded as follows:

Our reviewers have reported sufficient problems with this study to warrant a negative decision for publication. I am enclosing their critiques for your consideration. Although they agree in their recommendations not to accept the article, each finds the manuscript challenging. I am not sure their criticisms can be met in a manner that would permit a revision.

The subject is one about which there is a substantial division of perspectives. If you believe you can find ways to meet the objections of the reviewers without abandoning your fundamental argument, I would be happy to seek a second review.

Evaluator IIa

The comments of Evaluator IIa for Journal L began on the following promising note:

This paper begins beautifully. Skinner's speculative views on the basis for the attribution of human dignity seem well characterized, and an alternative view is clearly articulated. The writing style is clear, assured, and pointed.

These kind words seem to document the clarity of our presentation, but the illusion is short-lived. This evaluator goes on to question the validity of the empirical results of our study:

The experiments performed and the interpretation of them are problematic in relation to the general issue raised in the introduction. The manipulation of the independent variable—degree of perceived control—was not entirely successful, for the part of Skinner's assertion about perceived dignity that seems most to matter is that when there is no control, there is no perceived dignity. Hence, the failure to achieve the former condition weakens substantially the author's contention that they have somehow refuted Skinner's view on this matter.

We showed that the perception of dignity was significantly above zero even when perceived voluntary control of blameworthy behaviors was greater than zero. As we have said, there is no logical reason to think that this function should decrease with less voluntary control. What would that mean? Skinner certainly proposed monotonic functions. Therefore, one can reasonably argue that the intercept for blameworthy behaviors is at least as high as the values that we have documented. We argued in fact that the unwillingness of subjects even to concede that voluntary control could be pushed to zero by science was an argument against Skinner's argument for abolishing the concepts of freedom and dignity. Both of the above results indicate that the subjects will not accept either of Skinner's arguments as threats to the concepts of freedom and dignity.

This evaluator then goes on to say:

> This is an issue that deserves study, for it is of some importance to know more in a systematic way about the ways in which praise and blame are attributed to actors. The contrast the authors attempt to create between this research and the tradition of work on attribution theory is not entirely convincing, for after all, the judgments called for in this case, while focusing on the person, are based on but a single hypothetical incident. It would seem that a larger number of incidents and stimulus targets ought to be employed for any fair test of Skinner's view that null control produces a judgment of null dignity. But it also seems that this question is analytically separable from the question of whether human beings are in general disposed to grant a modicum of dignity to anyone, just in virtue of being human. This latter possibility would be fully consistent with social psychological theory on the character of ascribed roles, deriving from Ralph Linton. But it would seem to me also not inconsistent with Skinner's views, for he might argue that human beings have habitually and traditionally awarded grants of dignity where none are really warranted.
>
> In short, I think this paper starts far better than it finishes. It raises an important question in an engaging fashion. And yet the final result of the experimental inquiry is not to shed significant new light on this question.

This evaluator is trying to work three sides of the theoretical street. First, we are accused of using too specific a research situation. Second, we are criticized because our study did produce a result that was obvious. How is the question about the possibility of null dignity for null control separable from the issue of granting dignity just by virtue of being human (or the presence of some dignity with null control)? There seems to be a pervasive logic-tight compartment separating the scientists' beliefs in given human dignity and its relation to a graph as in Figure C.2 of Appendix C. Third, we are told that the complete exercise was futile anyway, because Skinner would have made the same prediction.

We are mystified by the comment that a person could award dignity when such is not justified. How can a researcher verify that a person has accorded dignity to another when it is not "really warranted"? One can perhaps discuss whether earned dignity is warranted, but not whether intrinsic dignity is warranted. In any case, we are talking about the reality of beliefs, and not the truth of those beliefs. We cannot imagine Skinner in a debate about whether a person truly has dignity, and therefore whether its accordance is "really warranted."

Evaluator IIIa

The next evaluator for Journal L reiterates the common theme:

Skinner has never argued that dignity must be earned by committing voluntary prosocial acts. Rather, he has contended that most people hold the *false* belief that dignity is a function of good and voluntary actions. In fact, Skinner argues that dignity, as used in everyday language, does not exist.

This is *our* point! We argue in addition that this argument of Skinner was not accurate because dignity is *also* accorded on the basis of the perceived attribute of being human.

This evaluator continues concerning the presumed Skinnerian argument relating dignity and voluntary choice (shown in Figure 1 of the first submissions) as follows:

Skinner would never assume this relationship because he does not describe human behavior in terms of perception.

As we understand the word "perception," this is what Skinner meant to "attribute" or " to give" or "to recognize" a person's dignity when that person voluntarily performs credible deeds. To say again: The issue is not about how Skinner himself interpreted causation of behavior, but about his view of what other members of society believe. Our argument with the reviewers is one of fact.

This evaluator has problems with the following sentence from our submissions in which we quote Skinner as saying "scientific analysis shifts the credit as well as the blame to the environment . . . (1971, p. 19). Because Skinner does not report data which might suggest or support this hypothesis, it must be based on casual observation or on deductions from his metaphysical position." With respect to these statements, this evaluator asserts:

> The authors do not present data relevant to this point either, although I think they are arguing that they do. Skinner is talking about a *scientific analysis*, not the kind of casual analysis the author's subjects probably used in their ratings of dignity.

What data are relevant here? We simply asserted that Skinner presented no data. He did no scientific analysis. We found no data in Skinner. Does this evaluator dispute this claim? Skinner could not mean that people do a scientific analysis before they develop a belief. He is merely describing a belief that he imputes to people in general. We are simply investigating that belief.

Next, this evaluator objects to our sentence that reads as follows:

> Therefore, the literature of dignity does indicate a prevailing belief in intrinsic dignity, unearned and independent of social roles.

His or her objection was as follows:

> The one (and only) reference given above on this point (Berger, 1970) is not ample enough testimony for this statement.

How many references would be ample, particularly if one is to discount casual observations? Our study was presenting such laboratory data for the first time.

Next, this evaluator has concerns about several matters pertaining to our methods:

> There are numerous problems with information given in the Method section of the ms. Among them are included:
>
> a. Improper headings (in fact, none) for the subjects and procedures sections.
>
> b. Subjects are not described in terms of their sex, ages or other relevant information.
>
> c. Separate and clear descriptions for Experiments 1 and 2 are not provided.
>
> d. Complete verbatim descriptions of the instructions and the six conditions (vignettes) have been omitted. Exactly how were the four descriptions of the circumstances in Experiment 2 edited?

The substantive nature of these criticisms is open to question. In any case, they could be easily corrected in a revision of the manuscript.

The next criticism concerns the statistical conclusion in which we found "significantly ($p < .01$) more subjects (70%) rating dignity above zero than below zero." He or she complained as follows:

There is no description of the type of statistical analysis from which this alpha level was derived.

This criticism is correct, but rather picayune. We had thought that the meaning of the statistics would be obvious.

Next, this evaluator raises concerns about the following paragraph in our conclusions:

The evidence from Experiment II thus supports the conclusion that subjects tend to accord some intrinsic positive dignity to persons who have not earned it through voluntary praiseworthy deeds. These results clearly contradict Skinner's contention that the function for praiseworthy behaviors will pass through the origin, and thus invalidate his practical argument against the concepts of freedom and dignity. Because some human dignity is thought to be intrinsic, independent of behavior, it is not threatened by even a science which aspires to discover all of the hereditary and environmental causes of human behavior.

The concerns of this evaluator for Journal L about the above quoted paragraph are as follows:

Although the author's data from Experiment 2 may show that college students assign dignity to people independent of behavior, these data do not in any way dismiss Skinner's ideas about freedom and dignity. These data do not bear on Skinner's point simply because Skinner believes the concepts of freedom and dignity to be illusory, pleasant fictions of the sociocultural educational process. In a sense, the authors are arguing apples and oranges with Skinner: They believe dignity to be a real thing and so treat the concept as such; Skinner believes just the opposite. How do these data about a "fiction" bear on Skinner's ideas about a scientific analysis of human behavior? As an alternative tack, the authors may wish to first demonstrate that dignity is, in fact, a very real human attribute before they seek to demonstrate how people think about it. I sincerely wish the authors best of success in their future endeavors to help us understand the concept of dignity and the manner in which people attribute it to others.

Again, we are faced with an evaluator who obviously does not understand the psychological questions asked in our study. We do not argue about whether freedom and dignity are illusory fictions, but about what people believe, and that is a legitimate issue. Skinner agrees that people believe in freedom and in earned dignity, but is totally silent about possible beliefs in an unearned dignity. This silence enabled him to construct an argument for why society opposes his brand of science. We simply argued that a belief in unearned or intrinsic human dignity is entirely inconsistent with his explanation for the dislike for strict behavioristic science.

We are *not* arguing with Skinner about whether there is such an entity as human dignity. Such a debate would be foolish, in contradiction to the view of this evaluator. How would one establish that dignity is "a very real human attribute"? Neither we, nor surely Skinner, would be a party to a nonempirical debate about whether human beings *have* an intrinsic dignity. But, a belief is a response, and especially Skinner would say that therefore it is "real." The issue is about behavior—whether people *act* like other people have such given dignity, either by helping behavior or verbal report. We are literally playing by Skinner's rules for behavioral science in making this argument.

The evaluator is in a world of his or her own about the issues in our submission. We are not debating apples and oranges. We expect to demonstrate later, by further research and argument, that a belief in intrinsic dignity is important for the improvement of our society. The very point of Skinner's *Beyond Freedom and Dignity* was, of course, to argue that the acknowledged beliefs in dignity and freedom were major *hindrances* to cultural improvement.

JOURNAL L, CYCLE B

Because of the errors by the evaluators, we decided to revise and possibly resubmit the report. On the basis of our past experiences, however, we desired some reassurances that our efforts would receive an open-minded hearing. Accordingly, the senior author wrote the following letter to the editor of Journal L:

> Thank you for your letter of August 8 in response to the Harcum and Rosen submission, "Perceived dignity as a function of perceived voluntary control of behaviors." Although you rejected the paper on the basis of two reviewers' comments, you agreed to seek a second review if we can meet the objections of the reviewers. We do anticipate a re-submission, but we have several concerns that we hope you will be kind enough to clear up for us.

For convenience, I will refer to the 1-page review as Reviewer A and the 2-page review as Reviewer B. Reviewer A seems to be bothered by the adequacy of our data, whereas Reviewer B is concerned more with the conceptualizations, indeed even with the relevance of our work to Skinner. The problem of relevance seems to be the more serious one. The submitted work is part of a program of several studies that we have done on this topic; obviously we should have cited some of them. Reviewer comments on the other studies have unfortunately often echoed those of Reviewer B, which we assert are off the mark. Your Reviewer A agrees with us on this, incidentally.

Please consider the first three specific comments of Reviewer B. The last line of our abstract admittedly should have been written more clearly, by inserting the qualification that we are referring to Skinner's view of society's view. Our meaning should have been clear, however, from the first full paragraph of Page 5. Here we clearly state that we are referring to "the beliefs of most people." By missing this point, Reviewer B misses the whole point of our paper. This is evident from his or her third specific point: Our data are relevant to *people's beliefs*, as we contend. Our data show that people do not believe the way that Skinner, *on the basis of no data* and as the result of *no* scientific analysis, contends that they do. Our point is that Skinner's treatment of this point is not only casual, it is cavalier—certainly not scientific.

In summary, we never argue, as Reviewer B contends in his comment 1, that Skinner argued "that dignity must be earned by committing voluntary prosocial acts." What we said on our page 6 and elsewhere, was that "people accord some level of dignity to others, unconditionally and noncontingently." Skinner denies that this is so. Because both of your reviewers deny this question of fact, they deny that our data are relevant.

Our concerns therefore revolve around this critical issue. If you do not agree with our interpretation of Skinner, who we specifically quote on the bottom of our Page 4, there is not much point in re-submitting our paper. Our view is that our data invalidate the whole thesis of Skinner's book.

We look forward to receiving your comment on the above issue. Thank you for your interest.

We received the following reply to our letter from the editor of Journal L:

Although I cannot assure you a more positive outcome, I believe the clarification and elaboration suggested in your second and third paragraphs are important. Do cite relevant work from your program of studies. It is essential that you establish your position as one based upon an empirical foundation.

State your case clearly enough to avoid the interpretive errors you attribute to Reviewer B, or at least so that the differences in perspective are resting upon data, whether or not this reviewer "believes them."

In short, I am not opposed to sustaining the "dignity" debate so long as it moves forward on the wheels of research. Obviously, without examining alternative paradigms there is the danger of self deception.

Encouraged by this reasoned response, we confidently submitted a revised version of our manuscript to Journal L.

Evaluator Ib

The editor of Journal L reported on our resubmission as follows:

I regret that the reviewers have been unable to find in your revision an adequate resolution of the problems identified in their first critique.

He did not add any comments to those of two evaluators. We do not know whether these were the same evaluators as before.

Evaluator IIb

This second evaluator for Journal L begins in a cavalier fashion:

The paper by Harcum and Rosen is generally interesting and well-written. However, I am not sure of the extent to which this paper represents a substantial contribution to the existing literature. I get the impression that the basic hypothesis, that others accord actors dignity even when their behavior is beyond their control, has been demonstrated previously. Any major contribution to the literature beyond this was not, in my opinion, demonstrated. Therefore, it is my recommendation that this issue, and those described below, be addressed in a revised paper and the paper resubmitted for review.

At least he or she agreed with our results. We regret that we had not encountered this evaluator earlier in our hunt for a publication outlet. It is ironic that this evaluator disagreed with so many others who felt that the issue had not been resolved by our studies. Unfortunately, we could not very well, at that time, cite the methodological and other objections of the previous evaluators.

The next point of this evaluator was as follows:

The relation of metaphysics, as a part of philosophy, to the scientific understanding of behavior seems tenuous. What is needed is not more philosophical analyses of behavior but empirical analyses (which is one of the stated reasons for the present study). More should be done to bolster the arguments for the empirical aspects of the present study than appealing to metaphysics as justification for the research.

We deny, of course, that we performed a philosophical analysis.

This evaluator added:

In paragraph 1 on page 4, Skinner is said to equate predictability with determinism. Admittedly, the quote cited by the authors seems to indicate this, but the point he is making is quite subtle. Skinner is not saying here (or elsewhere) that the two terms are synonymous; his point is that when we find human behavior to be more predictable (and hence controllable) we tend to reject the notion of self-determination.

The authors state that Skinner dismisses a literature of freedom. Actually, what he dismisses is explanations of behavior based on a *philosophy* (whether a philosophy of freedom or any other sort) when the only evidence for the philosophy is the behavior to be explained. Furthermore, in this same sentence I get the impression that it is being implied that because something may be intrinsic to humans, it is scientific. If this is not the intended meaning, it should be clarified.

The issue, of course, is what society believes, not the ontological question of whether they are correct in the belief. The literature of freedom is an empirical source of information about what society believes. Again, this evaluator missed our point that Skinner himself presented no data to bolster his philosophical, or theoretical, position about why society opposes the Skinnerian metaphysics. At the same time, Skinner ignored two lines of evidence against the Skinnerian view: (1) the religious and humanistic literature that affirms unearned human dignity; and (2) a voluminous philosophical and scientific literature by authors who apparently believe that they are rejecting Skinner's views on philosophical and scientific grounds. We challenged him on the battleground of empirical beliefs and practicality.

Evaluator IIIb

Several comments of Evaluator IIIb of Journal L concerned the exposition in the submission:

> The introduction appears to be a bit long. It could be shortened considerably and still retain its major points. The main hypothesis is (from the abstract) that an actor is accorded dignity or worth even when the behavior is ascribed to causes beyond voluntary control. Introductory material regarding this main point could be made in several fewer pages. The relevance to the major thesis of certain sections escaped me. Perhaps a careful re-working of the introduction with an eye towards brevity and relevance could resolve this issue.
>
> The reader may benefit if the Method section was divided into Experiment I and Experiment 2, each with its own Subjects, Procedure, Results, and Discussion section and a General Discussion section. As it now stands, I had some difficulty comprehending the exact nature of the procedures as the description frequently jumps back and forth, although the amount of detail given was quite reasonable. Also, inclusion of the rationale for some of the procedural details was helpful.
>
> More should be said about how the present data "clearly" refute Skinner's notion "that the progress of science threatens the concept of voluntary choice." In that this is a major point in the paper, more discussion is clearly warranted if the reader is to be convinced, especially the reader not closely aligned with the authors' position.
>
> In the last paragraph on page 18, the authors state that the true shape of the function is not critical. However, a considerable amount of their paper has been devoted to this issue. This apparent inconsistency should be resolved.

These points could be handled in a rewriting of the submission, because no fatal flaw has been discovered.

This evaluator also had some problems with the interpretation of the data:

> Inclusion of a table showing the "dignity data" may help the reader in drawing conclusions. Also, in the second paragraph on page 20 the authors note that 65% of the subjects rated dignity above zero. This means that 35% rated dignity below zero. Some reference and explanations of these results should be made.

The text of the manuscript at this point was referring to blameworthy behaviors under the condition in which there was the least perceived voluntary control. The conclusion about the ratings of negative dignity seems obvious to us: voluntary blameworthy behaviors produce reductions in perceived dignity. The interesting point is that 65% of the subjects accorded positive dignity to someone who committed a blameworthy act, not that 35% of the subjects accorded negative dignity to someone who performed a blameworthy act.

The evaluator continued:

> The statement, at the top of page 23, that "if dignity can be intrinsic and therefore unearned, the very thesis of his book collapses" is a bit strong and may overstate the consequences of these findings. The present findings do not necessarily suggest that radical behavioral theory is baseless. That persons accord others dignity even when the actor's behavior is beyond his or her control can be included within the radical behavioral framework. The behavior of according others dignity is a function of their environment (e.g., the values of the culture within which they have lived and are now living), and thus may be quite different for different persons.
>
> As indicated in the present study, some persons do and some persons do not accord dignity to others under various circumstances. This presents no difficulty for behaviorists; the fact that a person might accord a newborn dignity can simply be attributed to that person's history of reinforcement.

At least this evaluator accepts our conclusion that people, perhaps even behaviorists other than Skinner, believe in intrinsic dignity. But we never claimed, nor do we believe, that our research suggests that "radical behavioral theory is baseless." We concede that a belief in unearned human dignity may even be based entirely on a person's history of reinforcement. But, the belief exists, and that is the issue. For some reason, Skinner needlessly denied its existence. We readily agree that he was *not* forced to do so by his metaphysical stance. He chose to use this argument to explain the resistance of society to his strict behavioristic theory. Skinner could have argued that a belief in intrinsic dignity, regardless of source, could be overcome by proper reinforcement, of course. That would be theoretically possible, but a practical nightmare. We do not foresee how anything would be gained by such an exercise, except to make the rest of his formulation reasonable. It was simply a defensive reaction that should not have been taken as seriously as it was. To use such a rationalization for societal opposition to his formulations presumably made Skinner feel more comfortable. But, we suspect, it actually increased the opposition, because it led him to attack the cherished—and, to us, valuable to society—beliefs in human dignity. Obviously, such an attack by such a renowned social science researcher as Skinner had and still has, a major impact on how psychology is viewed by the public. This attack may have had a powerful effect on the current shift in emphasis in psychology to a more cognitive approach. We are simply refuting Skinner's interpretation of why society refuses to embrace his strict behavioristic theory, which he consistently equated with behavioral science itself.

Because we still did not believe that our arguments had been adequately considered by the evaluators, we again revised the manuscript and resubmitted it along with the following letter:

> I was quite disappointed to receive your letter of Feb. 21, informing me that the revision of the paper, "Perceived Dignity as a Function of Perceived Voluntary Control of Behaviors," by Harcum and Rosen, was rejected for publication in [your journal]. Your letter stated "that the reviewers have been unable to find in your revision an adequate resolution of the problems identified in their first critique."
>
> As I understand the reviews, however, the only unresolved problem mentioned in the last review which had been mentioned in the earlier reviews concerns the relevance of our data to behavioristic learning theory. In fact, we agree with both reviews that a belief in intrinsic dignity can be learned. We do *not* contend "that radical behavioral theory is baseless." We tried to make this clear (page 5 of our first revision) in a sentence that the last reviewer thought was "unnecessary in delineating the scope of the present research" (page 1, fourth paragraph of the last review). This sentence had been specifically added to clarify the misunderstanding in the first review. We agree with this reviewer that Skinner could easily accept the hypotheses of Figure 2, and these data supporting them, without conflict to his basic formulations about learning. Nevertheless, Skinner chose to base his entire book (BF&D) on premises about popular beliefs, with opinions unsupported by data. Our own empirical data specifically dispute Skinner's premises about the popular beliefs relating to freedom and dignity, which provided the basis for his attack on both. These data do not speak to Skinner's basic formulations about behavior theory, because he could have acknowledged a *popular belief* in intrinsic dignity, as well as he did acknowledge a popular belief in freedom. We have tried to make clear in the revision of the paper that the literal truth or falsity of these beliefs is not an issue.
>
> Because of the above considerations, I am surprised and confused by

the rejection of the paper. Your letter of Aug. 19, 1988 (attached) in response to my query of Aug. 23, 1988, clearly implied that a re-submission was in order because you agreed that Skinner *did* deny that "people accord some level of dignity to others, unconditionally and noncontingently." Our data do show that Skinner is wrong about this, and the last reviewer agrees in his penultimate paragraph. Trying to be as open-minded as I can, I can find no unresolved problems. The debate is simply between our data and Skinner's opinion about popular *beliefs* (responses in Skinner's system) concerning the origin(s) of human dignity.

On the chance that you will agree, after this clarification of our views, I have taken the liberty of resubmitting two copies of a revised version of the paper. These revisions take into consideration all of the sugges-tions from the latest reviewer. Thank you for your patience.

JOURNAL L, CYCLE C

Evaluator Ic

The editor responded to our second resubmission as follows:

I have reevaluated your manuscript, "Perceived Dignity as a Function of Perceived Voluntary Control of Behaviors," with the assistance of our Associate Editor [name]. We agree that the revised manuscript does not add sufficient strength to warrant publication. As you know there was very little support for its publication from our original reviewers. The competition for space in the journal is fairly severe and we must, therefore, make these hard decisions. We do appreciate the extensive amount of thought and work that you have expended on this subject and regret that we cannot give you a favorable judgment.

This letter was clearly not responsive to the issues raised in the cover letter.

JOURNAL M

Because there was obviously nothing to be gained by any further contact with Journal L, we submitted the research report to Journal M. The editor did not add to the comments of two reviewers.

Evaluator I

The first evaluator for Journal M concluded as follows:

Although the general topic being addressed has theoretical and philosophical interest, I do not think this manuscript warrants publication. My first comment is that it is not really appropriate for [this journal], and suggest a different outlet.

Concerning the manuscript contents, I just do not see the continuum being suggested between intrinsic dignity and change as a function of responsibility for pro- or antisocial actions.

Of course not! The graph of our hypotheses (Appendix C, Figure C.2) shows a horizontal line, labeled "Intrinsic Dignity," which indicated a positive level of dignity at zero personal responsibility; this level did *not* change as a function of personal responsibility for actions. Whatever this evaluator was responding to had no basis in our manuscript.

This review continued:

First, on the antecedent side, I suspect that many variables would influence ratings of dignity, from personal manner of dress and speech to apologies and confessions. What seems to be varied are perceptions of morality. If the question rated was "how moral is this person?", perhaps ratings of an infant would be more neutral, and quite likely the other data would be similar. This would be the case with ratings of any number of traits or states, given what was being manipulated. That is, there is not sufficient discrimination being made here. It might be contended that the authors are merely testing the statements of Skinner. But I do not think that justifies the methodology.

It is difficult to make a civilized response to the above paragraph. The first point represents an assumption that we propose to test later in our program, as we have said. But the later stages of our program—to test effects of dress and speech, for example—would be obviated if, as Skinner says, *all* of the variance is in the levels of credit for voluntary prosocial behaviors. Again we have an evaluator blithely asserting the correctness of our hypothesis concerning an interpretation of the dignity/voluntary choice function at a point above zero. We take the assertion at face value; we see no basis for doubting such a direct report on methodological grounds. This testimonial is not coming from a research subject, and therefore it should not be doubted on the basis of such issues as demand characteristics and social desirability.

If the y-intercept for zero voluntary behaviors is zero dignity, this evaluator's initial assumption is incorrect. That he or she even makes the assumption is evidence for our hypothesis of a dignity accorded on a basis other than intentionality of behavior. This affirmation of our hypothesis cannot be attributed to a need of the evaluator to make a response that he or she would intend only to be acceptable to the authors or the editors.

A possible relationship—or lack of it—between morality and dignity offers an interesting hypothesis for further study. But we can well imagine what an evaluator would say about a manuscript that asked subjects about morality and then claimed to have data that refuted Skinner's contentions about freedom and dignity. We presume that perception of morality is contingent upon value judgments, which Skinner vehemently deplored.

We are mystified by the evaluator's admission that we were "merely testing the statements of Skinner," but that such a goal does not justify our methodology. We have been taught to use the methodology that provides an adequate test of the particular hypothesis. This evaluator has not presented any argument that would invalidate our method. It is unfair for an evaluator to criticize us for not studying the research problem that he or she personally would have investigated, using a different methodology.

The final comment of this evaluator was as follows:

Finally, the authors ignore the vast literature on responsibility, blame, etc.

We have said that we did not see the necessity to get into the literature described above at the inaugural stages of our research program. What does the literature on responsibility and blame that is based on behavior have to do with the accordance of unearned dignity, based on sheer humanness without a behavior or a behavioral context?

Evaluator II

The second evaluator's remarks were as follows:

I don't find this manuscript at all acceptable. In the first place the writing is often beyond comprehension. For example, at the bottom of page 26 I found, "Therefore, human dignity is not threatened by a conception of science that some others hope will discover all the causes of human nature in terms of heredity and environmental factors. . . . " On page 27, I could not decipher the sentence beginning, "Therefore, in this context the scientific. . . . " I also could not readily re-construct the operations used in this research because the method section is so fragmented. The most clearly written section was the abstract.

We must admit to some problems of exposition here. We do not understand the difficulty in ultimately deciphering the meaning, given the context of an entire article.

This second evaluator for Journal M continued:

> I am also somewhat confused about the point of this research: Yes, Skinner believes that as behavior is shown to be a function of external circumstances a person is accorded less and less credit. And if the behavior is positive, then less and less dignity or worth is attributed to the person. Don't we all believe this? If a young assistant professor authors many valuable manuscripts with his or her advisor, don't we attribute less worth to the young professor than if he or she was the only author? Isn't this a fairly simple application for Kelly's discounting principle? But the authors go beyond this derivation. They focus on the Skinner quotation on page 5 of the manuscript (I examined three hard-cover editions of *Beyond freedom and dignity* and the pagination was not the same as the edition used for the manuscript under review.) and note that Skinner wrote "as the analysis of behavior adds further evidence, the achievements for which a person himself is to be given credit seem to approach zero." Strictly speaking, not even Skinner wrote that the credit would be exactly zero in this *passing* (!) remark, but the authors take the zero point quite seriously, and I frankly can't figure out why I should do likewise.

We were in fact guilty of citing incorrect page numbers for the Skinner quotations. We had cited pages from the soft-bound edition, rather than the hard-cover edition that we had cited in our reference. We offer no excuses for this error, and apologize for it.

If our language was inadequate, certainly the graph of our hypothesis should not have been. The issue raised by this evaluator about the relation between voluntary behavior and dignity reveals that he or she did not understand the text *or* the graph. This evaluator surely must be able to interpret a graph, or he or she would not be a consultant for a journal. How can an editor pass on such commentary to an author uncritically?

We contend that the *"passing"* remark was literally a cornerstone argument of Skinner's book. As we documented earlier, Skinner's argument was clearly stated in three publications (Skinner, 1955–1956, 1971, 1975) that spanned 20 years. Therefore, this evaluator's comment represented a gross lapse of scholarship.

As we have repeatedly asserted, Skinner's argument collapses if the intercept is not at essentially zero. Certainly, no serious scholar would propose that

Skinner does not deny voluntary choice. Therefore, his system must assume some specific value of dignity for zero voluntary choice, even if that value is zero—which is what he asserts. If a completely successful science becomes capable of explaining all behavior in genetic and experimental terms, would Skinner agree that the *conventional* concept of human dignity, in terms of something other than his notion of a magnificent machine, could still exist? If this were the case, the concept of dignity would not compete with the progress of science, because it would remain even if science were completely successful. Again, this is the critical issue in this research. We consider it important.

SUMMARY

This chapter reports some thirteen evaluations of a submission, returned from evaluators for five journals. It was judged not appropriate for a sixth journal. Although the empirical results of this study supported the previous results from different methodologies, the evaluative comments were much the same. In general, the evaluators were not willing, or able, to focus on the research problem as posed by the authors.

6

Confirmation

The fourth submission was basically an extension of Submission II. The subjects were populations of college students and direct-care providers in a mental hospital. In this study the subjects were asked for ratings of levels of agreement, instead of "yes/no" responses, about the dignity of a newborn baby and other persons under specified circumstances. Several new questions were added. The results of Submission II were supported with these changes in procedures.

Of the three journals that rejected this submission, two of them were more applied in orientation. We thought that we might have better success with publication in the applied journals because the issue is basically practical rather than theoretical. The first submission is reproduced as Appendix D. The article was eventually published by a fourth journal (Harcum & Rosen, 1992).

JOURNAL N

Evaluator I

The first evaluator for Journal N (the editor) responded as follows:

Your study is interesting, but there are a number of problems, both of definition and method. (See enclosed reviewers' comments.) In addition, the manuscript appears to be only marginally relevant for the practicing psychologist.

The alleged problems will be discussed in the context of the individual reviewers' comments. Although the issue of relevance represents opinion, to us it is obvious that the issues of intrinsic dignity and freedom should be of interest to any psychologist, particularly one who is engaged in human services.

Evaluator II

The second evaluator for Journal N was confused about the purpose of the study:

I applaud the interest in empirically testing theoretical premises, but I had some serious problems with this manuscript. First, I found the introduction and rationale for the study to be very confusing. The first paragraph outlining Skinner's position is hard to understand as currently written. What would this study prove, if anything? What importance would it have to the profession of psychology? So what if people state that they do believe in the idea of dignity? Is Skinner arguing in these passages against the concept/value of dignity in general, or against its empirical explanatory power? That is, behavioral psychologists have traditionally argued that some things worthy of study in their own right (e.g., philosophy) simply fall outside the purview of empirical psychological study. I also found myself wondering in the introduction whether any research other than Harcum's has any relevance to addressing these questions, e.g., attitudes about the disabled or victims of crime. Consideration of related ideas may help to flesh out the development of the topic. Beyond the conceptualization, I did not find the data and discussion to be convincing. On the whole, the respondents in both studies did not appear to feel strongly about the subject as shown by the large number of means near the scale midpoint. Multiple t-tests are difficult to interpret; analysis of data in terms of departures from midpoint seem problematic since respondents could have viewed this point several ways (neutral, neither, both, cannot say . . .) What would "significant" departure from the midpoint mean? I personally found the definitions of dignity and negative dignity given to the respondents to be very confusing. Another major problem concerns the issue of social desirability, which was not adequately assessed or discussed in this study. I do not doubt that Skinner would agree that dignity is a valued concept in our society. The fact that respondents seemed concerned about appearing in a favorable light does not mean to me that your premise is substantiated; merely that respondents may not have reported what they truly feel. It may be more interesting, and certainly more direct, to ask respondents more simply what they think about Skinner's ideas and why. The questions about pertinence to psychology remain, but perhaps the researchers can develop this further in future manuscripts.

We ultimately came to agree with this evaluator that the issue of social desirability was not adequately treated in our submission. Accordingly, we made major improvements in this respect in the final published version. Unfortunately, we did not have the foresight to add the extra analysis and discussion of social desirability when the paper was submitted to the next two journals.

It appears that this evaluator has only a sporadic concern with social desirability. Apparently, social desirability is not a major concern when the evaluators themselves propose "simply" asking direct questions of the research subjects. One can, of course, always question exactly what a subject means by marking a rating scale. We fail to see an important issue in this stated concern for the meaning of a neutral response. A significant departure from neutral indicates a belief depending on whether the item is checked in the positive or negative direction.

This evaluator obviously did not read our paper carefully. He or she does not understand what issue we have raised. We had said that we did not question the validity and value of Skinner's principles of learning, and we agreed that Skinner's metaphysical views cannot be disconfirmed empirically. Simply asking subjects what they think of Skinner's ideas would not in any way have justified a conclusion about Skinner's argument for the practical value of his metaphysical position, as opposed to the popular conceptions of freedom and dignity. It is rather difficult to take any pronouncements seriously from an evaluator who so misunderstands the rationale of the study.

We expect that by now the reader is as bored and annoyed as we are by the repeated criticism of several evaluators that our research did not refute Skinner's theoretical and metaphysical position. We tried to the very best of our abilities to make this clear in our submissions, especially in revisions after the earlier papers had been rejected, partly for this frequently stated reason. We can only surmise that there must be some cognitive set or defensive reaction (Harcum, 1988) to account for this consistent lapse of scholarship, or even reading comprehension. The evaluators seemed determined to force the issue into the well-worn path toward the bottomless pit of ontological debate over Skinner's metaphysical position.

Skinner's argument about freedom and dignity was a utilitarian one, which should ultimately permit an empirical resolution. The practical question concerns whether the humanistic assumptions of freedom and dignity are helpful or detrimental to the further progress of our culture. The thesis of our research program was that a critical element in the final answer to these questions is the fact of popular belief. As Harcum (1989) has pointed out, according to Skinner's (1958) own principles of learning, the instructor must start by assessing the knowledge state of the learner, and then proceed by shaping the desired behavior in small steps. Skinner attempted to institute a learning program for cultural improvement *without checking his assumptions about the initial state of the prospective learners.* Consequently, his intended learners—in this case the members of society—were not prepared to take the first giant step in his program. The analogy to psychotherapy is direct. As Harcum (1989) has argued, a voluntary commitment to the therapy must precede the use of rewards.

The personal reference to the senior author is unwarranted. We did, and do, exhibit the temerity to claim that no previous author had put forth the argument that we were making. We cannot be absolutely certain that there is no such priority. Any researcher who claims a new idea can never be certain that the idea is new, of course. The gratuitous claim of a priority without any documentation is an unfair trick that could effectively sabotage a submission. An evaluator should not make such a claim unless he or she can cite the earlier research, at least in general terms—some who, where, what, or when information about the alleged prior publication. Although several of the two dozen evaluators complained that there was literature that could have been cited, none of the evaluators referred to a specific publication that had made our point.

We could have, of course, inflated our reference list with tangentially relevant citations. Many authors (e.g., Chomsky, 1973; Rubenstein, 1971) have severely criticized Skinner's contentions about freedom and dignity on different grounds. But, we were reporting a research result, and not "Skinner-bashing" as some evaluators claimed. Clearly, we should not have even attempted to cite all of the authors who have previously written about human dignity, worth, or freedom. Many authors who have proposed an intrinsic human dignity could also be cited. Blanshard (Blanshard & Skinner, 1966) did so, in fact, but Skinner (Blanshard & Skinner, 1966) would not give scientific credence to such empirical support from so-called casual observation. Therefore, we have provided laboratory evidence for our hypothesis, which cannot be easily dismissed. If there is prior *laboratory* evidence for the popular belief in unearned dignity, then we have been remiss in not finding it. It is unfair and unprofessional, as well as poor science, for the evaluator to impugn our scholarship if he or she does not personally know of any prior laboratory evidence. This destructive tactic (Harcum, 1992), rather than an evaluation, is totally unwarranted for a gatekeeper of the science.

Evaluator III

The third evaluator obviously also did not understand the study, as can be deduced from the following comments:

> The rationale for this study is very weak. . . . Now, the scale relating to the word "dignity" defines this latter concept as "It is a property of persons of worth and esteem who are overtly valued by others." Skinner, on the other hand, defines "dignity" as follows: "We recognize a person's dignity or worth when we give him credit for what he has done" (from *Beyond freedom and dignity*, 1971, NY: Knopf). The authors go on to ask subjects to express attitudes, given the "set" that their definition of dignity provides, and then draw conclusions in opposition to Skinner's definition. But, of course, these are two different definitions and the resultant findings are quite irrelevant to Skinner's argument.

This evaluator thus accuses us of being so stupid as to define the term differently from Skinner, and then collect data based on the different definitions. We began our research with a deliberate attempt to use the same definition of dignity as Skinner, understanding full well that a common definition was essential. The alleged definition attributed to Skinner in the above quotation was actually not a definition at all, but an assertion *about the basis on which people assert dignity*, which is actually the basis of our quarrel with Skinner. Many objections to our studies have been based on concerns that we do not know on which bases society accords dignity. But, this is the goal of our research program: we need data to learn what determines worth in the eyes of the beholder.

Let us consider an analogy. We value the trees in our yards because they provide beauty, shade, oxygen, and so on. Several considerations can add together to determine what the trees are worth to us—say, in dollars. I might judge that the beauty of the trees is worth X dollars, the shade is worth Y dollars, and the wood is worth Z dollars. Suppose some biologist said to me that I must value the trees only for their oxygen-generating characteristic, and I should not value the beauty of the trees because it distracts me from studying their botanical structure and ecological value. We both may invest exactly the same degree of admiration for the trees, endowing them with the same worth, but for substantially different reasons. Would we save more trees if we convinced people that trees were not beautiful—that we should admire them only for their marvelous oxygen-generating morphology?

If Skinner was attempting to give dignity an operational definition, as simply the credit for performing praiseworthy deeds, then his argument is entirely circular and irrelevant. Such alleged use of operational definition is what one of our mentors in graduate school called "operationism gone sour." Better yet, it is not truly an operational definition at all, because there is no convergence of operations (Garner, Hake, & Eriksen, 1956). The point is that the *popular* basis of according dignity, which is the relevant issue, includes something more than giving credit for good deeds, performed voluntarily.

One of our questions asked the subjects if they would have defined dignity differently than the definition that was actually given to them. For neither group of subjects did the ratings differ significantly from a neutral response. Although this result is difficult to interpret, it suggests that the *subjects* did not disagree with our more inclusive definition.

Next this evaluator apparently seems somehow to agree with our argument:

> I do think that these authors have found that people would not be likely to agree with Skinner, particularly since they do not want to forego a belief in voluntary action. But, Skinner would doubtless say "Of course they don't agree with me, they have been conditioned to believe in voluntary actions and dignity. I am trying to teach them the scientific truth. People didn't believe the world was round once, either. People doubtless felt that science could not build a machine to fly. What has that got to do with my thesis?"
>
> On page 16, bottom half, much is made about the fact that "subjects clearly disagree with the idea that there is no such thing as voluntary choices of behavior." I think that this could be taken as evidence *in favor* of Skinner's writings, since this is what he *also* says is the case in the present. Thus, we read in *Beyond freedom and dignity* the following (p. 8): "Careless references to purpose are still to be found in both physics and biology, but good practice has no place for them; yet almost everyone attributes human behavior to intentions, purposes, aims and goals." This is what our authors have found, and yet take as evidence against Skinner's thesis.
>
> Both samples studied were heavily influenced by social desirability, a fact our authors do not find a criticism worth worrying about. The college students were heavily religious. Here again, it is a question of one's outlook on life—the Skinnerian or the Humanitarian. This is all that is "proved" in this study. . . . Skinner is not really countered seriously.

We did not consider our results to be nullified by a social desirability interpretation, but we were concerned about it. The wording of the evaluator would be incorrectly taken by a serious reader to mean that we completely ignored the issue. We did, after all, include social desirability items in our questionnaire and covered the issue in our discussion. When an editor takes such a comment seriously, it must be rather damaging to prospects for publication. This evaluator simply asserted our thesis, and contended that it is too trivial for publication: our results are not believable because of problems with such factors as social desirability, but, besides that, they are trite.

We did agree with Skinner that people tend to attribute much of human behavior to intentions. Therefore, we did *not* argue that such a finding refuted Skinner. Of course, the religious and the humanistic members of society do not agree with Skinner on their bases for according dignity. Our point is that Skinner said they do.

The final comment of this evaluator is as follows:

Final point: I can't see why this paper is submitted to [this journal] in the first place? This is not directly relevant to professional activities, excepting only in the sense that some professionals were used in the second sample.

We are distressed by this attitude. The perception of intrinsic dignity must be very close to unconditional positive regard (Rogers, 1959). The belief in voluntary choice is critical to much of psychotherapy (e.g., Harcum, 1989; Harcum, Burijon, & Watson, 1989). We suspect that the evaluator's problem is a failure to understand what our research is about.

Evaluator IV

The fourth evaluator for Journal N raised a new issue:

This is an empirical study designed to evaluate college students' attributions of dignity by means of a questionnaire. Part two of the study includes the attributions of human service providers including physicians, nurses and ward attendants. The Procedure section of the second study is refreshingly candid about the less than optimal conditions under which the measure was administered. They also point out that some of the social desirability items included in the first part of the study were omitted because of time considerations.

There are clearly some methodological concerns with this study as the authors acknowledge. The differences in administration between part 1 and part 2 of the study do raise questions of comparability. In addition the authors do not differentiate responses between nurses and physicians on the one hand and ward attendants on the other hand.

The evaluator does not suggest how any of these methodological concerns invalidate our results. So what, *for our conclusions*, if the conditions for students and service providers were different, or if physicians respond differently from ward attendants, as interesting in itself as that finding might be?

The next concern of this evaluator was as follows:

> The basic concern I have with this study is the extent to which it is of interest and significance to professional psychologists. Certainly, study one can be considered as a replication and extension of a prior study which has not yet seen the light of publication. One wonders if this extension of a study which is part of (or related to) two submitted publications warrants still another potential outlet. I do know the dilemmas of authors who need to obtain publications. On the other hand, I need to raise the issue of "milking" one's data. Alternatively, I need to raise the issue of publication overkill. I recognize that this may be hypothetical in that neither the 1989a or 1989b papers may be accepted for publication. I do commend the authors for their straightforwardness in noting their manuscript submissions, but the problem remains.
>
> Now for the second problem. Is this study particularly relevant to professional psychology? The tie-in seems to be the use of mental health providers. Yet the authors do not seem to explain how the results are relevant to the practicing clinician. Many of my colleagues will simply say "so what!" The authors need to think more about the implications for practice (if any). Otherwise, this is simply another correlational study which is only mildly interesting in general and less than mildly interesting and relevant to clinicians.

In a sense, this evaluation provides the best evidence, albeit from casual observation, that could be obtained for our hypothesis. Our studies merely demonstrate what every clinician knows to be true (e.g., Harcum, 1989; Harcum, Burijon, & Watson, 1989). This evaluator does not care that one of the foremost psychologists in the history of the discipline denied the fact.

With respect to multiple publications on this topic, this evaluator could not have known that the multiple publications were in response to rejections of the earlier submissions that were often based simply on alleged methodological objections he or she had already put forth in the evaluation. Therefore, the additional research was in response to previous criticisms. Because this evaluator did not know the facts about our previous submissions, he or she should not have pontificated about our motives. We resent the personal insult that we can achieve publications only through multiple variations of the same inferior research. Certainly, a more successful use of the near-replication approach in a cynical pursuit of publication would be the search for a more successful topic. A prestigious author would not have been subject to such prejudicial suspicions.

We believe in the potential of this research, and have received support in this belief from several evaluators, even some who rejected our first efforts. We both have sufficient familiarity with clinical issues to know the importance of beliefs about human dignity or worth. Just as Skinner devoted an entire book, plus several articles, to the destruction of the concepts of freedom and dignity—except on his own terms—clinicians build their therapies on such concepts (e.g., Erickson, 1973; Grusky, 1987; Prochaska & DiClemente, 1986; Yalom, 1980).

Bandura (1986) emphasizes the role of people's behaviors in building favorable or unfavorable conceptions of themselves. But, he cautions against a complete reliance on such a basis for evaluation: "This is not to say that personal valuation should derive entirely from how one behaves. *Humans should value themselves for their being* [emphasis added], but should self-evaluation enjoy total immunity from the nature of one's conduct?" (p. 516). Interestingly, Bandura did not pursue this idea, preferring to focus on the behaviors that regulate the perception of personal worth. For present purposes, however, we prefer to turn his question around: Should the nature of our conduct blind us to our worth for simply being?

Willerman and Cohen (1990) describe the contention of Ellis (1987) in cognition theory, that certain irrational beliefs create emotional problems for people. Examples of such beliefs are as follows:

> that one must be loved by everyone, that one must be supremely competent in all endeavors, and that one's worth is quite justifiably judged only by the quality of one's deeds (Bandura, 1986).
>
> People with such beliefs erroneously exaggerate the consequences of not living up to their lofty standards, which can lead to negative attributions of worthlessness. (p. 16)

The rationale of Ellis's therapy is that changing a person's cognitions will result in a change in that person's behavior. It seems to us that logically a great therapeutic value would accrue to the client who merely accepts the belief that he or she has value simply for being.

The several comments of this evaluator are so far off the mark that we were at first at a loss concerning a proper response. Only lately have we understood the basis of such comments. At first, in responding to the evaluators, we were victims of an understandable naivete. We responded to the criticisms as we had been trained to do: scientists settle questions with data when this is possible. Slowly, we began to understand that our problems were not produced simply by weak evidence for a phenomenon. Virtually everyone, when they were not playing the role of rigorous scientific referee, agreed with our basic thesis for a common belief in unearned dignity. Instead of evaluations, we had provoked defensive reactions (Harcum, 1988). Apparently, few representatives of the professional journals wanted to become associated with what Skinner, as self-proclaimed scientific prototype, labeled as unscientific. We are using the fact of the *necessity* for multiple publications as part of our indictment of the peer-review system. The resistance of the scientific community to our conclusions—and presumably the most qualified members of that community, as indicated by their selection as evaluators—dictated the additional research. Therefore, we have identified an important principle of peer review: Incompetent reviews lead to multiple resubmissions and additional new submissions on the same topic. A corollary is that incompetent reviews by overworked evaluators add further to the overload of other overworked evaluators. The gratuitous and unkind impugning of our motives by this evaluator was a proverbial rubbing of salt into our editorially inflicted wounds.

Finally, it does not build confidence in an evaluator when he or she misuses the term "milking data." We have always taken this term to mean reanalyzing one set of data in every conceivable way until the researcher discovers something that is statistically significant or important enough to report. This is not the same as collecting additional data, by different methods, because earlier evaluators were not convinced by the prior data. The latter situation is conventionally described in science as "conceptual replication," which is routinely applauded in textbooks on methodology.

JOURNAL O

The editor of Journal O rejected the article because it "does not fit within the scope of this journal." We thought that it was a reasonable submission because the abstracts of this journal appear in social, organizational, psychological, and social science summaries of the literature. This editor suggested submission to a different journal. Obviously, editors cherish the prerogative to establish the scope for their own journals. A particular editor knows his or her own criteria for appropriate submissions better than an author, of course. We did examine the statement of purpose and back issues of the journal before submitting our manuscript.

JOURNAL P

Evaluator I

This evaluator, the editor of Journal P, described the reviews as follows:

Enclosed are two reviews. Each is by a scholar for whom I have considerable respect, and I believe that each of them is sympathetic to what you are trying to accomplish. Reviewer A is, among other things, an expert on behavioristic doctrine, and on Skinner's writings in particular. I know for a fact that he is often critical of Skinner's positions. Reviewer B is a developmental psychologist who is well acquainted with issues related to social perception. As you will see, both reviewers conclude that there are major problems with the paper and both recommend rejection.

First, your test assumes that Skinner argued dignity is *only* accorded those who perform prosocial acts. This is a key assumption that is never really defended. I am not an expert on Skinner, but the fact that Reviewer A takes issue with this assumption gives me considerable pause. I think you will need to document this assumption very carefully—probably with direct quotes from Skinner—or expand the scope of your investigations.

There is really nothing more that we can say here. Our argument rests on the presumption that Skinner meant that in the eyes of society dignity is based *only* on the perception of intentional prosocial acts.

This evaluator continued:

My second concern is also conceptual. Reviewer A suggests that your use of the term "dignity" differs from that of Skinner. This is another key aspect of the study and you will need to document that your use is, in fact, consistent with Skinner's position. This is imperative if you want to tie the conceptual analysis so closely to Skinner.

How did the evaluator know that our use of the term was different? Skinner used a one-word synonym as a definition (i.e., "worth"), and we tried to tie our concept to that word as closely as we could. If we erred, it was in using the dictionary definition to clarify the concept for the subjects. Does the evaluator imply that Skinner was using other than a dictionary definition of dignity or worth? If Skinner were using his own idiosyncratic definition of dignity, then we have been taking his pronouncements too seriously. The evaluator is confusing the definition of dignity with the basis on which it is accorded. Although Skinner attempted to conflate the two, there are critical reasons to differentiate them.

This evaluator nevertheless continued to be concerned about our definition:

> My third concern is more empirical in nature. To be frank, I'm not sure your results mean what you suggest. When I tried to imagine myself as a subject, I noted that your definition was very formal and not quite the same as how I use the term. I then ran to my dictionary and found six definitions of dignity, the first of which is "intrinsic worth." If your subjects responded to the question with this definition in mind—rather than your more formal and cumbersome one—all of the results would make sense and they would pose no problem at all for Skinner. Thus, all of the results could be due to definitional differences between subjects (who use the common lay definition) and the experimenters (who use a very technical one).
>
> It is problematic that you never assess how subjects themselves use the term. And I'm afraid that, without this information, any interpretation of the data remains ambiguous. You attempt to defend against this by pointing to the responses to Question I 9, but I don't think this is sufficient. Subjects are notoriously mistaken in guessing how they would respond to such hypothetical questions.

We note that yet another evaluator is concerned that our dictionary definition is "not quite the same" as how he personally uses the term. But is this alleged difference in definition by our subjects substantive to the interpretation of our data? We find it ironic that the inclusion of "intrinsic worth" in the dictionary definition is used as an argument against our thesis. We could have attempted to refute Skinner by simply pointing out that his formulation was inconsistent with the dictionary definition of dignity. We doubt that such a tactic would have passed by any of the gatekeepers. And, rightly so, because the responses of the subjects are what matter here. The assertion that "all of the results could be due to definitional differences between subjects (who use the common lay definition) and the experimenters (who use a very technical one)" does not consider that the subjects responded as the experimenter predicted.

Assuming that the various members of society use the "dictionary definition" correctly, then a quantity of dignity must exist because it is intrinsic to the person and therefore does not have to be earned. This part of the definition of dignity, which we deliberately did not include in our formal definition, is however included by the subjects themselves. That is the very point of our study. Skinner's argument denies that the subjects will support the idea of unearned dignity. We ourselves find Skinner's position in this incredible. Even more incredible is the pervasive tendency of evaluators to buy into the argument at all, but especially when this point of view flies in the face of our data.

Thus, the analysis of this evaluator is hopelessly inconsistent, both internally and with the comments of other evaluators. First, let us consider the consequences if our research definition of dignity were substantively different from the Skinnerian and a "vernacular" definition. Presumably, according to this evaluator, Skinner was using a vernacular definition, in contrast to our formal and "cumbersome" dictionary definition. But, somehow, this evaluator then suggests that this definition now includes the term "intrinsic worth," which appears in the dictionary but we did not include in our formal, dictionary definition. As this evaluator said, if intrinsic worth was part of the definition given to the subjects, we could hardly be surprised if cooperative subjects recognized and reported its existence.

This evaluator also confused the definition of human worth with the bases on which it may be accorded. We agree with Skinner that society accords dignity earned by voluntary prosocial behaving. We disagree with Skinner that such societal belief in human dignity is objectively incorrect, that it is the sole basis of the perception of human worth, and that it is a barrier to cultural progress because it promotes opposition to science.

We argue that *another* basis for one human being to accord worth to another is an unearned dignity, accorded to each human being on the basis of his or her perceived humanness, or characteristic of possessing humanity. In this view, a person has worth by simply being. It does not depend upon possessing marvelous machinery, because it is accorded to retarded, handicapped, aged, mentally ill, and anyone else who may have defective "machinery." The relevant issue is not whether a human being actually *has* this given characteristic of innate worth—although we do personally affirm that belief—but that society as an entity *perceives* people to have such a characteristic, and is committed to the belief.

This evaluator agrees that our results indicate a societal belief in "intrinsic worth." Therefore, he is among the evaluators who believe we have shown such a belief in our subjects, and that this result poses "no problem at all for Skinner." He does not explain why this result is no problem for Skinner. Of course, it poses no problem for Skinner's metaphysics, but that is not our issue: our issue is Skinner's pragmatic argument against belief in freedom and dignity. Skinner said that perceived dignity, as defined and perceived by society, approaches zero as the perceived voluntary control of the behavior approaches zero. *The existence of an intrinsic (given) basis of dignity means that this statement is false.* Despite the fine concern for concepts and definitions, dignity or worth is still dignity or worth, regardless of the basis on which it is accorded.

Therefore, society does not oppose science because society perceives science as a threat to dignity. Even if Skinner's argument were otherwise correct, a completely successful science could not threaten the dignity that is given as an act of grace by one citizen to another, or to himself or herself. Because this characteristic of intrinsic dignity does not have to be earned, it is not dependent upon personal freedom to perform prosocial behaviors, or threatened by a science that *might* be perceived to threaten the concept of freedom. Moreover, because society believes human behavior to be controlled in part by free choices, it does not even view science as capable of threatening the concept of freedom.

The last paragraph in the above quotation from this evaluator betrays a shift from "you *never* [emphasis added] assess how the subjects themselves use the term" to "you attempted to do this in the responses to Question I 9, but I don't think this is sufficient." The evaluation should focus on the actual contributions of the study, not on all of the problems that remain after the conclusion of the study, particularly in a new area of investigation. Many scientists would claim in fact that the most valuable research raises fruitful new questions.

The next comment of this evaluator speaks to this point:

> Finally, it is damning that there is no coherent conceptual contribution that is developed in the Discussion section, at least for [this journal]. You return to discuss societal perceptions of science, and so on. But you never explain where these beliefs in dignity come from, and you never show that they flow *psychologically* from the definition you originally provide. You whet the reader's appetite but never deliver the goods. The result is that I left the paper wondering exactly what it is that I learned. I think it is important for you to fit this work into a larger context if it is going to have an impact in mainstream social psychology.

We really do not know how to respond to this assessment. Our stated goals did not include a conceptual contribution, except to show the incompleteness of Skinner's attempt. Our goals concerned applications and strategies for psychological science. The true issue is the major one dividing our profession (e.g., Kimble, 1984). As Nott (1977) pointed out, the issue was so important to Skinner that he wrote an entire book for the purpose of eradicating the beliefs in freedom and dignity from our society, especially from behavioral science.

Our data were clear. The massive resistance of the social psychology establishment was amazing, because, as best we can determine, most social psychologists blithely accept the notion of intrinsic dignity, and also base their theories on a concept of personal freedom. Apparently, some evaluators actually presumed our data, and thus failed to see our research as a contribution. But, others refused to accept our data as legitimate evidence for anything. We are convinced that the more significant problems in this area concern the basic subjectivity of science—the foibles of scientists—rather than issues of fact and logic.

Our logic, as well as our scientific training, tells us that it is reasonable to demonstrate the existence of a phenomenon before beginning to search for its cause. We have demonstrated a phenomenon in ways that should be acceptable to the scientific establishment. The convergence of our laboratory evidence with casual observation should be a distinct scientific advantage, rather than the handicap so many evaluators have claimed. The demonstration of this phenomenon is worthy in view of the practical issues concerning beliefs in freedom and dignity, and because it opens new avenues of research.

At the risk of appearing petulant, we wonder about the relationships that so many other evaluators saw between our research and a "wealth" of other studies. If the relationship is so close and obvious, we wonder why so many evaluators are "confused" by our study. We submit that the confusion may be fostered by the futile attempt to force our results to fit inappropriately into previous bodies of research and comfortable theoretical categories.

The final comment of this editor was as follows:

> I am sorry that I cannot accept your paper. It is very nicely written and I found it quite interesting. I am afraid, however, that it is not conceptually meaty enough to justify publication in [this journal]. I do wish you the best in finding another outlet.

Evaluator II

The second evaluator for this journal was also seriously concerned about the definition of dignity:

> Skinner's usage of dignity refers to the process of assigning "credit" or "worth" to others' behavior as a function of how opaque the causes are for their behavior. When the causes of an individual's behavior are made more explicit (e.g., by discovering ulterior motives, etc.), we tend to assign less credit or we withhold credit altogether. Thus, we admire people to the extent that we cannot explain what they do and their

behavior deviates from the norm in a socially desirable way. [As Skinner points out, the word "admire" actually means "marvel at" (p. 58)].

We certainly agree that the evaluator has done an excellent job of para-phrasing Skinner. But here we again encounter the frequent confusion between Skinner's statement of the basis on which dignity is accorded and the definition of dignity. The point is that Skinner was operationally defining dignity as the admiration accorded a person for voluntarily performing creditable behaviors. We would not allow our undergraduate students to employ this device. Some convergence is needed. The point of our research is that Skinner and his followers believe such admiration for voluntary prosocial behaving is all that is involved in dignity, and compound the error by assuming that is the way the rest of society would define or accord dignity. On this false presumption, Skinner built his practical case against the concepts of freedom and dignity. Skinner did not eliminate the global concept of dignity by attempting to reduce it to his conception of credit dignity. He made a case against a belief in dignity *as he narrowly defined it operationally*, and then used this as an argument to oppose the value of a concept of dignity as society conceptualizes the term. This does not work for us.

In the paragraph quoted above, the evaluator described Skinner as *equating* the assignment of dignity to the admiration of a person who has performed creditable deeds on the basis of no known environmental cause. Obviously, this evaluator reads Skinner as stating that dignity is accorded *only* on the basis of such admiration; the actual assertion of an equation clearly and unambiguously precludes another possibility. There is no other reasonable way to read this paragraph, or Skinner's prose either, despite the contentions of several evaluators.

This evaluator continues with a concern for the definition of dignity:

The authors of the present manuscript think of dignity differently; and they define it differently (p. 5). But that's a semantic quibble with Skinner, not a competing hypothesis that can be adjudicated empirically.

We have answered this criticism above. This is not a semantic quibble, because it concerns the entire issue of operational definitions. Skinner's *operational* definition does not even converge with the dictionary defini-tion, which says that a person could be admired for something other than voluntary creditable behaviors. This definitely is a competing hypothesis with Skinner. Our subjects accorded dignity, using their own (society's) definition, to persons who could not have performed marvelous or inscru-table behaviors.

Of course, our subjects may have lied or deceived themselves. This trite observation is only truly relevant if the evaluator can provide a reasonable basis for suggesting it. Was there some specific flaw in our research design to suggest that lying would be appropriate? Can it be that everyone believes that a belief in intrinsic human dignity is socially desirable, but that no one actually believes that a concept of the same intrinsic human dignity actually exists?

This evaluator continues in a familiar vein:

> In addition, Skinner never said society accords dignity or worth to an individual *only* because the person is seen as voluntarily performing prosocial behaviors. It's much more a matter of degree.

As we have said the "only" is required by Skinner's text, because his whole argument rests upon the assertion of zero dignity for zero choice. Moreover, the language of this evaluator's own comments verifies our interpretation: "we admire people to the extent that we cannot explain what they do." To insert the word, "only" before "to the extent" in the above phrase is totally redundant, as it usually would be in Skinner's text. It would only add emphasis. We consider this fine-grained analysis of syntax to mask—and not very well—an obstinate attitude.

In the last sentence in the above quotation, this evaluator suggests that overall dignity is the result of differing relative amounts of credit dignity and other kinds of dignities. How is this a criticism of our argument?

The last comment to be quoted is unfair:

> The authors also introduce a new term that Skinner never used: "negative dignity." They define it, and then go on to test its utility. This seems curious, inasmuch as what the authors say they are up to is testing an argument proposed by Skinner.

Skinner apparently did not see this implication of his formulation: If dignity is zero for zero credit, it must fall below zero for various levels of blame. Skinner himself made the concept of "negative dignity" necessary. It is unfair to criticize us for attempting to deal with an implication of Skinner's formulation that he did not treat in the original formulation. This evaluator manufactured baseless criticisms, without coming to grips with the issues.

Finally, this evaluator criticized our use of the term "Likert scale":

> On a more technical level, the 7-point measure employed is referred to as a Likert scale. It is not a Likert scale: Likert scales need to be developed using an iterative procedure.

Following common practice, we used the term in the generic sense of a 7-point rating scale.

Evaluator III

As was so often the case, this evaluator begins on a positive note, and then lapses into familiar criticisms:

> The study reported in this paper is an interesting one, and has the potential to be an useful contribution to our understanding of human beliefs and behavior. However, the paper itself has some serious problems, and may need to be rethought.
>
> The most serious problem emerges in the first sentence. The authors state that Skinner (1971) suggested that the widely held idea of human dignity hinders progress in human welfare because it opposes a science of behavior. This conveys to me that Skinner believed that people resist utilizing new techniques and strategies of behavioral science because the techniques necessarily challenge their ideas of human dignity and freedom. People do not like the idea that behavior is not controlled from within, but from environmental contingencies. That is to say, people believe in dignity and free choice even though behavioral science can explain much of behavior without resorting to such constructs. If this is indeed the case, then I would expect that Skinner would not be surprised that people believe in dignity; and further, he would expect that people in this country particularly, would believe that dignity is a quality of the human being, an inalienable right of inherent worth.

We believe that this reviewer is correct until he gets to the end of the quotation. Indeed, we would not have been surprised if Skinner had argued that the members of our society shared an erroneous belief in "an inalienable right of inherent worth" (except that would have precluded his argument for why society rejected his particular science of behavior).

This evaluator continued:

> Further, Skinner is presented as arguing to change the "scientific position" (see also the results for statement III 1 on page 13). Therefore, surveying people's opinions about dignity is not going to challenge what has been presented as Skinner's position, especially if those people are not scientists.

Statement III 1 in our submission reads as follows: "As science learns to understand better the environmental causes for a person's actions, I believe that eventually there will be no need to account for any actions in terms of a person's voluntary wishes." Both the college students and the direct-care providers agreed with this statement, to a statistically significant degree. We say again, the issue is not whether Skinner or these research subjects are correct about some ultimate reality, but about their perception of *what society believes* about freedom and dignity. Skinner simply asserted as fact what he thought society believes. We asked these representatives of society what they believe. Surely, it makes no sense for empirical scientists to trust Skinner's intuition over our subjects' empirical data, even though it involves direct report, unless there is some very strong reason to question our data. Moreover, our own subjective impression of society's beliefs is exactly the opposite of Skinner's interpretations.

This evaluator was also concerned about alleged definitional problems:

It is not made clear in this paper what precisely Skinner meant by the word 'dignity.' The authors do suggest that Skinner contends that "in the view of society dignity must be earned," but they do not say what Skinner believed individuals would say about dignity. The distinction I see is between the views of the individual, his or her own personal opinion, and what that person would say our society in general would say. The distinction, then, is between private opinion and public opinion. How do we as a society accord dignity? Asking individuals how they accord dignity is not going to answer that question.

This last assertion supports our belief that evaluators on occasion spew out assertions that they have not thought much about. Surely, asking individuals how they accord dignity must be at least *one* reasonably valid way to discover how the global society would accord dignity. Is this a blanket repudiation of survey research? What is a better empirical way? Of course, one can always raise the issue of whether the subjects' response to a questionnaire represents their true beliefs. But, what is the reason to raise the question in this particular research? To assert that some subjects will always lie, or for some reason produce false reports, is just plain foolish. We trust that our subjects' verbal reports of their beliefs is a better indication of what they truly believe than Skinner's simple assertion of his belief about what they believe.

We cannot help feeling that we are encountering an atypically critical set of evaluations for this particular research. We do not believe that survey data from other topics in social psychology are routinely rejected because the subjects' responses might not reflect what they, as members of society, believe. Our conclusion is bolstered by the number of evaluators who have asserted that our data represent a trivial, obvious conclusion. Nevertheless, such evaluators find a different reason to reject our data—as valid, but irrelevant conceptually. We believe that these reviewers are overly chary of publishing *data* that claim to refute a Skinnerian formulation.

This evaluator continued:

> These problems with the logic of the paper might be corrected by a more thorough review of Skinner's position, detailing exactly what Skinner suggests about individual's beliefs, how that relates to societal beliefs and what precisely Skinner means when he talks about dignity, perhaps comparing that to what the common understanding is (that is, what does Webster say dignity is?). Then, it is important to lay out the logic of the study, what premises the authors are challenging and how their methods examine those premises.

This, of course, is precisely what we had done. The following is the exact text of the introduction that was submitted for this particular evaluation:

Skinner (1971) argues that the concept of human dignity hinders progress in human welfare because it produces opposition to a science of human behavior. He believes that the concepts of both human freedom and human dignity are alternatives to behavioral laws, providing acceptable reasons for behaviors which society does not understand because the sources of control are hidden or internal. *According to Skinner (1974) "There is no place in the scientific position for a self as a true originator or indicator of action" (p. 225). Skinner (1955–56; 1971) argues that the discovery of scientific laws reduces the number of unexplained behaviors, and thus reduces the need for these cherished concepts, because dignity, as well as freedom, would have to be zero if all of the behavioral laws were known* [emphasis added]. Presumably, blameworthy behaviors would not detract from perceived dignity if they were perceived as completely determined by the environment. As the number of undesired responses which were perceived as voluntary increased, the perception of dignity would decrease.

In several studies, Harcum and his co-workers (Harcum & Rosen, [Appendices B and C]; Harcum, Rosen, & Burijon, 1989) hypothesized that people accord some dignity to others which does not have to be earned by voluntarily performing prosocial acts. They predicted that some minimum level of such intrinsic dignity would be awarded by one person to another simply because people are perceived as having this human trait. They also predicted that for blameworthy behaviors the perceived dignity would decrease as the behaviors were more often ascribed to greater voluntary choice, resulting in the perception of negative dignity. *Populations of college students and adult members of community service organizations did accord dignity to those persons whose behavior was entirely controlled by environmental circumstances. These results offer an empirical contradiction to Skinner's contention that in the view of society dignity must be earned* [emphasis added].

The previous results may indicate merely that Skinner over-generalized. The generality of assertions on both sides indicates the need for data from more subjects, preferably from different populations.

Study 1
Study 1 was basically an extension of the earlier study by Harcum and Rosen (1989b) [Appendix B] which used college students and members of community service organizations as subjects [emphasis added]. The main difference in the present studies was that Likert-scale items replaced the previous yes/no questions in order to provide graduated degrees in the attitude measurements which were to be correlated with the subjects' personal characteristics. Also, more information on the personal characteristics of the subjects was obtained.

We had presented Skinner's complete argument. Therefore, the deficiencies in the presentation of the Skinnerian argument were not caused by inadequacies of our explanation, but by weaknesses in the argument itself. The evaluator assumed, without checking, that any deficiencies were the fault of the authors.

Next this evaluator complained about the presentation of the paper:

A second major problem I have with the paper has to do with the presentation of the methods and result section. The authors reproduce their study in detail, rather than simply describing the method. For example, it does not help me to understand the study to know that the first page of the questionnaire was a consent form and that subjects had to tear it off and turn it in separately. Nor does it help me to know that the second page asked for their age and gender. Knowing what page these items occurred on only confuses me. Further, while the authors do give me each question, verbatim, they do not tell me what the theoretical significance of each question is, what Skinner's prediction would be and what their own prediction is. If the questions are important enough to be presented in the methods, then the hypothesis and predictions should also accompany them. Even more confusing is that in the result section the authors refer to questions by section and number, expecting me as a reader to turn back to find out what exactly that question was so that I can understand what the numbers in the results section really mean. This makes the paper not very "reader friendly." I would suggest that the authors present the methods very briefly, as a general overview of what they did, who the subjects were and that they used a questionnaire format, and what the general sorts of questions were that were asked. Then, in the results section, the authors should present each question, or set of related questions, what the Skinnerian position would be, and what the results are. This would reduce the cognitive load on the reader, and clarify the purpose of the study.

Some of these changes would probably improve the presentation. They are not bases for rejection, however.

After several complaints about the organization and presentation of the paper, this evaluator concluded:

A third major problem with this paper is that the authors introduce new ideas and issues in their conclusion. They talk about Skinner's metaphysical views, which they have not mentioned before, and that they do not describe. The authors suggest that Skinner's insistence on Behaviorist guidelines for behavioral science have somehow inhibited the value of behavior modification and environmental engineering. What is not clear is why they make this assertion in a study on personal beliefs about dignity. The authors conclude by stating that the results of this study refute Skinner's argument for the practical value of his metaphysical position. This argument was never presented, or even obliquely referred to in the introduction. Therefore, I have no way of assessing the validity of that assertion. The authors also assert that Skinner's attempts to shape new attitudes have met with strong resistance. But, again, I am uncertain as to what attitudes Skinner is attempting to shape and what evidence there is for the resistance the authors mention.

We answer the above criticisms by referring to the above quotation of our entire introduction, with emphasis on the relevant sentences. The above comment from this evaluator in fact provided the main reason for presenting the entire introduction of our submission. It seems that the evaluator is responding to some other article than the one we submitted. The highlighted sentences indicate, first, a "mention" of Skinner's metaphysical position, then a presentation of his argument, and, finally, a rationale for the submitted study. The statement that Skinner's argument was not "even obliquely referred to" is revealed by these emphasized lines as cruelly false. This evaluator either hastily scanned our paper, or wrote the evaluation a month later, or possibly both. He or she wrote some very strong criticisms of our work without checking them against the manuscript for accuracy.

The last quotation from this evaluator bolsters the argument that we have presented the rationales of our studies competently. This evaluator, and apparently others as well, had not taken sufficient care to understand what this research is all about. At this point we simply ask our readers to ask themselves if they understand the connection between "environmental engineering" and our "study on personal beliefs about dignity." We also note that our first paper on this topic (Harcum, Rosen, & Burijon, 1989), was published in May, 1989, well before this submission was submitted to Journal P in November, 1989, and cited in the submission. Actually, that article gave the rationale of the study in about three journal pages. An evaluator who had made himself or herself familiar with that article would be much less confused by the rationale of this submission.

Several specific comments of this evaluator will now be mentioned:

The authors present a definition of "negative dignity." Does Skinner have such a construct, and, if so, what is it? If not, why is such an idea presented?

Skinner did not present a concept of negative dignity directly, although he did mention the effects of blame. This is a shortcoming of Skinner's formulation, rather than a needless elaboration of ours.

Next, this evaluator commented:

In the second study, the authors mention the very serious problem of burn-out among helping professionals. This is very interesting, and it needs to be elaborated on, particularly explaining how it fits with the main hypotheses.

Our point, which we thought was obvious, was that a burned-out worker would accord no intrinsic dignity to a patient.

Next, this evaluator commented:

On page 15, the authors say that "the gender of the respondents was not a variable." They mean, I believe, to say that they did not analyze this variable. If this is the case, they should not mention gender or they should explain why they do not discuss the results.

We did analyze the variable, and concluded that gender did not influence the results on this questionnaire. Because we did not in fact expect gender to be a variable, there was no point in discussing it.

Presumably, the editor was influenced by the nonsense in this evaluation. These accusations, taken at face value, would be compelling reasons to reject the article. We received no indication that this editor had any problem with the review, however.

JOURNAL Q

The only evaluator for Journal Q was the editor, who responded as follows:

Based on my reading of the paper, I do not believe that [this journal] is the appropriate outlet. I would suggest that you consider submitting it to [another named journal].

SUMMARY

A fourth submission was evaluated by four journals, three of which were very applied in nature. Because the evaluators were generally confused about the rationale of the study, we quoted the actual introduction to the submitted article. The writing in the quoted introduction documents that we were charged with omitting certain critical information that was ostensibly read by the evaluators.

7

Need for Appeal

Evaluators are often personally quite willing to accept the notion of intrinsic human worth or dignity, only if it is called by a more scientifically acceptable name, or if the evidence for it comes from casual first-person observation or intuition. This paradox has enormously important implications for an applied science of behavior. Our beliefs about important issues concerning human nature are achieved ingenuously through everyday personal experiences. Moreover, these views seem to be largely impervious to change even in the face of formal scientific evidence and are not allowed to mingle with scientific beliefs. This interesting generalization apparently holds for the gatekeepers of the scientific literature as it does for the rest of us. Thus, some scientists and gatekeepers of scientific literature actively search for excuses to discount and disbelieve our laboratory evidence for the same belief in intrinsic human worth about which they themselves personally do not hold the slightest doubt.

We cannot know whether this phenomenon applies to a more general class of beliefs than those concerning freedom and dignity. This paradox may be restricted to the special circumstances when a renowned scientist is involved in the controversy. The motivation in this case may be restricted to the need to avoid a challenge to Skinner's pragmatic argument against freedom and dignity. These evaluators seem to accept Skinner's contention that the only way to be truly scientific is to follow his definition of what constitutes acceptable science, and what does not. Obviously some human responses are more amenable to his methodology than others.

As a related matter, we do not believe that all submissions to individual psychological journals are examined with the same care and with the same rigorous criteria of scientific accountability. In fact, we believe that the submissions described in this book were generally subjected to criteria that were substantially harsher than a reasonable norm for the individual journals. We document this last assumption by a subjective comparison of the present evaluations with the implicit norms provided by the published articles in the individual journals, which were presumably the products of many of these same evaluators. We will not attempt to document this claim by pointing to specific examples from the published literature. In our view, however, its truth is easily verified by a quick examination of the published literature in the journals relevant to this area of research.

Many of the comments in the preceding historical account do not in fact represent good science, but patronizing posturings about science. Apparently, some evaluators do not even consider it necessary to read carefully a submission that has the temerity to favor beliefs in freedom and dignity over the formulations and assertions of Skinner. Seemingly, to some the mere fact of such a challenge is proof of ineptitude in science.

The evaluations of our attempts to document the reality of beliefs in intrinsic human dignity tend to fall into two categories of bases for rejection. The first category includes those evaluations that agree with our interpretation of Skinner's pragmatic argument, but do not agree that our data are strong enough to refute Skinner. The second category of evaluators concluded that our data are most convincing, and that we have actually measured something important, but what we have measured is somehow totally irrelevant to Skinner's contentions.

THE METHODOLOGICAL PROBLEM

The evaluators who take the tack that we have methodological problems assert that we have not really demonstrated anything except response biases. Basically these evaluators are saying that although people typically rate others as having intrinsic dignity, none of them really believes that others do in fact have such unearned worth. These evaluators attribute these positive ratings to other factors such as social desirability, demand characteristics, and the like.

Such criticisms are impossible to refute with certainty in this or any other research on such topics that involves the methodological problems of direct report. Such criticisms often can be placed in the "universal general deficit" category (Beaver, 1982, p. 200). There are some technically legitimate criticisms that can always be leveled at any research with essentially no fear of disproof. Harcum (1992) called such a reviewing ploy the Carp and Quibble Tactic. Because the criticisms are technically always correct, they forestall a rebuttal from the author. For example, a control group is never fully equivalent to an experimental group in every aspect that a hostile evaluator might callously assert is relevant. Other similar examples are the reservations that everyone must have about the true validity of any test or measurement, the trite criticisms concerning size and representativeness of the subject population, the subjects' personal interpretation of the questions, and the legitimacy of the statistical analysis.

Beaver (1982) charged that evaluators cite such deficiencies as a reason for rejecting papers that, for example, they might vaguely remember as similar to earlier published research. This is a deliberate defensive maneuver, designed to eliminate protests by the authors with unanswerable verbalized criticism. The charge of duplicating earlier work, on the other hand, can be challenged and, furthermore, the reviewer must cite the earlier work.

We endorsed the assertion that to accord intrinsic dignity is a socially desirable response. But, in the published version of our fourth submission (Harcum & Rosen, 1992), we provided empirical evidence against the proposition that our results could be entirely explained in terms of social desirability artifacts. Specifically, even after we corrected our data for social desirability, we found that populations of college students indicated disagreement with the statement asserting zero dignity to a newborn baby. They gave a rating of 2.48 on a scale in which 1 indicated complete disagreement and 4 indicated a neutral attitude. The disagreement was even slightly greater after the adjustment for social desirability than before. Similarly, a population of care-givers in a mental hospital gave an adjusted rating of 2.86 on the same scale. Therefore, using a direct-report procedure, we found clear evidence for a belief in intrinsic (unearned) dignity that was not produced by social desirability response bias.

Because the significant positive correlation between our social desirability measure and the tendency of both groups of subjects to accord dignity to a newborn baby was not a manifestation of the same attribute, what does the correlation mean? We think that the obvious implication is that the two attributes are outward manifestations of a person who is well socialized.

Let us continue a formal answer to the question by considering the opposite proposition, that the two concepts are the same. What would be the implication of concluding that an accordance of dignity is merely a socially desirable response? This would mean that the accordance of social desirability is perceived to be either an ideal or a social norm. *At least it is identified as an existing concept to be dealt with or used.* It may even be a concept that almost everyone overtly endorses, but privately or subconsciously rejects.

The formulation that Skinner offered is actually mediational. Because of certain hidden, internal responses, the person develops a negative attitude toward science, and therefore manifests various overt oppositional behaviors to science. Given the assumptions that Skinner attributed to the members of society, the ultimate opposition to science is logically inescapable. Here Skinner gave remarkable credit to the lay and professional communities to be able to work out the clever formulation that he attributed to them. We must say, parenthetically, that one of the arguments *against* Skinner's position is that within the substantial collection of trained minds of our professional evaluators, many cannot, or will not, even understand his formulation about what the unsophisticated member of society is supposed to think.

Suppose, for the sake of argument, that the majority of our subjects consciously or unconsciously lied to us. This supposition would be most damaging to our case, but it is not really a plausible interpretation of our results. To accept this supposition would require a consistent reason for many subjects to lie. To say that it was the result of demand characteristics in the experiment, without specifying the nature of the demands, would be circular, merely indicating that the critic is just not prepared to accept our results.

Even if our subjects did not initially believe in the truth of an intrinsic dignity, the sheer availability of the concept provides an alternate basis for escaping Skinner's supposedly inescapable conclusion. If the subjects are capable of these logical operations, then they can use our formulation to avoid the need to oppose behavioral science. Why would subjects not use the logical loophole available to them? Which would be more objectionable: belief in intrinsic dignity or belief in science? On the basis of simple intuition, it seems to us that people are more likely to be consistent in reporting an actual belief than in lying or self-deceiving themselves about it. Thus, the sheer magnitude of the result is compelling to us, although we understand that this cannot be a strong conclusion.

As Shaver (1987) has discussed, the response set of social desirability can involve not only conformity to perceived social norms, but also conformity to perceived attributes of the experimenter—a part of the demand characteristic of the experiment. This mind set can be reduced by decreasing the personal demands on the subject from the research procedures, by masking the value implications of the research questions, and by making statistical corrections for social desirability tendencies. We have attempted to reduce this problem by such methods.

There are several bases to argue that our questionnaires were not ego-involving in a way that would encourage approval-oriented responses. First, they were not presented as attempts to assess characteristics of the subjects, but merely to determine the subjects' opinions on dignity. The verbatim instructions of Harcum, Rosen, and Burijon (1989) were as follows:

> We are studying people's opinions about whether human behavior is caused by voluntary choices, by a person's environment, or by both of these possible factors together. We also want to find out what causes you to believe that someone has dignity or worth. Finally, we want to find out if a person's behaviors influence your perception of his or her dignity, and if this judgment is also influenced by whether you believe that the person did what he or she did because of a deliberate, voluntary choice. (p. 260)

Moreover, in the Harcum, Rosen, and Burijon (1989) Study II, the issues were discussed for the students, indicating that different psychologists, as possible role models, would respond differently. The course instructor and the researcher provided conflicting role models, in fact. Harcum, Rosen, and Burijon thought that this discussion "obviated the variable of appeal to authority" (p. 263). Moreover, the researchers advised the subjects in a "special note" that "different people will probably have different ideas about the sources of dignity and that 'what we want is for you to respond according to how you personally believe'" (p. 261). Also, Harcum, Rosen, and Burijon reported that "all test booklets included the phrase emphasizing that 'each person must be correct in his or her own judgments'" (p. 263).

Finally, the questionnaires were completed anonymously. This practice does not eliminate socially desirable responses, of course, but it does reduce the subjects' tendency to make such responses.

RELEVANCE OF THE DATA

The second category of evaluators believes that our data do reflect some entity, but prefer to call that entity something like "general positivity," "likableness," or "moral evaluation." In short, they say that whatever it is that the subjects are reporting they believe in, it is not intrinsic dignity, despite what the subjects *themselves* call it. Somehow, the argument goes, the entity we have documented is the same as these other entities, and thus not the belief that Skinner was discussing. Therefore, they argue, our data are not relevant to Skinner's formulation.

The evaluators are thus attempting to fit what Skinner has called dignity, or worth, into some existing bodies of literature under different labels. To accomplish this, or at least to show the relevance of these other literatures, is certainly a legitimate and probably ultimately productive goal. But to use such tenuous arguments as a basis for rejecting our results seems to block an avenue for further progress with our different approach.

We used the same words as Skinner to define the concept, and augmented them with a dictionary definition of those words. Although it is, of course, a logical possibility that our subjects were using different meanings for those words than either we or Skinner, that does not seem likely. In fact, it seems rather hubristic of an evaluator to suggest that these subjects are not using the proper words—or using the words improperly—because there are similar concepts in the social psychology literature and therefore the data should be interpreted in those familiar terms. We submit that the onus is on the evaluators to show that such concerns are relevant to an evaluation of our results. We do not understand why our results cannot be taken at face value, while still understanding that much additional research is necessary before we can fully understand and exploit the vital roles of the beliefs in freedom and dignity in our society.

In this context, some of the comments by the editor of Journal D are worth repeating. He said:

> It does not strike me as interesting to discover that people who perform approved acts also are seen as having more "worth, excellence, value," etc. Nor is it interesting *per se* to find that hardly anyone reports that a baby could be so unfortunate as to not elicit supporting and defending behaviors; would you expect people to say that such unfortunate babies be immediately abandoned, which seems to be the only alternative given the broadness of your definition of dignity. I wouldn't know what to think of your subjects had they answered otherwise than they did. . . . Skinner was (and remains), whatever you may think of his theory, an acute observer of human behavior, and would not likely have missed the obvious point that in this and other societies we accord the old, the young, and the helpless some forms of respect and dignity. . . . What might be more interesting to discover is whether people feel that mere humanness conveys intrinsic worth, something that natural law theorists have preached for centuries, but that is under attack in a society that does seem to value mere utilitarian worth. And it might be interesting to look at what features of any of humanness convey this intrinsic value. For example, how far does one have to depart from normality before one is seen as less fully human in this intrinsic sense. These kinds of issues are, of course, very much relevant to present day discussions of treatment for the terminally ill, for treatment and death issues of those born with severe birth defects, and even of abortion. What does it mean to be human? What rights do people assume that people have merely by being human?

The above observations and assertions are, of course, from only one observer, albeit an editor of a psychology journal. He basically agrees with every one of our arguments except insofar as we interpret our results to refute Skinner. Specifically relevant is his confident assertion that it is an "obvious point that in this and in other societies we accord the young, the old and the helpless some form of respect and dignity."

There are three important points in this connection. First, this person probably *does* believe in the intrinsic dignity that he emphatically affirms. To argue that this direct verbal report merely reflects social desirability, or some other response bias, is to strike at the very heart of the concept of peer review, as we have said. Are we blithely to dismiss the sincere declarations of a journal editor in the performance of his editorial duties?

The second point is that this editor perceives others as also believing in such a basis for according dignity. This second point is understandable because of the obviously large proportion of persons in this and other societies who have professed a belief in intrinsic dignity, including many prestigious authors (e.g., Lewis, 1954). Given the frequency with which our subjects profess such belief, presumably these positive reports must often occur in casual conversation.

An interesting point of this evaluation process of four journal submissions is that not a single evaluator ever expressed doubts that members of our society believe in the existence of an unearned basis for according some positive value to other members of society. Some evaluators have in fact, as above, given impassioned support for their personal belief in this concept, although they may have preferred to label it in a way that does not have a connotation that opposes Skinner.

The third point to be made from this evaluator's comments is that the research on these topics is important for society. This aspect of the comments is very gratifying given the comments of some evaluators who have questioned the practical value of this research for practitioners of psychology. As this evaluator said, "These kinds of issues are, of course, very much relevant to present day discussions of treatment for the terminally ill, for treatment and death issues of those born with severe birth defects, and even of abortion." Unfortunately, this evaluator showed that he did not understand that these issues were the focus of our submitted research, as the following comment from the evaluation reveals:

What might be more interesting to discover is whether people feel that mere humanness conveys intrinsic worth, something that natural law theorists have preached for centuries, but that is under attack in a society that does seem to value mere utilitarian worth.

We do not understand how this evaluator can propose this alleged superior alternative to our study after reading our submission. We expressly stated the purpose of our study in the abstract of our submission: "The main research hypothesis was that persons accord an intrinsic dignity to others which does not have to be earned through praiseworthy behaviors performed voluntarily." Can it be that this evaluator did not understand that both we and Skinner equate the concepts of "dignity" and "worth"? That hardly seems likely; we literally made the equation in the first sentence of the abstract, which immediately preceded the sentence stating the hypothesis to be tested. Frankly, we do not see the justification for rejecting our submissions because the evaluators do not understand what they are about.

EVALUATOR STYLE

In addition to complaints about the substance of these evaluations, we often had reason to complain about the style in which the evaluations were written. Following Harcum (1992), we use the term "imperial" to describe many of the reviews, because in general the evaluations were not what we would expect from our peers in terms of the care or in the style of writing. If the reviews were indeed written by our nominal peers, they certainly did not appear so. Rather, as a group with only occasional exceptions, they could be characterized as imperial in the worst sense—unapologetic incompetence, often delivered in an imperious manner.

Roediger (1987) refers to the tendency of evaluators to slip into a "reviewer's mode" or response set to be hypercritical in reviewing a submission. In the case of the present evaluations, this mode has lapsed into the lower level of sophistry. It represents an innocent use of fallacious reasoning that is lacking in genuineness, naturalness, and simplicity.

THE NUMBERS GAME

A question has been raised in this book about the actual proportions of the members of society who believe as we say or as Skinner said. This issue is not as important as it may seem, although our papers did deal with it through the necessary statistical analyses. Clearly, our demonstration of a substantial proportion of the society that believes in intrinsic dignity is a refutation of Skinner's formulation.

But, upon further reflection, it is not truly relevant whether the greater proportion of society believes as we claim or as Skinner claimed. The important point is that a substantial proportion of our subjects did at least acknowledge a belief in a concept of intrinsic dignity. A purist, however, might argue that this is not irrefutable proof because the subjects might have merely reported such a belief and not truly believe in such a basis for according dignity. By such profession they identified or affirmed a possible category or concept of intrinsic dignity. Presumably, they also judged that it was socially desirable to hold such a belief.

The acknowledgment of such a category destroys Skinner's logical argument against the concepts of freedom and dignity. Whether a person *does* believe in intrinsic dignity, he or she *can* believe in such a concept in order to preserve a belief in dignity in the face of a science that could be seen as threatening it. Therefore, there is also a logical alternative to Skinner's plan to remove opposition to science. Instead of eliminating the concepts of freedom and dignity, the alternative is to affirm not only an earned basis for according dignity, but also an unearned basis. Our alternative to Skinner's plan therefore is to: (1) affirm a soft determinism, so that dignity can be preserved by a principle of extenuation for antisocial behaviors; (2) affirm freedom of choice, so that dignity can be earned; and (3) affirm intrinsic dignity, so that dignity does not have to be earned. Let us encourage society to affirm an intrinsic dignity for all human beings, instead of following Skinner's plan to abolish the concepts of freedom and dignity for all.

The advantage to society of these affirmations of freedom and dignity seem obvious to us. By definition, people are more likely to aid those whom they perceive as having dignity or worth. In the context of psychopathology, this view is strongly supported by Rogers (1964, p. 163): "The therapeutic relationship is not devoid of values. When it is most effective it is, I believe, marked by one primary value, namely, that this person (the client) has *worth*." *Unconditional* positive regard implies that the accordance of dignity is not contingent upon the perception of voluntary prosocial behaviors.

THE CONCEPT OF DIGNITY

We agree with several evaluators that we are not able to list all of the factors that enter into a judgment of dignity. Undoubtedly those factors include or overlap some of the factors involved in judgments of general positivity, likableness, or moral evaluation. But, to be consistent with our interpretation of Skinner, we have used the terms "dignity" and "worth" in the sense of the broad dictionary definitions.

We do not question the need for further study of the attributes of one person that induce another to accord that person dignity. In fact, this is the ultimate goal of our program. The first step, nevertheless, is to document that one such basis is perceived humanness. We agree with several researchers that this attribute could be labeled dignity, worth, general positivity, or some other term that does not require that it be earned by voluntary prosocial behaviors. The substantive issue is whether all admiration of people stems from their good behavior, voluntarily performed, or from their existence as marvelous machines, or simply from their possession of a thing called humanity. The irony of this evaluation process is that some evaluators have considered the point too obvious to publish documentation, while others have considered our evidence inadequate because of methodological criticisms that are trite but not truly substantive. As Garcia (1981) said, the basic issue is whether minor methodological deficiencies destroy the validity of the conclusions.

The issues here concern the beliefs of society about dignity and worth. We asked groups of persons, who are part of that society, to rate how much dignity or worth was incorporated in hypothetical persons under selected conditions. *It is not for the evaluators to say that the subjects were conceptualizing dignity incorrectly, or that the subjects did not know what they were doing.* Surely, if the subjects had been given more information about actor characteristics and situational context, they would have rated differently. Exactly how they would do this educated rating provides questions for further study. Very likely, the ratings in our studies were influenced by the use of contrived vignettes and hypothetical persons, instead of actual newspaper accounts. Although our subjects rated the dignity of an actor within a rather impoverished context, Skinner's original formulation was in fact totally devoid of any limiting context.

Our major problems with the evaluators apparently entail the difficulty in finding some way to show that our data, which indicate the common expression of the belief in some factor called unearned or given dignity or worth by our subjects, are related to Skinner's concept of dignity. Because we are using the same words, and letting the subjects do the ratings in those terms, they must be referring to dignity or worth, whatever that may be for them. We do not know exactly what it is, but we know that it is there because our subjects told us so. Individually, they may be confused in that the entity they are calling dignity is only social desirability, or collective illusion, or general positivity, or likableness. But it is not *earned* dignity, and that is the point.

Whatever this concept is, it is not threatened by a science of behavior, as Skinner claimed, because it is not dependent on unexplainable behavior for its existence. Therefore, we do not have to get rid of this concept in order to have a science of behavior, even if Skinner's conception of science were correct—which obviously we do not accept (Harcum, 1988).

A belief in given dignity is a response. It may have been learned or developed through reinforcement or imitation. At this point exactly how it may have been acquired is not crucial. The nature of the belief is not crucial, or even that the belief is identical for each respondent. Interestingly enough, not a single evaluator ever said, "I do not agree with you that the members of our society believe in an intrinsic dignity that does not have to be earned by voluntary prosocial behaviors." In fact, several vehemently stated the belief we were attempting to demonstrate.

We predicted that people would report that they did have such a belief. To impugn a positive report, one must resort to some sort of interpersonal dynamics that might represent logical possibilities, but not necessarily realistic ones. The argument ultimately reverts to an admission that subjects recognize some generally accepted category of positive values about people that does not come from their voluntary behaviors. This concept is therefore not threatened by a science of behavior that destroys the concept of voluntarism. The only thing remarkable about this is that Skinner denied it, and others have uncritically gone along for years with his assertion.

A TENTATIVE EXPLANATION

Evaluators seem to be looking for the complication and the exception instead of the basic generalization. This is analogous to a familiar example in problem solving. When asked to complete the letter sequence OTTFF, young children easily give the correct answer, S. College graduates, on the other hand, are baffled, because they tend to make exotic hypotheses and overlook the possibility of the first letters in the spelled numbers representing a counting sequence. We accuse the evaluators of showing such intellectualization, avoiding the simple and obvious in favor of the complicated. Possibly the mechanism is motivated avoidance (Harcum, 1988), distraction from work overload (Harcum, 1992), an overzealous extension of their training in critical analysis, overly critical thinking when shifting into the reviewing mode (Roediger, 1987), or something else. We rule out personal bias because frankly we doubt that we are personally acquainted with any of these evaluators.

We suspect that this critical mind set was potentiated by the fact that we were unknown authors—at least to social psychologists—and we were strongly attacking the work of a highly prestigious and famous researcher and author. Even if our submissions were submitted to blind review, the authorship could hardly be doubted. To see this, the reader is invited to examine the references cited in the articles in the appendices. These citations clearly reveal that we had conducted several studies on these problems, whereas no one else had previously even raised the issue in print, as best we can determine.

Perloff and Perloff (1982) suggest that authors should pay cash to evaluators for their evaluations in order to enable the evaluators to use sufficient time and attention for meritorious reviewing. But this plan would probably also have undesired effects. For example, the prestigious researcher would be less likely to perceive the process of evaluation as a public service to the profession, and would be less attracted to the remuneration, which would in all likelihood be rather modest. Therefore, the evaluators might not be as overworked, but they would probably be less experienced in research and less skilled in evaluating submissions. Thus, the answer is not in securing evaluators, but in increasing their accountability.

The evaluators were certainly not even-handed in their concern for scientific rigor. For example, we were severely criticized several times for insufficient attention to the definition of dignity and to the validity of our attempts to measure beliefs about it. But not a single editor or evaluator took Skinner to task for writing a major book and several articles about dignity and not offering more than a single-word (i.e., "worth") definition for it. We do not argue that they should have done so, because we do not fault Skinner for his laconic definition of dignity. Perhaps somewhere in print an author has previously taken Skinner to task for not adequately defining what he meant by "dignity." We are not aware of one. We argue, however, that such omissions in the numerous printed reactions to Skinner's classic book clearly indicate that the definition was not a problem in the context of his argument. At this point we raise the disturbing question about why so many of these reviewers and editors now view the definition as crucial to the acceptance of our results, instead of suggesting new avenues for research. In the context, Skinner's definition was totally adequate; ours was actually more so. As we have said so many times, our disagreement with Skinner is not a matter of the definition of dignity, but the bases on which it is accorded by one person to others.

We did nevertheless provide subjects with a dictionary definition of what the word "dignity" means. We asked the subjects to answer questions about it in several ways, all of which converged on the same conclusion: these citizens believe in what we have called unearned or intrinsic dignity. We never encountered an evaluator who said, "I am glad that someone has finally provided data to refute Skinner's unfounded assertions about freedom and dignity." This fact is particularly interesting in view of the large number of writers who were greatly distressed and violently opposed to Skinner's proposal to eliminate freedom and dignity, and also the great number of authors who hailed his book as one of the most important of the period. On the positive side, as a fall-out from these evaluations, there have been several indications of encouragement about the possibility of helpful outcomes from this research program. There have also been some possibly helpful suggestions for further research and where to look for relevant data and theory.

DIGNITY AND BLAME

Recently, we were embarrassed to report (Harcum & Rosen, 1990c) an oversight in our preparation of the various submissions we have discussed. It concerns the implication of Skinner's argument in the case of antisocial behaviors. In this case, the progress of science shifts the blame from the person to the environment, thus decreasing the loss of dignity to be expected from the performance of perceived voluntary misdeeds. Although we can hardly blame the editors and evaluators for missing a point that we ourselves initially missed in our research, we note that this inconsistency in the Skinner argument was also overlooked by over two dozen experts who evaluated our submissions. This is at least consistent with our belief that the evaluators often did not truly come to grips with our research problem or results.

As best we can discover, this point of criticism had not been previously expressed in the 35 years since the argument was first advanced, and over 20 years since the argument was widely disseminated in Skinner's classic book. It is interesting to speculate why so many writers, including our evaluators, have focused on Skinner's metaphysics and largely ignored his practical argument against freedom and dignity. The historical avoidance of the freedom and dignity issue may have been caused by the same factors that produced the negative reactions of our evaluators. When confronted with this issue, the evaluators proposed that our concept of intrinsic dignity was not importantly different from several concepts already in the research literature. But none were willing to make an extensional connection between such research and Skinner's formulation. Our explanation for this is that many authors were quite willing to attack Skinner on metaphysical issues, which were not resolvable empirically, but singularly unwilling to question him on empirical grounds—presumably because he established the scientific rules. Skinner was able to run a practical bluff for over 30 years because no one prior to our first submission in 1987 was willing to call him on it, or was able to achieve publication of such a challenge. Because of Skinner's expertise as a laboratory researcher, behavioral scientists may have been afraid to question his conclusions about empirical fact. When he turned away from his database in attempts to design a better culture, he was only occasionally challenged (e.g., Smith, 1973). As best we know, no one prior to our first submission had ever attempted to refute with data Skinner's practical arguments against freedom and dignity. Perhaps some had tried but fell short of publication because they were less persevering than we.

We charge that the members of the profession were generally afraid of being labeled as unscientific if they attempted to refute Skinner's formulations against freedom and dignity with empirical data. We charge that the evaluators for this reason were afraid to endorse our results and conclusions. Such fear is inimical to a supposed self-correcting science.

IMPLICATIONS FOR SCIENCE

Society opposes science for the simple reason that many of its members actually buy into Skinner's conception of science. Those who conceptualize science in terms of strict behaviorism do not perceive the loophole of intrinsic dignity, and therefore oppose science as they understand it. Or, to say it another way, they feel that if the science of human behavior is as reductionistic as described by Skinner, they want no part of such a science anyway.

Others simply do not like Skinner's metaphysical position for whatever legitimate professional or personal reasons. Therefore, they oppose it, whether or not they have worked out a good logical argument to support their views. In any case, the sheer existence of opposition to Skinner's views on freedom and dignity is not viable evidence for the validity of Skinner's formulation. First, it would be necessary to rule out several alternative explanations, as proposed above. Thus, this book fulfills its purpose of redirecting our thinking to the true cause of opposition to Skinner's view of science. The answer is in terms of weaknesses in that view itself, not some complicated argument about intrapersonal dynamics, as Skinner suggests.

Paradoxically, however, Skinner's example does illustrate the true character of science. Modern notions about the nature of science involve the central role of certain characteristics of scientists as persons. The sets and biases of scientists with respect to acceptable methods and philosophies control the direction of research and therefore the progress or stagnation of their science. These predispositions of evaluators become important because they become heuristics for solving the press of multiple submissions and limited journal space. Therefore, the current system of peer review increases the possibility that such dispositions will inhibit progress, because the individual evaluator is likely to be a successful product of the traditional scientific presuppositions.

A PROPOSAL

The existence of a phenomenon in the peer-review process has been demonstrated: some editors and reviewers for journals that report psychological research tend to use a set of heuristics for solving the problems of selecting research for publication (Harcum, 1992). Although it is not possible to make an accurate estimate of the frequencies of usage for each heuristic, the frequencies do indicate that such use is a sufficiently indigenous part of the reviewing system to warrant remedial action.

We propose that evaluators give greater priority to new ideas, even if they have reservations about some methodological details of the study. The purists and doubters still have an opportunity to express their concerns later in signed publications. One may argue, with some justification, that all submissions and evaluations should be published. But, as Roediger (1987) pointed out, there is no point in publishing, for example, the case histories of women who allegedly vomit frogs just because someone wants to make the claim. To be sure, there could be some advantage to open publishing of everything. When the results are valid, even if not productive in opening new awareness of research, other scientists would know of false starts, and also false blocks to progress. The present book does in fact provide one example of what might be learned by a practice of open publication.

Glenn (1982) made two worthy suggestions for improving journal evaluations: (1) send evaluators' comments to the authors for rebuttal before the editor makes the decision to reject; and (2) limit the number of manuscripts per year to be handled by a single editor. While endorsing both proposals, we would like to emphasize the first one, because, in one sense, it does not matter how many evaluations a person performs if he or she does them all well. Unfortunately, our experience with Journal L, described in Chapter 5, does not bode well for the success of such a procedure. But, perhaps our situation was somewhat unusual in that we were attacking the work of a prestigious author.

Finke (1990) joined other authors who believe that the editorial process would benefit from an exchange of arguments between evaluator and author:

> editors should give authors an opportunity to reply to a reviewer's negative comments before reaching an editorial decision, especially when the reviews are mixed. This would minimize the problem of having a quality paper rejected because some of the reviewers are uninformed, overly demanding, or misunderstand the paper. The reviewers, in turn, could be invited to respond to the author's reply, if desired. (p. 670)

Colman (1982) suggested that an editor who does not himself or herself have the specialized knowledge to evaluate the evaluator's criticisms of a submission should send the criticisms to the authors for rebuttal. If the authors respond, then their rebuttals should be sent to an independent judge, along with the original submissions and the evaluator comments. As Colman concludes, "This procedure would perhaps eliminate some of the more blatant injustices of the peer-review system and act as a corrective to referee error" (p. 206).

Bornstein (1990) proposed a legal model for the evaluation of submissions to journals. The philosophy of the legal model displaces the concept of an even-handed assessment of the strengths and weaknesses of a submission, with the concept of the reviewers as prosecutors, frankly devoting themselves to challenging the value and validity of the author's conclusions. Because the reviewers would be instructed to criticize the submission, with the knowledge that their comments could be directly challenged by the authors, neither blind reviews nor anonymous reviews would be necessary or desirable. Bornstein (1990) described the details of the model:

> Following the legal model, the "burden of proof" (i.e., the burden of demonstrating that a manuscript was seriously flawed) would rest on the reviewer(s), and a study would be considered "innocent until proven guilty" (i.e., publishable until shown to be significantly flawed).
>
> By having an associate editor always make the initial judgement regarding acceptance or rejection of a manuscript, the mechanism for "appeal" of a decision perceived by the author as unfair would be clear. Such an appeal would be handled by the journal editor and would consist of the initial critique and rebuttal, along with the associate editor's decision letter and a further (brief) follow-up rebuttal by the author. (pp. 672–673)

The major advantage of this system, according to Bornstein (1990), is as follows:

> When an adversary model is used, manuscripts could not be rejected on the basis of incorrect or subjective assertions made by reviewers (a situation that, unfortunately, does occur under the present system; see Bradley, 1981; Garcia, 1981; Mahoney, 1985). (p. 672)

The conclusion is possibly naive. Presumably, the journal editor is still the judge of whether a submission is "significantly flawed."

Harcum (1992) proposed an office of ombudsman, to be associated with one of the associations of psychologists, which would evaluate charges of unfair, incompetent, or otherwise flawed evaluations. The present problems of evaluation would probably have been reduced or eliminated if there were such an official ombudsman to support meritorious appeals of journal decisions. In the case of the submissions in question, the ombudsman would have long ago made the judgment that we now ask our readers to make. Have we, as the authors of proposed articles, been guilty of further burdening an already overburdened research-evaluation establishment by wrong-minded perseverance in seeking publication of this research? Or has the peer-review system been a victim of its own failures to produce competent evaluations? If the authors are merely guilty of "journal shopping," they could be discouraged by the ombudsman evaluation. No one would want to develop a reputation as a journal shopper. Instead of adding an extra burden to the peer-review process, the ombudsman concept would reduce the workload through increased efficiency. It should produce a better feeling in authors about the process, through a reduction of frustration.

Our documentation supports the pessimistic conclusion of Blisset (1982), however, that the basic problem of satisfactory evaluation of journal submissions goes deeper than simply defective evaluation processes. Blisset said, "The problems are content problems and go to the nature and structure of the disciplines involved" (p. 204). Therefore, simple changes in peer-review practices, such as the use of appeal panels and evaluation of evaluators, will not solve the problem. None of these changes will compensate for poorly trained, closed-minded professionals in the field, from whom evaluators may be selected.

A BELIEF WITH SURVIVAL VALUE

Before concluding this book, we wish to add a few paragraphs about the practical implications of the repeated rejections of our submissions. We assume that our long-range research objectives concerning the factors controlling the perception of freedom and dignity would be beneficial to society. Our program was immeasurably hindered by publishing setbacks. Not only was the publication of our first results delayed, but we were forced to conduct additional studies in further attempts simply to establish the existence of beliefs in intrinsic dignity. The program was further delayed by seemingly endless rewrites of the various submissions. The multiple resubmissions added further to the heavy workload of editors and evaluators, as well as the secretarial, administrative, and other support staffs, which—to us at least—are severely limited in the time available for such services.

All of our effort to date is worse than useless if the readers of the published work and this book are not convinced by our argument for the practical relevance of the issue of freedom and dignity. We must deal with the possibility that the recommendations to reject were correct, even if the reasoning was incorrect. Are we correct in advocating a need for beliefs in freedom and dignity, as well as in demonstrating the reality of the beliefs? Therefore, an additional issue involves what behavioral scientists *should* believe, rather than what society *does* believe. In one sense, does it truly matter which belief is the more popular? The important question is: In the best interest of our culture, whose minds should be changed, if either view is to be changed? Should we convert the humanists to Skinnerians or Skinnerians to humanists, or none of the above? To use Skinner's proposed criterion, which practice would increase the likelihood of survival for our culture?

We have no dependable criterion measure for answering this question. We do have some relevant data, however, based admittedly on casual observation of unreliable indicants. The first indicant is the fact of current survival of the belief in intrinsic dignity. Although we do not know that the existing practices and beliefs will ultimately survive, we can use the fact of present existence to suggest that they must have enjoyed at least some short-term advantages. Skinner himself used such an argument. Therefore, the evidence for the current belief in an intrinsic human dignity suggests that such a belief has been beneficial for some persons in some circumstances.

Presumably also, Skinner's belief was helpful to him at least (Elms, 1981). In this sense, then, the relative numbers of people holding a given belief would be relevant to the issue of which might be more useful. A belief in a completely deterministic world may decrease the sensed loss of dignity through personal failure, but it does not produce a positive sense of personal worth. Skinner's proposal was to accord a person dignity because he or she, as a human being, is a marvelous piece of machinery, without volition to do good or evil. This seems a very poor substitute for believing that every human being has worth—that just by virtue of being human, a person has value, whether or not he or she retains the marvelous functioning of the body.

The second indicant is, as suggested by Skinner, a determination of which practices seem to be working in the culture. Clearly, for example, the use of reward-contingencies has been effective in behavior modification and educational programs. There is cause for caution, however, because of the concern for replacing intrinsic motivation with reward-oriented motivation (Deci, 1971; Kohn, 1990). The danger is that no beneficial behaviors will be manifested unless the person expects a tangible, externally based reward. Despite the dangers, which could be reduced by proper education, one must endorse the proper use of learning principles.

There is also evidence for the effectiveness of approaches based on the concepts of personal intentions and efficacy. Examples can be cited, for example, from applications to psychotherapy (Erickson, 1973; Harcum, 1989), business (McClelland, 1985), and general culture (May, 1969). Various successful missionary and humanitarian aid programs are based on the concepts of human dignity, especially for those who have not been able to earn it, and who would be unlikely to be able to reciprocate at a later date. Frequent newspaper accounts amply document this conclusion.

Because beliefs in both intrinsic and earned dignity are not incompatible, both sources of dignity are available to the thinking of a person who chooses to believe in them. Such a person obviously has an additional reason to help another—which should be beneficial to society. The dual view permits a person full access to the principles and techniques of learning, plus additional principles and techniques of humanistic psychology that are not available to the strict determinist.

We need research on which attributes cause people to accord dignity to their neighbors. A peer-review system that has systematically impeded the progress of research in this direction, by bringing to bear seemingly all of the documented flaws of the system against it, has not served the science or the society well.

SUMMARY

This book has described the case history of several journal submissions to illustrate some common practices in the reviewing process that can thwart the publication of worthy information, especially from innovative research. The analysis supported several suggestions for improving the system, including instituting an office of editorial ombudsman that would support meritorious appeals. Currently, there are no guarantees that an appeal will be taken seriously—or even that it will be read. The ombudsman could urge the editor to reconsider a decision. Nothing would infringe on the right and responsibility of the editor to make final decisions, however. Evaluators should be the gatekeepers of an improved science, more open to new ideas.

This book closed with a discussion of the scientific implications of the decisions to reject these submissions. The decisions hindered progress in convincing society that it would be improved if it maintained and strengthened our beliefs in freedom and dignity.

Appendix A

First Submission:
Direct Test

ABSTRACT

This study investigated the relationship between the degree to which a person's behavior is ascribed to voluntary choice and the level of dignity ascribed to that person, to test Skinner's (1971) contention that the function originates at zero dignity for zero choice. In Study 1, 91 students in introductory psychology answered questions about themselves, their beliefs about voluntary versus environmental control of behavior, and their bases for judging dignity. Then they attempted to describe their views of the functional relationship between voluntary control and human dignity, for prosocial and for antisocial behaviors. Most subjects indicated belief in voluntary choice, and some in intrinsic (unearned) dignity, but most could not relate choice and dignity quantitatively. The study was repeated, using 27 students in a personality class, for whom the theoretical implications of various functional relationships were discussed before the functions were drawn. Results contradicted Skinner's formulation.

THE PERCEIVED FUNCTIONAL RELATIONSHIP BETWEEN INTENTIONAL BEHAVIOR AND HUMAN DIGNITY

One of the most important propositions of our time is the proposal of B. F. Skinner (1971) that the science of human behavior has been hindered by the false beliefs of many that there is a positive functional relationship between two entities called personal freedom and human dignity. In Skinner's view of society's beliefs, the function for prosocial behaviors begins at the origin, with zero

First submission of "Popular versus Skinnerian views on the relation between human freedom and dignity" to Journal A. For final publication, see Harcum, Rosen, and Burijon (1989).

personal freedom corresponding to the perception of zero human dignity. As the prosocial behaviors are ascribed to greater degrees of voluntary control, the amount of perceived dignity increases. Thus, according to this belief system, all human dignity is earned through the voluntary performance of prosocial behaviors. Consequently, in Skinner's conception of society's view, without personal freedom to make voluntary prosocial acts, there can be no dignity.

Thus, according to Skinner's formulation, the members of society fear that any reduction of personal freedom will naturally result in a corresponding reduction of human dignity. In order to protect the cherished concept of dignity, he argues, people therefore tend to oppose anything which threatens the concept of personal freedom.

Skinner argues that behavioral science is inexorably reducing the domain of personal freedom in human behavior by providing environmental and genetic explanations for behaviors previously ascribed to personal choice. Therefore, he asserts, science comes to be perceived as the foe of, first, personal freedom and, second, human dignity. This interpretation is offered to account for society's failure to embrace his strict behavioristic metaphysics, which deny the existence of any personal freedom of choice. Without choice, by Skinner's reasoning, people will be forced to give up the notion of personal dignity.

The purpose of the present report is to investigate the actual relationship between perceived freedom of choice and the perception of personal dignity. Skinner's metaphysical position rests on his unsupported belief that the public believes that personal dignity depends solely upon the existence of freedom of choice.

Skinner is able to maintain his view of society's beliefs because he essentially disregards the literature on freedom and dignity as not scientific (Blanshard & Skinner, 1966). Perhaps data based on casual observation should be ignored by the scientist; laboratory data would be more convincing to some, even if not more conclusive. Harcum and Rosen [Appendix C] tested the hypotheses represented in Figure 1. [This figure has not been reprinted in Appendix A—it is the same as Figure C.2 in Appendix C.] The primary hypothesis is that the subjects will accord a degree of positive (intrinsic) dignity to a person who has not earned it through the voluntary commission of prosocial acts. Further, the level of dignity can be augmented by prosocial behaviors and decreased by antisocial behaviors. College students were asked to read short vignettes describing prosocial and antisocial behaviors performed under six presumed levels of personal choice. Their ratings of dignity for the various conditions confirmed the general tenor of the hypotheses in Figure 1 [Appendix C, Figure C.2], but there were too few data points to identify the shapes of the curves, and too few ratings near zero personal choice to determine with precision the intercept on the dignity axis.

The main purpose of the present study is to test the hypotheses of Figure 1 [Appendix C, Figure C.2] using a more direct procedure. The subjects will literally be asked to draw their conception of the functional relationship between the ascribed degree of personal choice in the selection of a behavior and the amount of perceived dignity accorded the behaving individual. The primary hypothesis is that persons are accorded an intrinsic level of dignity which does not have to be earned, and this level of dignity is merely augmented by perceived voluntary performance of prosocial behaviors and diminished by perceived voluntary performance of antisocial behaviors. Thus, the major prediction is that the functions will intersect the y-axis (perceived dignity) at a value significantly above zero, for those persons judged not to be personally responsible for their behavior.

Secondary goals of the study were to investigate beliefs about the relative influences of personal choice versus environment on behaviors, and what attributes of persons cause them to be accorded dignity.

STUDY 1

Subjects

The subjects were 91 students in Introductory Psychology serving as part of a course requirement.

Method

The subjects were tested in a group. Each subject was given a test booklet with consent forms attached. The instructions told the subjects:

> We are studying people's opinions about whether human behavior is caused by voluntary choices, by a person's environment, or by both of these possible factors together. We also want to find out what causes you to believe that someone has dignity or worth. Finally, we want to find out if a person's behaviors influence your perception of his or her dignity, and if this judgement is also influenced by whether you believe that the person did what he or she did because of a deliberate, voluntary choice.

The subjects were then asked to read and sign the consent form and detach it from the test booklet. All agreed to participate.

Part I of the test booklet asked the subjects to indicate their gender, race, whether they considered themselves culturally different from the majority of students of their sex and race, whether or not they were religious—defined as belief in God(s) and frequent worship—and the likelihood of their choosing a career in human services.

Part II, Section A asked the subjects to indicate their beliefs about whether "meaningful daily behavior (that is, excluding simple reflexes like the knee jerk) could be influenced by the deliberate, voluntary intentions of a person, in contrast to the possible influence of environmental forces." On a scale ranging from 0% (entirely environmental) to 100% (entirely voluntary), with 50% indicating half environment, half voluntary, the subjects were asked to indicate their beliefs for these situations: (1) "most people in general throughout life"; (2) "the person who's (*sic*) behavior is generally as influenced as much as it is possible in reality for behavior to be influenced by environmental forces";

and (3) "the person who's (*sic*) behavior is generally as influenced as much as it is possible in reality for behavior to be influenced by deliberate personal intentions."

In Part II, Section B, each subject was asked to write a description of "what circumstances, events, states, etc., determine your judgements about whether or not you will judge another person to have dignity or worth." A dictionary definition of "dignity" was given, along with the following operational definition:

> From a scientific standpoint, the only way that one can establish whether or not a person in fact has worth or value as a human being is to find out whether he or she is thought by others to have such worth. Objectively, a person has worth if someone perceives that he or she has it.

Then the subjects were asked to draw, on a provided blank graph matrix, a functional relationship indicating their beliefs about the relationship between the "assumed percentages of influence on behavior by voluntary intentions" (ranging from 0 to 100%) and the "percentage of maximum possible perceived dignity" (ranging from +100%, through 0, to −100%), one for behaviors considered "beneficial" and one for behaviors considered "harmful." The subjects were told in a "special note" that "we understand that different people will probably have different ideas about the sources of dignity" and that "what we want is for you to respond according to how you personally believe." As an experimental variable, one-third of the subjects were told the following: "Nevertheless, given the definition of dignity, each person must be correct in his or her own judgements. Therefore, your criteria are unquestionably correct for you and your judgements, whether or not they happen to agree with those of anyone else." Another third were told, "For example, the eminent humanistic psychologist, Carl R. Rogers, contends that each person has some dignity just by being or existing, independent of whether or not his or her behaviors are socially approved." A final third were told, "For example, the eminent behavioristic psychologist, B. F. Skinner, contends that the only way a person can have dignity is to earn it by performing socially approved acts."

The subjects were asked to draw a function for the complete range of the abscissa "in a hypothetical sense if necessary," even if they did not believe that the full range of voluntary control was possible. The instructions were summarized as follows:

> You should now have drawn two lines relating the two scales of the graph. You have one line for "beneficial" behaviors and another line for "harmful" behaviors. You may have just one line for both if your view is that the lines should be identical. If your two lines are identical, label the line "both beneficial and harmful." Now, check the line, or lines, to determine if they represent what you mean. Whenever a line rises above zero, it means that you would admire such a person and consider him or her to be an asset to society; whenever a line

falls below zero, it means that you would despise such a person and consider him or her to be a detriment to society.

The instructions in the test booklet invited students to ask questions if they did not understand the task, but not, of course, about what their personal answer should be.

Results

Belief in Voluntary Control. We predicted that the subjects would avoid the extreme values for the items indicating voluntary control of behavior. The subjects indicated that for most people in general, the behavior is 56.0% controlled by voluntary choice. No subject gave a 0% or 100% response to this item. The person who is generally as influenced as much as it is possible in reality for behavior to be influenced by environmental forces is thought to be controlled only 32.6% by voluntary choice. Only one person gave a 0% response to this item. The person whose behavior is generally influenced as much as it is possible in reality for behavior to be influenced by deliberate personal intentions is thought to be influenced 74.5% by voluntary choices. Only one subject gave a 100% response.

Essays on Dignity. When writing the brief essays describing what they considered endowed a person with dignity or worth, 12 (13.2%) of the subjects responded with the statement that dignity is always present in each human being. The 13.2% who mentioned intrinsic dignity is significantly different from the 0% predicted from Skinner's argument: $t(90) = 4.11; p < .001$.

Function Drawing. When the subjects attempted to draw curves relating perceived dignity to the degree to which the prosocial or antisocial behaviors were thought to be caused by a voluntary choice of the person, the results revealed no consistent pattern. Many subjects produced a result which was idiosyncratic and unintelligible to the researchers. The most frequent result (*viz.*, $N = 11$) was, however, a "Skinnerian" response in that both functions for Harmful and Beneficial behaviors started at the origin of the graph. Nevertheless, this result represented a small minority (12.1%) of the subjects, compared to the 100% predicted by Skinner's formulation.

Experimental Manipulation. The experimental manipulation of references to authority could not be evaluated meaningfully because the dependent variable (the functional relationship) was so erratic.

Individual Differences. Several of the subject characteristics correlated with the beliefs about voluntary control. Women tended to rate higher than men the level of voluntary control for the person with the most control: $r = -.291; p = .003$. Ratings of the likelihood for entering human services were correlated with the judgements about the general level of voluntary control for most people throughout life: $r = -.258; p = .007$. Of course, the ratings for the general category of control were correlated with the other two: general vs. least: $r = .573; p < .001$; general vs. most: $r = .672; p < .001$. However, the least category was not correlated with the most category: $r = .144; p = .228$.

Discussion

These results indicate a virtually universal belief in both voluntary human choices of behaviors and in a degree of environmental control. None of the students seemed to be concerned about any problems in resolving possible conflicting connotations of the two concepts. These results would be more or less expected by everyone.

The results from the written narratives about the basis of awarding dignity, in which 13.2% of the subjects mentioned intrinsic dignity, are surprising in view of some previous results of Harcum and Rosen [Appendix B], which revealed that about 35% of the subjects would write narratives supporting the view for intrinsic dignity. We attribute this difference in results to the way the questions were asked, because it could have been interpreted to be asking what *behaviors or conditions* caused one person to be accorded more dignity than another. Nevertheless, there was evidence in favor of a belief in intrinsic dignity.

The lack of consistency among the subjects, in drawing the functional relationship between perceived voluntary control and perceived dignity, was disappointing. It was not possible to determine whether this lack of consistency was caused by an inability of the subjects to understand the task, to their attitudes on the subject, or both. In either case, we can draw the tentative conclusion that Skinner is not correct in attributing a consistent, thought-through attitude on these issues to the members of society; if the belief systems were sorted out, the task would be understandable. Thus, the sheer incoherence of the results tends to refute Skinner; the subjects do not conform to his formulation. We suspect, in fact, that the subjects giving the "Skinnerian" response were merely producing the simplest curves that would satisfy the instructions. Because this interpretation cannot be proved, further study is needed.

STUDY 2

The second study was designed to secure a population of subjects for whom the function-drawing task would be understood and meaningful. Instead of using rather naive subjects, the method was to select subjects from a more sophisticated and knowledgeable population, and to discuss frankly the issues and options with them before the task was completed.

Subjects and Method

The method was very similar to that of Study 1, with two major changes: (1) The subjects were 29 members of an advanced class in personality theory for which introductory psychology was a prerequisite, tested during regular class hours; and (2) the issues under investigation were thoroughly discussed with the students, as part of the educational experience of the course, before they attempted to draw the functional relationship between perceived voluntary choice and perceived dignity.

The manipulation of appeal to authority was not used because of the discussion, which obviated the variable. All test booklets therefore included the phrase which emphasized that "each person must be correct in his or her own judgements."

The study was conducted during a regular meeting of the class at a time when the instructor was introducing the approach of B. F. Skinner to personality theory. Therefore, the discussion of issues and theory were a part of the educational experience for the course. In the presence of the course instructor, who was basically behavioristic in his approach to theory, the experimenter, who is basically cognitive in his approach, discussed metaphysical and theoretical issues involved in the conceptions of how presumed choice and dignity might be related. He emphasized how various psychologists would presumably respond, and he interpreted the implications of different possible subject responses. He answered questions to clarify the task, but emphasized that the only "correct" answer was a true reflection of the individual student's own beliefs. The course instructor, because of his different theoretical persuasion, was an effective monitor to assure that all issues were fairly discussed and that the students were not led by the experimenter to any particular response.

Results and Discussion

Estimated Voluntary Control. The means of the estimated percentages of control by intentional choice were as follows: (1) most people in general = 49.9%; (2) least influenced by intentional choice = 29.7%; and (3) most influenced by intentional choice = 69.9%. These values were quite similar to the results from the larger, less selective population in Study 1.

Bases of Dignity. The statements of what gives a person dignity revealed 12 subjects who awarded dignity just because a person exists (*viz.*, "everyone has it"). This was the most frequent response (41% of the subjects). Other answers were distributed among such earned bases as having good personal qualities and actions, good self-esteem, and motivation for self-actualization. Because Skinner would predict a response of 0% for the intrinsic worth statement, the 41% result may be considered significantly different from zero: $t(29) = 4.56$; $p < .001$. Therefore, Skinner's contention is again refuted with this sample of subjects.

Choice/Dignity Function. Although 27 subjects satisfactorily completed the task of relating perceived voluntary control and perceived dignity, there was nevertheless great variability. Therefore, the representativeness of average curves was questionable. The result for beneficial behaviors was an ascending straight line intersecting the ordinate at about 27% of maximum positive dignity. The median was at 20% positive dignity. For harmful behaviors a descending straight line intersected the ordinate at about −2% of maximum negative dignity, with a median of 0%. These average results however actually could be said to be representative specifically of the results of only three subjects. Of the remainder, twelve subjects drew both of the intercepts above zero, five drew both intercepts through zero, and the remaining subjects represented various other possibilities.

The box score thus tends to contradict Skinner; whereas only five subjects responded as he presumed, 12 subjects responded as we predicted. The stronger evidence, however, comes from an evaluation of the intercept for beneficial behaviors. Considering only the perceived dignity for 0% voluntary control, there were eight responses of zero dignity, 17 responses of positive dignity, and two responses of negative dignity. It should be noted that the deviations from zero were not due to sensory-motor limitations, because the smallest positive values were at 7 and 8%. Eight of the positive responses were in fact at 50% or greater.

A simple t-test was performed to compare the mean intercept on the ordinate to the 0 intercept predicted by Skinner. The result was significant: $t(24) = 4.53$; $p < .001$. Thus, Skinner's assessment of the public belief system is not substantiated, and therefore his practical argument against the concepts of freedom and dignity is without substance.

The fact that the intercept for Harmful behaviors was not greater than zero, and not equal to that for Beneficial behaviors, is an embarrassment for the present theory, described in Figure 1 [Appendix C, Figure C.2]. Logically, persons not responsible for their actions should not be held accountable for them, and thus there should be no difference at the y-intercept between the Harmful and Beneficial responses. Perhaps subjects cannot truly conceive of such completely environmentally determined behavior. In any case, an extrapolation to the left, if that were meaningful, would indicate a crossing of the curves at a point above zero.

Subject Characteristics. The correlation between gender and voluntary choice for the most extreme case was about the same as in Study 1, but opposite in sign. It was not significant, presumably because of the smaller number of subjects: $r = .249$; $p = .097$. Therefore, the issue of possible gender differences requires further study. Again, the estimates of voluntary control correlated significantly, except for the situations representing the least and the most extremes of voluntary control.

Two subject characteristics correlated significantly with whether their curve drawings tended to support Skinner or the authors' hypothesis. Subjects more likely to choose a career in human services were more likely to support our hypothesis: $r = .391$; $p = .024$. Also, subjects attributing greater voluntary choice in the most extreme case tended to support Skinner's hypothesis: $r = -.421$; $p = .016$.

GENERAL DISCUSSION

Both of these studies give clear support to the notion that college students believe in the existence of voluntary control of behavior. Skinner does not disagree with this fact, but merely with the objective truth of the belief.

The narrative descriptions of the subjects in both studies indicate that a substantial minority of them report a belief in intrinsic, unearned dignity. Skinner's formulation does not make a place for such a belief.

The evidence from the perceived functional relationship between behavior and dignity is the most damaging to Skinner's position. Whereas he ascribes a particular belief system to society members in general, a large sample of college students in Study 1 was unable to reproduce such a response on demand. It does not seem too important in this context whether this failure was caused specifically by an inability to understand the task, or by a prior failure to have thought through the relationship. At best, the belief system is not as universal, fixed, and verbalizable as Skinner claims.

The task was shown to be meaningful in Study 2. In the second study, the subjects generally responded according to present expectations, and contrary to Skinner's formulation.

The results of both of these studies refuted Skinner's contention, for which he presented no empirical evidence, that all perception of having dignity must be earned by prosocial behaviors. Because this contention was a major practical argument for the abolition of the concepts of freedom and dignity, as working against a science of behavior, Skinner's attack on these cherished concepts is opposed by laboratory evidence as well as casual observation.

Appendix B _____

First Submission:
Yes/No Questionnaire

ABSTRACT

This study tested the contention of Skinner (1971) that dignity, or worth, must in the view of society be earned by voluntarily performing prosocial acts. The main research hypothesis was that persons accord an intrinsic dignity to others which does not have to be earned through praiseworthy behaviors performed voluntarily. College students and adult members of the community completed questionnaires about themselves and their beliefs concerning the origins of human dignity. In each subject population, many respondents indicated that they would accord dignity to newborn infants who could not have earned it. The results thus supported the main hypothesis. Other subject responses revealed, as predicted, that perceived dignity is in addition augmented or decreased by voluntary praiseworthy or blameworthy behaviors, respectively.

PERCEIVED DIGNITY OF PERSONS WITH MINIMAL
VOLUNTARY CONTROL OVER THEIR OWN BEHAVIORS

Skinner (1971) argues against the concepts of human freedom and dignity, contending that together they form a practical barrier to the science of human behavior and therefore to progress in human culture. His reasoning is based upon his personal conception of science. With respect to freedom, Skinner (1955–56) maintains: "But science insists that action is initiated by forces impinging upon the individual, and that caprice is only another name for behavior for which we have not yet found a cause" (p. 53). Skinner (1955–56) has consistently maintained

First submission of "Perceived dignity of persons with minimal voluntary control over their own behaviors" to Journal C. For final publication, see Harcum and Rosen(1990b).

therefore that science is acceptable to general society only as long as it is just partially successful in accounting for human behavior. He argues that the barrier to scientific programs occurs because science, in discovering the determinants of behaviors, thereby replaces the concept of voluntary choice, which is cherished by the people. To halt this replacement process, society opposes further progress in science. Thus, as science becomes more effective it arouses public opposition, because it conflicts with the traditional humanistic views of human nature. Skinner (1955–56) summarizes his reasoning as follows:

> Every discovery of an event which has a part in shaping a man's behavior seems to leave so much the less to be credited to the man himself; and as such explanations become more and more comprehensive, the contribution which may be claimed by the individual himself appears to approach zero. (p. 52)

The issue with respect to dignity is whether or not society believes that all human dignity, or worth, is contingent upon the ability of a person to perform prosocial behaviors voluntarily. In Skinner's view of society's beliefs, as more prosocial behaviors are ascribed to greater voluntary control, there is an increase in perceived dignity. If all human dignity must be earned through performance of voluntary praiseworthy behaviors, there can be no dignity without the capability of making such voluntary acts. Thus, a reduction in the perception of personal freedom as science discovers the relevant behavioral laws consequently reduces human dignity. In order to protect the cherished concept of dignity, society then tends to oppose Skinner's strict behavioristic metaphysics and his concept of science.

Although Skinner does not specifically discuss the relationship between freedom and dignity for blameworthy behaviors, his formulation does imply an inverse relationship between dignity and greater voluntary control of such behaviors.

The purpose of the present article is to challenge these contentions of Skinner about society's metaphysical beliefs. Skinner (1971) presents no empirical evidence to support his opinion about the impracticality of the concepts of freedom and dignity. Moreover, he disregards the so-called "literature of freedom" (Skinner, 1971, p. 31) as unscientific. We oppose this view because data from casual observation should not be ignored by scientists, even if such observations are based on the writings of non-scientists, such as artists or other humanistic scholars. This literature does provide frequent evidence of society's belief in the intrinsic dignity of persons. On the presumption that laboratory data provide more convincing evidence, however, our purpose is to add such evidence.

The basic issue is whether or not persons with no opportunity to control their own behaviors by an alleged internal mechanism are perceived by their peers as possessing dignity, as we claim, or not, as Skinner claims. The definition of dignity is critically important. Skinner (1971) simply equates "dignity" with "worth." To operationalize this definition in a way that should be appropriate to Skinner's argument, we define dignity in terms of affirmative responses to a person by others.

Specifically, we argue that a person has dignity if other persons show admiring and supportive behaviors toward that person.

In the context of blameworthy behaviors, we follow Harcum, Rosen, and Burijon (1989) who proposed a concept of "negative dignity," which is the logical opposite of dignity. A person with negative dignity would not be esteemed or supported by others. Greater numbers of blameworthy behaviors would produce decreases in dignity, possibly enough to produce a state of negative dignity. Presumably society would perceive itself to be better off without a person having negative dignity.

Some empirical data are already available. Harcum and Rosen [Appendix C] asked college students to rate the dignity of hypothetical actors in short vignettes which described both prosocial and antisocial behaviors performed under six presumed levels of voluntary choice. These subjects accorded some positive (intrinsic) dignity to a person who had not earned it through voluntary social acts. Also the perception of dignity was augmented by voluntary prosocial behaviors and decreased by antisocial ones. Harcum and Rosen [Appendix D] also asked college students and direct-care providers to rate the dignity of newborn infants, who could not have earned it, and to rate other factors relating to the judgement of human dignity. Results again supported the concept of intrinsic dignity, and also the increase and decrease of dignity with voluntary prosocial and antisocial behaviors, respectively.

Harcum, Rosen, and Burijon (1989) asked college students to draw complete graphs which described the students' beliefs about the functional relationships between voluntary control of praiseworthy and blameworthy behaviors and the students' attributions of dignity and negative dignity. Unsophisticated beginning students were not able to perform the research task, presumedly because they could not understand it. Therefore, even if Skinner's reasoning about society's beliefs are minimally correct, these beliefs are not consistent and articulated. When Harcum et al. used a group of more advanced students, for whom the issues were discussed before the task was attempted, the results clearly con-tradicted Skinner's contention. These more sophisticated subjects supported the hypotheses of a perception of dignity even when a behavior was not ascribed to voluntary choice. Spontaneous comments by both the unsophisticated and the sophisticated subject groups indicated a tendency to award intrinsic dignity in the absence of voluntary behaviors.

The present study attempts to provide additional evidence to disconfirm Skinner's unsupported contention about public beliefs concerning freedom and dignity. Such evidence will destroy his practical argument against the value of freedom and dignity in social action. As many have argued (e.g., Harcum, 1988), society will benefit from a more, rather than less, humanistic approach to behavioral science. The present study tests in a different way the hypotheses of Harcum and Rosen [Appendices C and D]. The subjects will be asked whether or not they will accord dignity to individuals having certain characteristics. The main hypothesis is that persons are accorded intrinsic dignity which does not have to be earned. Secondary hypotheses are that dignity is augmented by perceived voluntary prosocial behaviors and reduced by perceived voluntary antisocial behaviors.

STUDY 1

The method of Study 1 differs from the previous research in that the subjects are asked direct questions about a hypothetical person (a newborn infant) who would not have had the opportunity to earn dignity by voluntary prosocial performance or to lose it by voluntary antisocial performance.

Method

Subjects. Three groups of college students served as subjects. The first two groups were students in the first and second semesters of a one-year course in introductory psychology. These groups, identified as C.S. 1 (N = 72) and C.S. 2 (N = 161), respectively, served as part of a course requirement and were tested in special sessions outside of class. A third group (C.S. 3, N = 110) consisted of advanced students tested in class as part of the regular coursework in four courses: Experimental Psychology; Social Psychology; Physiological Psychology; and Sexuality.

Procedure. All students were given a questionnaire booklet in which the top page was a consent form, which explained that the study would ask certain questions about their personal characteristics and about their beliefs concerning human dignity. It guaranteed anonymity and assured the students that they could refuse to answer any question and discontinue the study at any time. No student declined to participate.

The instructions defined dignity as follows:

> Dignity: A person has dignity to the extent that he or she has worth, excellence, value, usefulness, or is held in esteem, as indicated when other persons show such behaviors toward that person as overtly supporting, rewarding, admiring, saving, defending, and/or honoring.

Subjects were asked to try to answer all of the questions, and to feel free to comment if "yes" or "no" answers did not adequately communicate what they believed. The first questions asked for gender, race, and probable major in college. The subjects were also asked if they thought that their cultural experience was different from the majority of students of their sex and race in the class. If "yes," they were asked to describe such possible differences.

The questions about dignity, to be answered "yes" or "no" with space for comments, were as follows:

1. Can a baby be born somewhere today who will have such an unhappy combination of characteristics (such as sex, race, religion, ethnic or socio-economic origin, mental disability, physical disability, etc.) that he or she will have no (zero) dignity?
2. Can a person increase his or her dignity by performing acts approved by society?

3. Can a person decrease his or her dignity by performing acts condemned by society?
4. Can a person lose all of his or her dignity (i.e., reduce it to zero) by performing acts condemned by society?

The next two questions asked about "negative dignity," defined as follows:

Negative dignity: Negative dignity is the opposite of dignity. A person has negative dignity to the extent that he or she is unworthy, detrimental, injurious, harmful, and/or is a liability or failure, as indicated when other persons show such behaviors toward that person as overtly opposing, punishing, despising, expending, attacking, and/or discrediting.

5. Can a baby be born somewhere today with such an unhappy combination of characteristics, as in 1 above, that he or she will have "negative dignity"?
6. Can a person develop "negative dignity" by performing acts condemned by society?

Results

The percentages of "Yes" responses to the six questions are shown in Table B.1, along with the prediction for each question. The percentages were very similar across the three groups of college students for each question, with the largest $\chi^2(2) = 1.25; p > .70$. The summarized results for all subjects in the sixth column are very close to the averages across groups of the three individual percentages, despite the differences in Ns. Consequently, the differences among the college groups were ignored in subsequent evaluations of these data.

The predictions were supported by answers to each question except Question 4, which denies that a person can lose all dignity by performing condemned acts. This result is apparently inconsistent with the responses to Question 6 which agrees that a person can develop negative dignity by condemned acts. Perhaps Question 6 could be read as equivalent to Question 3, to indicate that dignity could be *developed* in a negative direction (i.e., decreased), but not *achieved* in an absolute sense.

The answers to the main question, Question 1, support by a large majority of these respondents the argument for an intrinsic, unearned dignity. Further evidence is provided by the spontaneous comments of the students, as shown in Table B.2. Each of the eight comments in the table was made by at least 3% of the subjects. The comments are ranked according to the percentages of respondents making the comment. When a subject made more than one comment, the second comment simply clarified or amplified the first. Clearly, the preponderance of comments support the concept of intrinsic dignity.

Efforts to relate subject characteristics to the various responses about dignity did not produce any general conclusions.

Table B.1

Predictions and Percentages of "Yes" Responses by Subjects in Two Studies to Six Questions About Dignity

Question	Prediction	Study 1				Study 2	
		C.S. 1	C.S. 2	C.S. 3	ALL	Serv. O	G. Club
1. Born zero	NO	23	17	21	21	37	67
2. Praise increase	YES	85	86	85	85	92	93
3. Blame decrease	YES	84	84	89	86	94	87
4. Lose all	YES	33	30	29	31	46	56
5. Born negative	NO	30	23	32	29	45	59
6. Gain negative	YES	80	74	76	78	80	93

Discussion

With the one noted exception, the results were as predicted from the Harcum and Rosen [Appendix C] hypothesis. The most important result is the subjects' report that a person with minimal voluntary control over his or her behaviors is still accorded dignity. Therefore, Skinner's (1971) contention, that society accords dignity only to those who voluntarily perform prosocial acts, is contradicted by these data.

Because college students are obviously a relatively small and select sample of possible research subjects, the impact of these data is to refute the generality of Skinner's claim, rather than to establish a phenomenon. More and different samples of subjects are necessary for any attempt to establish the generality of the Harcum–Rosen hypothesis.

STUDY 2

In order to establish generality for the conclusions in Study 1, in Study 2 two additional groups of subjects were administered essentially the same questionnaire used in Study 1.

Method

Subjects. One group of 52 subjects consisted of a service organization (Serv. O), primarily of white men. A second group of 46 subjects was a garden club (G. Club), exclusively of white women, which also was dedicated to community service. Because many of the subjects declined to give their ages, mean ages were not determined, although clearly the average age for each group was substantially greater than that of the college students. Undoubtedly, there were other differences. Instead of listing a college major, these subjects were asked to give their occupations.

Table B.2
Percentage of College Students in Study 1 Making Spontaneous Comments Within Each Category*

Category	Percentage
1. Dignity is always present	35
2. Dignity comes from self-appraisal	29
3. Dignity is inborn	11
4. Everyone has potential to earn dignity	7
5. Dignity is earned, not inborn	4
6. Dignity lies in reasons for actions	4
7. Dignity can be zero for terrible acts	3
8. Negative dignity is only in eyes of society	3

* Includes only comments by at least 3% of subjects. Subjects could make comments in more than one category.

Procedure. Both groups of subjects were administered the questionnaire during regular meetings of their organization. The procedure, conducted by the senior author, included the signing of consent forms, instructions, and de-briefings in a manner as equivalent as possible to that for the college students.

Results

The results of Study 2 are given in the last two columns of Table B.1. Although the differences between the two groups were significant only for Question 1: $\chi^2(1) = 8.51$; $p < .004$, this meant that the results for these groups could not be combined in the further analysis.

For the three groups of subjects in both studies, the results for the six questions in order were: 1—$\chi^2(2) = 43.95$ ($p < .001$); 2—$\chi^2(2) = 3.91$ ($p > .10$); 3—$\chi^2(2) = 2.92$ ($p > .20$); 4—$\chi^2(2) = 12.07$ ($p < .01$); 5—$\chi^2(2) = 15.49$ ($p < .001$); and 6—$\chi^2(2) = 6.03$ ($p < .05$). For all six questions, there was a progressive increase in "Yes" responses relative to the college students for the Serv. O and G. Club subjects, respectively. This generalization is most relevant to the most important question, Question 1, for which the G. Club subjects actually produced more "yes" than "no" responses. Although the result on this question for this group is more affirmative than predicted, the value (i.e., 67%) is still substantially less ($t(42) = 4.60$; $p < .001$) than the 100% claimed by Skinner (1971). The consistent differences between college and older groups could merely reflect a greater acquiescence set for the older groups, although there is no independent evidence for this.

The three groups of subjects are in good agreement that praiseworthy and blameworthy behaviors increase and decrease dignity, respectively.

Again, we were unable to relate any of the personal characteristics of the subjects to their attitudes about dignity.

The spontaneous comments of these populations of subjects were too rare to permit a table such as Table B.2, or indeed any generalization. We can offer no serious proposal about the cause of this difference in the number of spontaneous comments relative to the college students. The most frequent comment in the Serv. O group—made by only three subjects, however—was C1: Dignity is always present.

Discussion

This study gives clear support to the notion that older adults also believe in voluntary control of behavior, and, moreover, that they employ this concept in assigning dignity to individuals.

The earlier results of Harcum and Rosen [Appendices C and D] and Harcum, Rosen, and Burijon (1989) are supported by these results which employ a different research tactic and include different populations of subjects. Not only are the concepts of freedom and earned dignity, and a relationship between them, firmly associated in the minds of the subjects, but also the subjects believe in a level of dignity which is intrinsic at birth and therefore is not contingent upon the ability of a person to initiate behaviors voluntarily.

Study 2, along with Study 1, thus refutes Skinner's contention, for which he presented no empirical evidence, that dignity can only be present if it is earned by voluntary performance of prosocial behaviors. Because this contention was the basis for his practical arguments against the concepts of freedom and dignity, as contrary to a science of behavior, the basis of his argument is refuted by both laboratory evidence and by casual observation (Blanshard & Skinner, 1966).

Appendix C _____

First Submission:
Vignettes

ABSTRACT

This study investigated the functional relationship between the perceived dignity of an actor in a vignette and the degree to which his or her blameworthy or praiseworthy behaviors were judged to be produced by voluntary choice. In two experiments, college students read two vignettes representing, respectively, examples of praiseworthy and blameworthy behaviors. Each vignette was assumed to have occurred under six different circumstances, each representing a different degree of voluntary control over the behavior by the actor. The main hypothesis was that an actor is accorded dignity or worth even when the behavior, whether prosocial or antisocial, is ascribed to causes beyond voluntary control. The results of the first experiment were supportive of the hypothesis, but not conclusive. The second experiment conclusively supported the hypothesis and clearly refuted the contention of Skinner (1971) that dignity must be earned by prosocial acts which are ascribed to voluntary choice.

PERCEIVED DIGNITY AS A FUNCTION OF PERCEIVED VOLUNTARY CONTROL OF BEHAVIORS

In his provocative book, *Beyond Freedom and Dignity*, B. F. Skinner (1971) advanced arguments for the abolition of the concepts of freedom and dignity in human behavior, at least in terms of humanistic connotations for those terms. His attack on the concepts involved two related assertions: (1) freedom is merely an illusory concept, because all behavior is completely determined by hereditary and environmental influences; and (2) the very idea of freedom is a practical barrier to

First submission of "Perceived dignity as a function of perceived voluntary control of behaviors" to Journal H. For final publication, see Harcum and Rosen (1990a).

progress for a science of human behavior, because science inexorably finds causes for behaviors that would otherwise be attributed to voluntary choice, thus superseding this cherished concept and consequently arousing opposition to further scientific progress. Because the first assertion is unprovable, as Skinner himself admits (1971, p.96), it is not of major concern in this study. Although Skinner has received the most attention on this first assertion (Weigel, 1977; Machan, 1974), we are concerned with the second assertion because it can be empirically evaluated. Neither Skinner nor apparently anyone else, as far as we can discover, has attempted to verify empirically the second assertion.

Skinner (1971) argues that ignorance of the causal mechanisms of human behavior has permitted many laity and also professionals to inject a false concept of personal choice in explaining the behavior. But, he says, this cannot continue: "This escape route is slowly closed as new evidences of the predictability of human behavior are discovered. Personal exemption from a complete determinism is revoked as a scientific analysis progresses, particularly in accounting for the behavior of the individual" (p. 19). This is a rather strong assertion in view of the admittedly moot issue of voluntary choice vs. determinism; the shrinking domain for personal choice as science progresses certainly does not require that the further progression of science eliminate completely a viable concept of intentional behavior.

Skinner (1971) carries his argument against a voluntary control of behavior yet further. He argues that scientific progress not only obviates the idea of freedom to choose behaviors, but, as a further natural consequence, it exposes the conventional concept of human dignity as a mental impediment, because people accord dignity to those who perform prosocial acts through personal choice. Therefore, he argues:

> Any evidence that a person's behavior may be attributed to external circumstances seems to threaten his dignity or worth. We are not inclined to give a person credit for achievements which are in fact due to forces over which he has no control. . . . But as an analysis of behavior adds further evidence, the achievements for which a person himself is to be given credit seem to approach zero, and both the evidence and the science which produces it are then challenged. (p. 41)

On the basis of this argument, Skinner (1971) achieves his final conclusion that the so-called literature of human dignity " . . . thus stands in the way of further human achievements" (p. 55).

On the basis of the above arguments, Skinner assumes that the beliefs of most people would represent a functional relationship between perceived dignity and perceived voluntary control of praiseworthy behaviors about as shown in Figure C.1. The function intersects the ordinate at zero (the origin), representing a perception of no dignity when there is no voluntary control of the behavior. Presumably, the function monotonically increases as the behavior is ascribed to greater voluntary control. Skinner does not specifically discuss a possible relationship for blameworthy behaviors, but his formulations clearly imply a func-

Figure C.1
**Functional Relationship (Credit) Between Society's Judgment of the Dignity
of the Person and the Degree to which that Person's Behavior is Apparently
Caused by Personal Choice, According to Skinner (1971). (Note: Skinner
does not specify the form of the relationship other than that it is monotonic
and intersects the ordinate at zero.)**

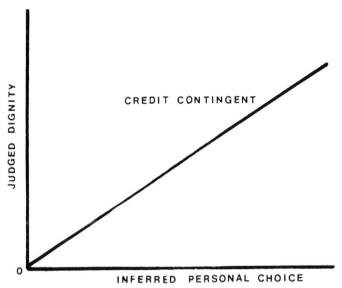

tion starting at the origin and decreasing with greater influence of voluntary
control. He says, " . . . scientific analysis shifts the credit as well as the blame to
the environment . . . " (1971, p. 19).

Because Skinner does not report data which might suggest or support this
hypothesis, it must be based on casual observation or on deductions from his
metaphysical position. He dismisses what he calls the "literature of freedom"
(Skinner, 1971, p. 27; Blanshard & Skinner, 1966) as not properly scientific,
despite the admonitions of other scholars (Blanshard, in Blanshard & Skinner,
1966) that many great writers and thinkers have endorsed freedom and dignity
as intrinsic attributes of human beings. This mode of thinking has in fact
increased as a result of the modern disorganization of society, according to Berger
(1970), because modern thinking has changed from identifying a person in
relation to cultural norms and institutional roles and instead identifies the person
as a part of humanity essentially independent of such norms and roles. "Dignity,
as against honor, always relates to the intrinsic humanity divested of all socially
imposed roles or norms. . . . The implicit sociology views all biological and
historical differentiations among men as either downright unreal or essentially
irrelevant" (Berger, 1970, p. 342).

Figure C.2
Hypothetical Relationship between the Inference of Voluntary Control of Behavior and Society's Judgment of the Dignity of that Person

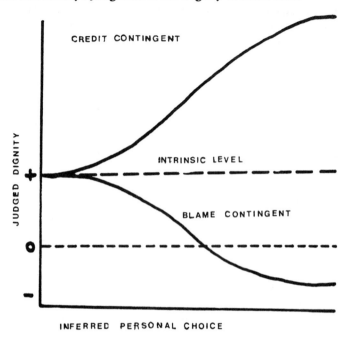

Therefore, the literature of dignity does indicate a prevailing belief in intrinsic dignity, unearned and independent of social roles. On the basis of this belief, in addition to our own casual observations, we have arrived at a quite different hypothesis from Skinner. Our hypothesis leads to the predictions illustrated in Figure C.2. We hypothesize that, because of the socialization process, people accord some level of dignity to others, unconditionally and non-contingently. That is, all dignity does not have to be earned through creditable behaviors, performed voluntarily. A minimum level of intrinsic dignity is awarded simply because of a person's humanity, because they are human beings. This level of intrinsic, unearned personal dignity thus indicates a y-intercept at greater than zero dignity, instead of at zero as Skinner predicts. We further predict that the function will be sigmoid, because of a secondary hypothesis that it approaches limits at either extreme.

Figure C.2 introduces the concept of "negative dignity," the exact opposite of dignity. For blameworthy behaviors, the perceived dignity decreases as the behaviors are ascribed to greater degrees of voluntary choice, ultimately resulting in the perception of negative dignity, because a person who performs antisocial deeds from personal choice is not admired. The two sigmoid functions in Figure C.2 represent the predictions for the present study of the public's beliefs about the relation between dignity and voluntary choice of behaviors.

Method

In two experiments the method was basically the same. Two stories were written to describe respectively an antisocial (blameworthy) and a prosocial (praiseworthy) act. Both stories began with identical sentences describing a workman driving a cement truck on a mountain road, who came upon a stalled bus loaded with 33 children. The second sentence for the praiseworthy act had the driver drive over the cliff, killing himself but saving the children. The blameworthy sentence had the driver crash into the bus, saving himself but killing the children. For each story the subjects were given six conditions or circumstances under which the story was assumed to have taken place, representing six degrees of voluntary choice involved in the driver's decision. For example, the following description of circumstances appeared as Situation 2 in Experiment I and Situation 4 in Experiment II. "The driver had only a split second to think about the situation, and therefore did not have time to weigh fully the consequences of his responses." This was designed to represent a relatively low level of voluntary control, which the data later confirmed.

The subjects were students in introductory psychology, fulfilling a course requirement. There were 33 subjects in Experiment I and 277 subjects in Experiment II.

In Experiment I, for each story under each circumstance, each subject was asked to rate on a scale of 0 to 10 "the degree to which the driver could exert voluntary control over his own actions," and also on a 7-point Likert scale of –3 to +3 "your evaluation of the driver himself." The minus values indicated "degrees to which the driver is judged to be despised, harmful, and a liability. Positive values indicate degrees to which the driver is judged to be esteemed, useful, and worthy." One-half of the subjects read the praiseworthy condition first and the other half saw the blameworthy condition first. The order of specific circumstances was the same for the two stories, but there was no mention of this in the instructions.

In Experiment II, the procedures and instructions were changed somewhat in order to focus the subjects' attention more specifically on the evaluation of the driver rather than upon his specific behavior under the various specified circumstances. The subjects were divided into four approximately equal groups, with the separate groups judging the degree of voluntary control or the degree of esteem, for the praiseworthy or for the blameworthy behaviors, respectively.

The instructions were essentially the same as for Experiment I except that they emphasized how "you," the subject, would rate the dignity or estimate the degree of voluntary control for each circumstance and emphasized that the behavior in the story was typical of the driver, as follows: "While this story represents only one episode in the life of the driver, consider his behavior as typical of his responses throughout his life; his dignity or worth as a person should represent the sum total of everything you consider appropriate."

These subjects were also told that the specific circumstances were presented in no special order, and that they could go back and re-read and change answers if they desired. Instead of rating the specific circumstances of voluntary control, the appropriate groups of subjects used a magnitude estimation procedure, with the first story assigned a value of 100. In order to provide a circumstance representing an intermediate degree of voluntary control for this reference point, a condition judged to be intermediate in Experiment I was used for this standard. This required a different fixed order of circumstance descriptions in Experiment II relative to Experiment I. In the following list, the first number is the order of a situation in Experiment I and the second number is the order of that same circumstance in Experiment II: 1 = 2; 2 = 4; 3 = 5; 4 = 3; 5 = 6; and 6 = 1. Actually, four of the six descriptions of the circumstances were edited slightly for Experiment II.

Results and Discussion

The results of Experiment I are shown in Figure C.3 which plots the mean dignity ratings as a function of the mean ratings of voluntary control for each Circumstance. The numbers by the data points indicate the order in which the circumstances were presented. Clearly, praiseworthy behaviors which were attributed to a greater degree of voluntary choice produced ratings of positive dignity, whereas blameworthy behaviors attributed to a greater degree of voluntary choice produced ratings of negative dignity.

Unfortunately, the subjects tended to avoid ratings of zero voluntary control, even for the Circumstance written specifically to produce such a rating which was as follows: "The driver had time only to respond reflexly (*sic*), without thinking, and therefore responded the same as anyone else would have in the same situation." The averaging process, of course, virtually precludes a value at zero, because all responses must have values of zero or above. Therefore, any serious attempt at an extrapolation to the y-intercept would not be appropriate. The curve of blame is very slightly above zero dignity at the closest point to zero voluntary control, but not significantly so. In fact, the subjects were equally divided in rating dignity above and below zero at that point. This is suggestive of the hypotheses, but not conclusive. Although the curve of praise is empirically above zero dignity at the point of least rating of voluntary control, there is no strong basis to argue for or against a further drop to zero dignity at the y-intercept. Nevertheless, even the slight rating of positive dignity at the first two points for an actor committing an antisocial act with an appreciable degree of intentionality is encouraging for the hypothesis, and definitely indicates the advisability for further study.

Because of the limited range of points, their small number and their irregularity, it is not profitable to speculate about the true shape of the functional relationships. In fact, the question of the true shape is not a critical issue. By visual inspection, the praise curve appears to be positively accelerating, whereas the blame curve appears more sigmoid.

Experiment I does not provide an adequate test of the main hypothesis which predicts an intrinsic, unearned dignity. The first problem is, of course, the absence of data points sufficiently close to zero voluntary control. The second problem is the use of a single vignette as a basis for assessing the dignity of the *person*, rather than the *act* itself. This potential problem was identified, and a solution was attempted

Figure C.3
Mean Rating of Dignity as a Function of the Mean Rating of Voluntary Control for Both Prosocial
and Antisocial Acts in Experiment I

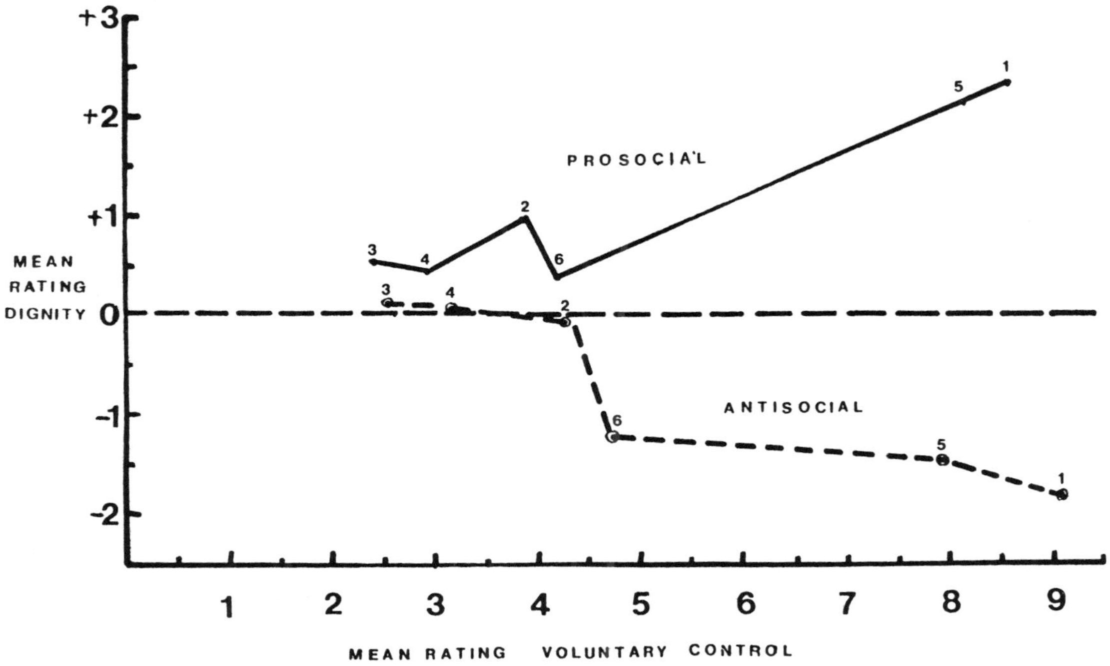

by including specifically in the verbal instructions to the subject, the admonition to judge "the worth or value of the person. Judge the person himself, and not the act itself or the result of the act."

The results of Experiment II are shown in Figure C.4, which is plotted much the same as Figure C.3, except that the abscissa now represents magnitude estimations of the degree of voluntary control. The general appearance of the data is as before except that the data points for the estimations of less voluntary control of antisocial behavior now fall noticeably above zero dignity, converging with the array of data points on the curve of praise. A conservative test of the hypothesis concerning a y-intercept above zero dignity would be achieved by testing whether the three points closest to zero choice on the curve of blame show significantly positive dignity, because the progression of these points is still rising. Moreover, it is reasonable to expect the two functions to converge at some point on the y-axis. It would not be reasonable to expect the two functions to cross, or for the blame curve to decrease with less voluntary control.

An examination of the dignity data for the single circumstance of least estimated voluntary control for blameworthy behavior reveals significantly ($p < .01$) more subjects (70%) rating dignity above zero than below zero. If one collapses the data for the three Circumstances closest to zero voluntary control for the blame stories, the difference from zero is again significant ($p < .01$), and even more convincing.

The difference in the numbers at the data points for the two experiments provides inferential evidence against a major effect of order. The consistency of results for similar circumstances in the two experiments does provide inferential evidence for the validity of the variable of voluntary control.

Again the blame curve appears slightly sigmoid, and the shape of the praise curve ambiguous. This possible difference remains a problem for further study.

GENERAL DISCUSSION

Whereas the results of Experiment I were equivocal with respect to the main hypothesis, the results of Experiment II provide clear support for it. Although there were several improvements in method for Experiment II, the most important ones probably were the written emphasis on judging the actor, not the act, and the removal of the necessity for changing sets by having to rate the actor for both blameworthy and praiseworthy situations.

This difference in experimental results implies a distinction between this research on the perception of dignity and research in attribution theory. Whereas this line of research focuses on the evaluation of the person, presumably based on many responses over many years, the attribution research assesses culpability or credit for a given instance of behavior. Although the functional relations would in all likelihood be similar in slope, the level of intrinsic dignity would differ because of the problem of assessing a person on the basis of a single act. In fact, one subject made such a comment. A subject would have to be rather alert not to be distracted from the logical conclusion that the driver has dignity because all individual humans have dignity.

Figure C.4
Mean Rating of Dignity as a Function of the Mean Magnitude Estimation of Voluntary Control for Both Prosocial and Antisocial Acts in Experiment II

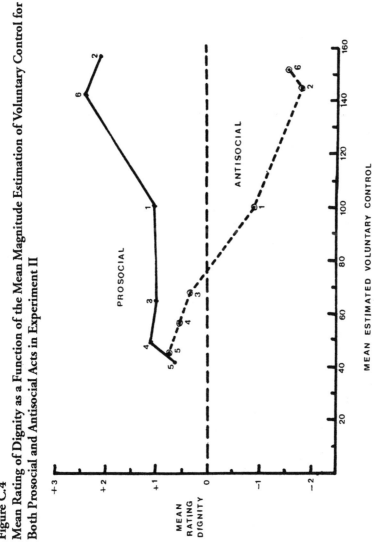

The study of Kahneman and Tversky (1973) shows that subjects will not use relevant stored information to solve a problem when they are given other irrelevant information that actually cannot be used to solve the problem, thus distracting from the rational basis of decision that is available. This is a difficulty with the indirect approach to studying attitudes. But it seems rather fruitless to ask the direct question, because of potential problems with social desirability and demand characteristics. The role of social desirability and demand characteristics is, of course, a ubiquitous question whenever one attempts to make inferences about human attitudes. Previous unpublished data [Appendix D] do not, however, indicate a relationship between social desirability and ratings of dignity. Moreover, if social desirability and demand characteristics were factors in the dignity ratings, they should have been equally effective in Experiments I and II. The lack of a significant effect on the y-intercept in Experiment I indicates no effect of these variables. Finally, the purpose of the study was in fact to discover the subjects' conformity to presumed internalized standards of social evaluation. Empirically and practically, the helping behavior is more relevant than an inferred attitude even if behavior and true attitude did happen to be different.

It may also be relevant that the word "dignity" was never used in Experiment I, but it was used once in the written instructions of Experiment II, in the added sentence quoted in the methods section above.

The evidence from Experiment II thus supports the conclusion that subjects tend to accord some intrinsic positive dignity to persons who have not earned it through voluntary praiseworthy deeds. These results clearly contradict Skinner's contention that the function for praiseworthy behaviors will pass through the origin, and thus invalidate his practical argument against the concepts of freedom and dignity. Because some human dignity is thought to be intrinsic, independent of behavior, it is not threatened by even a science which aspires to discover all of the hereditary and environmental causes of human behavior.

Thus, freed of this one irrational fear at least, we can give ourselves wholeheartedly to the scientific study of human attitudes. While we advocate a liberal view of what scientific methods are acceptable, we do also encourage the use of the best methods available in a specific context. The present results indicate that Skinner's (1971) prediction of human behavior from his casual observations was off the mark. Thus, we have demonstrated the validity of Skinner's contention that the results of "casual observation . . . must be corrected or displaced by a scientific analysis" (p. 17).

Appendix D

First Submission: Confirmation

ABSTRACT

This study tested Skinner's (1971) assertion that society accords dignity or worth to an individual only because the person is seen as voluntarily performing prosocial behaviors. Therefore, society opposes science because progress in science eliminates interpretations in voluntary terms, and, as a direct consequence, it obviates dignity. The present hypothesis was that subjects accord an intrinsic dignity to newborn infants who could not have earned any dignity through personal performance. College students and direct-care providers at a state mental hospital indicated, by rating their agreement with direct questions, the criteria they would use to accord dignity to others. Results for each group of subjects supported the hypothesis. Therefore, Skinner's practical argument against the concept of human dignity is refuted.

PERCEPTION OF HUMAN DIGNITY BY COLLEGE STUDENTS AND BY DIRECT-CARE PROVIDERS

Skinner (1971) argues that the concept of human dignity hinders social progress and human welfare because belief in the concept produces opposition to a science of human behavior. He believes that the concepts of both human freedom and human dignity are used as alternatives to behavioral laws. They provide acceptable reasons for those behaviors which society does not understand because the sources controlling the behavior are hidden or internal. According to Skinner (1974), "There is no place in the scientific position for a self as a true originator or initiator of action"

First submission of "Perception of human dignity by college students and by direct-care providers" to Journal N. For final publication, see Harcum and Rosen (1992).

(p. 225). Skinner (1955–56; 1971) argues that the discovery of scientific laws reduces the number of unexplained behaviors, and thus reduces the need for these cherished concepts, because dignity, as well as freedom, would have to be zero if all of the behavioral laws were known. If dignity can be earned only by voluntarily performing prosocial behaviors, there must be freedom if a person is to acquire dignity. Without a history of voluntary prosocial behaviors, by this reasoning a person would have to be accorded zero dignity.

Although Skinner does not mention blameworthy behaviors, presumably blameworthy behaviors would not detract from perceived dignity if they were perceived as completely determined by the environment. As the number of undesired responses which were perceived as voluntary increased, presumably the perception of dignity would decrease.

Harcum, Rosen, and Burijon (1989) hypothesized that people accord some dignity to others which does not have to be earned by voluntarily performing prosocial acts. They predicted that some minimum level of such intrinsic dignity would be awarded by one person to another simply because people are perceived as having certain human traits, and this is one of them. Harcum et al. also predicted that for blameworthy behaviors, the perceived dignity would decrease as the behaviors were more often ascribed to greater voluntary choice, possibly resulting in the perception of negative dignity. They asked college students to indicate their beliefs about freedom and dignity by drawing graphs to represent the functional relationship between voluntary control and perceived behaviors. Students in introductory psychology courses could not understand the task, however. This was interpreted by Harcum et al. to represent a problem for Skinner's argument. Even if Skinner correctly assessed society's reasoning, the thought processes were not introspectively available to even college students. Although college students may not be mature enough to have thought through this possible relationship, Skinner does not put age or maturity conditions on his interpretation.

Harcum et al. repeated this study with advanced students but explained the task and the issues before the task was administered. These students did accord dignity to those persons whose behavior was entirely controlled by environmental circumstances. Both groups of students were also asked to write brief essays describing what characteristics they considered important in their perception of dignity or worth. In fact, 13.2% of all the subjects wrote that dignity is always present (i.e., intrinsic) in each human being. The subjects also indicated on further questions a strong reluctance to concede even that a human behavior could actually be produced without a voluntary component.

In another study designed to investigate functional relationships between perceived dignity of a person and the degree to which that person's blameworthy or praiseworthy behaviors were ascribed to voluntary choice, Harcum and Rosen [Appendix C] had college students read two vignettes representing, respectively, praiseworthy and blameworthy behaviors, with each vignette presuming six different degrees of voluntary control. The main hypothesis was that a person is accorded dignity or worth even when the behavior is presumed to be caused by circumstances beyond voluntary control. The results supported the hypothesis.

A later study by Harcum and Rosen [Appendix B] found that three different populations of subjects accorded dignity to persons who could not have earned it by voluntarily performing praiseworthy behaviors. Specifically, these subjects reported that they would accord dignity to a newborn infant, who would not have had the opportunity to perform any social acts, either praiseworthy or blameworthy. About 79% of the 343 college students and 52% of the 98 subjects in two older groups responded that a newborn baby has dignity. Moreover, the most frequent spontaneous comments by the subjects reflected a belief that no person is without some dignity. These results offer an empirical contradiction to Skinner's contention that in the view of society dignity must be earned.

Although the previous results clearly are contrary to Skinner's (1971) assertion, they may indicate merely that Skinner overgeneralized. He may have been basically correct about society's view on the functional relationship between freedom and dignity. This hardly seems likely when one considers that Skinner has provided no laboratory data, in contrast to the several empirical studies from this laboratory. Nevertheless, the generality of assertions on both sides indicates the need for data from more subjects, preferably from different populations. This was the primary purpose for the present studies.

STUDY 1

Study 1 was basically an extension of the earlier study by Harcum and Rosen [Appendix B] which used college students and members of community service organizations as subjects. The main difference in the present studies was that Likert-scale items replaced the previous yes/no questions in order to provide graduated degrees in the attitude measurements which were to be correlated with the subjects' personal characteristics. Also, more information on the personal characteristics of the subjects was obtained.

Method

Subjects. The subjects were 96 college students enrolled in an introductory psychology course who volunteered in order to fulfill a research participation requirement.

Questionnaire. The first page of the questionnaire booklet was a consent form which was to be read, signed, detached, and returned separately. The form informed the students that they would be asked to give their age, gender, an estimation of the probability that they would choose a career in human services, and their beliefs on several topics. They were assured anonymity, and reassured that they could refuse to answer a question, and discontinue at any time.

The second page asked for their ages, genders, and the likelihood that they would "choose a career of some sort in human services," to be expressed as a percentage.

The remaining pages consisted of the questions about their personal attitudes. The first nine questions were concerned with dignity. Dignity was defined by

Harcum and Rosen [Appendix B]: It is a property of persons of worth and esteem who are overtly valued by others. Subjects indicated their agreement with the various statements on a scale of 1–7, with 1 representing "Strongly Disagree," 4 representing "Neutral or Neither," and 7 representing "Strongly Agree."

The questions were as follows:

Section I

1. A baby born somewhere today can have such an unhappy combination of characteristics (such as sex, race, religion, ethnic or socio-economic origin, mental disability, physical disability, etc.) that he or she at birth has no (zero) dignity.
2. A person can increase his or her dignity by performing acts approved by society.
3. A person can decrease his or her dignity by performing acts condemned by society.
4. A person can lose all of his or her dignity (i.e., reduce it to a net of zero) by performing more or stronger acts condemned by society than acts approved by society.
5. If a person cannot control his or her own life because he or she is powerless to make choices, due to a lack of freedom or other circumstances beyond his or her control, the person has no dignity.
6. If a person cannot change his or her own life situation because he or she cannot give up the many comforts he or she presently enjoys in life, the person has no dignity.
7. I cannot conceive of a situation or circumstance in which a person would not have some dignity.
8. People who attribute more dignity to others are those that have more dignity themselves.
9. I would have defined dignity differently from the definition given on the first page, and this would have affected my answers.

The next four questions concerned negative dignity. Negative dignity was defined as before [Appendix B]: The opposite of dignity, in an unworthy person who is overtly despised and discredited.

Section II

1. A baby born somewhere today can have such an unhappy combination of characteristics (such as sex, race, religion, ethnic or socio-economic origin, mental disability, physical disability, etc.) that he or she at birth has negative dignity.
2. A person can achieve negative dignity (i.e., reduce dignity to a net below zero) by performing more or stronger acts condemned by society than acts approved by society.
3. I do not believe that there is such a thing as negative dignity.

4. I would have defined negative dignity differently from the definition on the preceding page, and this would have affected my answers.

The next ten questions concerned other attitudes, as follows:

Section III

1. As science learns to understand better the environmental causes for a person's actions, I believe that eventually there will be no need to account for any actions in terms of a person's voluntary wishes.
2. While filling out this questionnaire, I wondered what the researcher expected of me.
3. While filling out this questionnaire, I wondered how my responses might appear to others.

Items 4–9: These six items tested the degree to which the subject tends to give socially desirable responses—those which would generally be perceived as good responses by most people. The purpose is to determine whether the subjects are tending to respond in ways that make them look good, rather than perhaps fully truthful ways. In this group, items 4–9 were taken from the Crowne and Marlowe (1960) social desirability scale. The specific items were selected because they were judged to be best for our purpose. Although the items on the original test were answered as a true/false dichotomy, the Likert scale was employed for these items on the present test.

10. I consider myself to be religious because I have a sincere belief in a Supreme Being(s) and engage in some form of personal or organized worship.

Finally, a modified form of the Crowne and Marlowe (1960) test of social desirability was administered. The modification consisted of replacing the items used in the previous section with new items generated by the authors. The new items were intended to measure social desirability in the context of a college education.

Procedure. Students appearing at a designated time for a study advertised as research on "Beliefs About Human Dignity" were told that the study would question them about some personal characteristics and beliefs. All subjects signed the consent form and remained for the duration of the study.

The questionnaire booklet added the instructions to answer "by placing an X on each scale line from 1 to 7. If you feel that your answers do not truly convey what you believe, feel free to comment on the back of any page." After all questionnaires had been handed in, the subjects were de-briefed.

Results

The means and standard deviations of ratings for the questions on dignity and science are given in the second and third columns of Table D.1. The means of responses that are significantly different from a neutral response of 4 are indicated. The crucial questions for the main hypothesis of the study (i.e., Statements I 1, I 5, and III 1) all give strong support for that hypothesis. These subjects deny that a

Table D.1
Means, Standard Deviations, and Significance Levels of Ratings on Dignity and Science by College Students and Direct-Care Providers

	Question	College		Direct-Care	
		M	S.D.	M.	S.D.
I.	1. Born zero	2.55#	1.69	2.79#	1.89
	2. Increase*	5.13#	1.40	4.73#	1.72
	3. Decrease	4.99#	1.57	4.80#	1.88
	4. Lose all**	3.94	1.61	4.53#	1.77
	5. No power**	2.32#	1.38	3.13#	1.97
	6. No change**	3.79	1.52	2.70#	1.46
	7. Affirm dignity	4.85#	1.81	4.38	2.11
	8. Attribute	4.75#	1.38	4.57#	1.71
	9. Defined dignity differently	3.97	1.74	4.13	1.77
II.	1. Born negative	2.48#	1.71	2.80#	1.78
	2. Gain negative	4.25	1.76	4.69#	1.73
	3. No negative*	4.30	1.73	3.77	2.03
	4. Defined negative differently	4.05	1.53	4.09	1.60
III.	1. No voluntary**	1.90#	1.13	2.74#	1.86

* $p < .05$ for difference between groups
**$p < .01$ for difference between groups
\# significantly different from 4.0 at $p < .01$

person can have zero, or less than zero, dignity at birth, and that science will ever abolish the need for explanations in voluntary terms.

These subjects also believe that dignity can be gained and lost by a person's actions, but they are not consistent in deciding about changes in negative dignity, or that a person can ever lose all dignity.

These subjects have no strong opinions for or against the given definitions of dignity and negative dignity.

The subjects gave a neutral response to Statement III 2 on their concern for what the experimenter expected (M = 3.96; $p > .01$). They were concerned with how their responses would appear to the experimenter (M = 3.42; $p < .01$). The Social Desirability items were keyed so that the larger numbers reflect greater social desirability. The subjects did tend significantly ($p < .01$) to give social desirable responses (M = 5.06). They also considered themselves to be religious (M = 5.23; $p < .01$).

Discussion

These results support the hypothesis that college students accord intrinsic dignity which does not have to be earned. At least, they say they do. Is this just another socially desirable response? In one sense, it does not matter in this case what the individual subject believes, if that subject believes that the rest of society finds a belief in intrinsic dignity to be desirable. If everyone reports a belief in intrinsic dignity in order to conform to a perceived norm, the perceived norm is certainly contrary to Skinner's assertion.

The remaining question concerns the generality of this norm. To what extent does it apply to special populations? Study 2 was undertaken to answer this question.

STUDY 2

Study 2 was essentially a repetition of Study 1 with a sample of persons who were currently working as direct-care providers. The direct-care employees of a state mental hospital provide an excellent specialized population for testing our hypotheses and assumptions. Such persons have had extensive experience with individuals who have not been consistently effective in making personal choices, thus presumably with less internal control of behavior. If direct-care employees of the hospital also regard persons with minimal skills at earning dignity through prosocial behavior as having worth or dignity, then powerful evidence is added to our argument. If, however, the hospital employees should be unlikely to accord dignity to others, our generalizations would be curtailed. Such an outcome would also suggest the need for guided training programs for the direct-care personnel, to prevent this aspect of a "burn-out" problem. We expected, however, that this population would give more humanistic ratings because of their commitment to human services.

Method

Subjects. The subjects were 139 employees of a state mental hospital whose duties included direct services to patients. The population included both genders, and substantial ranges in both age and educational levels. Respondents included, for example, physicians, nurses, and ward attendants.

Questionnaire. The questionnaire was identical to that of Study 1, with two exceptions: (1) instead of reporting the likelihood of a career in human services, the respondents reported percentages of time spent in direct patient care; and (2) because of time limitations, the final page of social desirability items was omitted.

Procedure. Prior to initiating the study, the senior author met with several groups of administrators and supervisors in order to explain the study, to answer questions about it, and to solicit their cooperation. Both researchers and hospital employees understood that the research was to be accomplished on a time-available basis so as not to interfere with patient care. In particular, it was understood that the research was contingent upon the approval of the supervisors. In fact, on several occasions the collection of data had to be postponed in a given building because of exigencies related to patient care.

The above considerations dictated that the conditions under which the questionnaires were distributed, answered, and collected were not well controlled. Typically, the questionnaires were handed out by a research assistant at the beginning of a shift, completed by the employee when time was available, and returned to the assistant at the end of the shift. The research assistants were senior psychology majors and recent graduates in psychology of the authors' university. Despite a general uneasiness at the lack of control of the testing situation, we have no specific reason to believe that these data do not adequately reflect the beliefs of the direct-care providers.

Complete feedback on the research was provided by an article written by the authors for the hospital newspaper. Telephone numbers of the authors were included so that questions could be answered.

Results

The results of the study are given in the fourth and fifth columns of Table D.1. The results show, as predicted, that these subjects attribute dignity to persons who could not or have not earned it through good deeds. For example, the subjects disagree with Statement I 1 that an infant who could not earn dignity does not have it. Similarly, the subjects deny in Statement II 1, that an infant can be born with negative dignity—that is, can be a detriment to society. Also, Statements I 5 and I 6 indicate that a person without power to control his or her own life still is accorded dignity. Although in Statement I 7 the subjects do not significantly agree with the direct affirmation that everyone always has dignity, the tendency is in that direction.

The subjects do agree that a person can lose some dignity by his or her own behaviors, as indicated by responses to Statements I 2, I 3 and II 2.

The possibility of zero or negative dignity is not consistently supported. Responses to Statement II 3 are neutral about whether negative dignity is possible. There is agreement with I 4, that a person can lose all dignity, and agreement with II 2, that a person can achieve negative dignity.

Statements I 9 and II 4 were merely checks to determine whether or not the subjects believed and could use our definition of dignity and negative dignity. Results indicated no problem with our definition.

Statement I 8 was used on the chance that something interesting might be revealed. A strong response of agreement or disagreement would have been interesting. The general statement that people with more dignity attribute it to others was expected and found.

Statement III 1 tests a specific assertion of Professor Skinner (1971). He argues that people tend to oppose science because they fear it will eventually discover that all behavior is the result of environmental influence, thus eliminating any possibility for explaining a person's actions in terms of their own voluntary choices. Because there can be no dignity without free choices, Skinner argues, both concepts of free choice and dignity must be eliminated because they are not scientifically valid. As we predicted, however, the subjects clearly disagree with the idea that there is no such thing as voluntary choices of behavior.

Statements III 2 and III 3 were used to indicate the extent to which the subjects were responding according to how they thought they should be responding, or how their responses might appear to others. These items, along with Statements III 4 through III 9 were used to get some idea of the accuracy with which the subjects were expressing their own attitudes about dignity, as opposed to what they thought they should be expressing. The subjects were concerned with the experimenter's expectations (M = 4.72; $p < .01$), but neutral about how their responses would appear (M = 4.35; $p > .01$). These responses in both cases were significantly higher ($p < .01$) than for the college students.

The care providers were concerned with social desirability (M = 5.48) to a significant degree ($p < .01$). They were significantly more concerned with social desirability than the college students: $F(93, 132) = 1.78; p = .004$.

Statement III 10 indicates a religious population of respondents (M=5.31). They were not significantly different from the college students, however: ($F(94, 133) = 1.06$; $p = .768$.

The age of the respondents was related to several responses. The older subjects were more likely to agree that a person could enhance or decrease his or her dignity level by personal actions. They were also more likely to agree with Statements I 7 and I 8, indicating a greater tendency to accord dignity. The older subjects also tended to disagree with the concept of negative dignity (Statement III 4) and with the idea that a person's behavior is controlled by the environment (Statement III 1). The older subjects also were more concerned about how their responses would appear to others (III 2, III 3, and III 4 through III 9).

The gender of respondents was not a variable.

The percentage of time spent in direct service to patients was related to disagreement with the idea that a person could have no dignity (Statement I 7) and to agreement that the environment causes a person's behavior (Statement III 1). Because the older subjects tended to spend less time in direct contact with patients, presumably because of more administrative responsibilities, this fact should be considered in interpreting the results. Although the average respondent spent more than 73 percent of his or her time in direct service, almost ¼ of them in fact spent full time in direct service.

Discussion

Because most of the students who were surveyed with this same questionnaire were freshmen or sophomores, there are several obvious differences from the hospital population that should be considered in any comparison. For example, the average

age of the college students was 19 years, whereas the hospital population had reached an average age of about 37 years. The differences in life experiences represented by the age differences are very likely important. Clearly, the hospital population had a wider variation in educational experience.

There was also a difference in the way the tests were administered. Whereas the students came to an arranged group testing session, the hospital employees completed the questionnaire during working hours as time was available. Frequently the instructions were given by their supervisors, rather than the experimenters directly. Such arrangements were necessary so as not to interfere with the primary function of the hospital staff. Also, by definition the entire hospital population was involved in human service careers; only about 50% of the students anticipated entering such careers.

In spite of the large demographic differences between populations, nevertheless the fundamental conclusions to be reached were the same for both groups. For any statement for which there was a significant difference between the groups, the difference was merely that the college students tended to be more extreme (i.e., certain) in holding to the same view as the hospital group. Probably this is caused merely by age differences, with the older subjects being more conservative.

The hospital subjects also tended to be more concerned with making the socially correct response. This could be due to age, experience, or both. Also, because of the method of administration of the questionnaire, the hospital staff might not have been as confident in the anonymity of their responses from their supervisor. This could account for the more conservative responses.

The results themselves are important from what they tell specifically about the direct-service personnel at the hospital. Despite undoubted experiences which could lead to disillusionment and cynicism, those employees nevertheless, as predicted, exhibit a positive view of people, including a belief in a viable human will. While this result, in itself, may not be remarkable, it is noteworthy that we did not in fact find the reverse.

GENERAL DISCUSSION

There are several ways in which the present results are valuable. The first is the value of the scientific results themselves. Skinner (1948, 1971) has been an influential proponent of human engineering of environments and behavior modification. While his contributions have undoubtedly been great in these areas, the achievement of their full value has been prevented, in our view, by Skinner's insistence on strict Behaviorist guidelines for the development of psychological science. Although Skinner's basic metaphysical views cannot be proven false, his strategy for applying them is open to serious criticism, in terms of the assessment of current beliefs of the population. Therefore, his attempts to shape new attitudes have met, and will continue to meet, strong resistance from more humanistic professionals, and from the population at large which is, we conclude, very humanistic in orientation to psychological problems.

The true barrier to helping behaviors arises when persons feel that they must accept or reject Skinner's propositions on an all-or-none basis. Therefore, they may reject all of his formulations, including the valuable, established ones. The present research shows that Skinner's thinking can be rejected in part. The validity and value of his principles of learning are not questioned. While his metaphysical views are disputed by many, they cannot be empirically disconfirmed. The present results do however refute his argument for the practical value of his metaphysical position, as opposed to the popular conceptions of freedom and dignity.

Bibliography

American Psychological Association. (1983). *Publication manual of the American Psychological Association* (3d ed.). Washington, DC: Author.

Bandura, A. (1986). *Social foundations of thought and action*. Englewood Cliffs, NJ: Prentice-Hall.

Beaver, D. D. (1982). On the failure to detect previously published research. *Behavioral and Brain Sciences, 5*, 199–200.

Berger, P. (1970). On the obsolescence of the concept of honor. *Archives Europeennes de Sociologie, 11*, 339–347.

Betancourt, H. (1990). An attribution-empathy model of helping behavior: Behavioral intentions and judgments of help-giving. *Personality and Social Psychology Bulletin, 16*, 573–591.

Blanshard, B., & Skinner, B. F. (1966). The problem of consciousness—A debate. *Philosophical and Phenomenological Research, 27*, 317–337.

Blisset, M. (1982). Peer review and the structure of knowledge. *Behavioral and Brain Sciences, 5*, 203–204.

Bornstein, R. F. (1990). Manuscript review in psychology: An alternative model. *American Psychologist, 45*, 672–673.

Bradley, J. V. (1981). Pernicious publication practices. *Bulletin of the Psychonomic Society, 18*, 31–34.

Chomsky, N. (1973). The case against B. F. Skinner. In F. W. Matson (Ed.), *Without/Within: Behaviorism and humanism* (pp. 58–79) Monterey, CA: Brooks/Cole.

Colman, A. M. (1982). Manuscript evaluation of journal referees and editors: Randomness or bias? *Behavioral and Brain Sciences, 5*, 205–206.

Crowne, D. P., & Marlowe, D. (1960). A new scale of social desirability independent of psychopathology. *Journal of Consulting Psychology, 24,* 349–354.

Cummings, L. L., & Frost, P. J. (1985a). Epilogue. In L. L. Cummings & P. J. Frost (Eds.), *Publishing in the organizational sciences* (pp. 781–784). Homewood, IL: Irwin.

Cummings, L. L., & Frost, P. J. (1985b). Two case studies of author/journal interactions: An acceptance and a rejection. In L. L. Cummings & P. J. Frost (Eds.), *Publishing in the organizational sciences* (pp. 509–780). Homewood, IL: Irwin.

Deci, E. L. (1971). Effects of externally mediated rewards on intrinsic motivation. *Journal of Personality and Social Psychology, 18,* 105–115.

Dennett, D. C. (1978). *Brainstorms.* Cambridge, MA: MIT Press.

Ellis, A. (1987). The impossibility of achieving consistently good mental health. *American Psychologist, 42,* 364–375.

Elms, A. C. (1981). Skinner's dark year and *Walden II. American Psychologist, 36,* 470–479.

Erickson, R. C. (1973). "Free will" and clinical research. *Psychotherapy: Theory, Research, and Practice, 10,* 10–13.

Finke, R. A. (1990). Recommendations for contemporary editorial practices. *American Psychologist, 45,* 669–670.

Fiske, D. W., & Fogg, L. (1990). But the reviewers are making different criticisms of my paper! Diversity and uniqueness in reviewer comments. *American Psychologist, 45,* 591–598.

Frost, P. J. (1985). Responding to a rejection: An author's view of the rejection of an academic manuscript. In L. L. Cummings & P. J. Frost (Eds.), *Publishing in the organizational sciences* (pp. 766–773). Homewood, IL: Irwin.

Garcia, J. (1981). Tilting at the paper mills of academe. *American Psychologist, 36,* 149–158.

Garner, W. R., Hake, H. W., & Eriksen, C. W. (1956). Operationism and the concept of perception. *Psychological Review, 63,* 149–159.

Glenn, N. D. (1982). The journal article review process as a game of chance. *Behavioral and Brain Sciences, 5,* 211–212.

Grusky, Z. (1987). The practice of psychotherapy: A search for principles in an ambiguous art. *Psychotherapy, 24,* 1–6.

Harcum, E. R. (1988). Defensive reactance of psychologists to a metaphysical foundation for integrating different psychologies. *Journal of Psychology, 122,* 217–235.

Harcum, E. R. (1989). Commitment to collaboration (CTC) as a prerequisite for existential commonality in psychotherapy. *Psychotherapy, 26,* 200–209.

Harcum, E. R. (1990). Methodological vs. empirical literature: Two views on casual acceptance of the null hypothesis. *American Psychologist, 45,* 359–366.

Harcum, E. R. (1992). *Impeerial review.* Manuscript submitted for publication.

Harcum, E. R., Burijon, B. N., & Watson, N. (1989). Need for a theoretical justification of humanistic commitment components in behavior therapy. *Psychological Record, 39,* 493–500.

Harcum, E. R., & Rosen, E. F. (1990a). Perceived dignity as a function of perceived voluntary control of behaviors. *Journal of Psychology, 124,* 495–511.

Harcum, E. R., & Rosen, E. F. (1990b). Perceived dignity of persons with minimal voluntary control over their own behaviors. *Psychological Reports, 67,* 1275–1282.

Harcum, E. R., & Rosen, E. F. (1990c). The two faces of freedom and dignity: Credit or extenuation. *Psychological Reports, 66,* 1295–1298.

Harcum, E. R., & Rosen, E. F. (1992). Perception of human dignity by college students and by direct-care providers. *Journal of Psychology, 126,* 27–36.

Harcum, E. R., Rosen, E. F., & Burijon, B. N. (1989). Popular versus Skinnerian views on the relation between human freedom and dignity. *Journal of Psychology, 123,* 257–267.

Harnad, S. (Ed.). (1982). Peer commentary on peer review: A case study in scientific quality control. Cambridge: Cambridge University Press.

Harvey, J. H., & Harris, B. (1975). Determinants of perceived choice and the relationship between perceived choice and expectancy about feelings of internal control. *Journal of Personality and Social Psychology, 31,* 101–106.

Harvey, J. H., Harris, B., & Barnes, R. D. (1975). Actor-observer differences in the perceptions of responsibility and freedom. *Journal of Personality and Social Psychology, 32,* 22–28.

Harvey, J. H., & Weary, G. (1984). Current issues in attribution theory and research. *Annual Review of Psychology, 35,* 427–459.

Janis, I. L. (1971, November) Groupthink. *Psychology Today, 5,* 43–46; 74–76.

Kahneman, D., & Tversky, A. (1973). On the psychology of prediction. *Psychological Review, 80,* 232–251.

Kimble, G. A. (1984). Psychology's two cultures. *American Psychologist, 39,* 833–839.

Kimble, G. A. (1990). To be or ought to be? That is the question. *American Psychologist, 45,* 558–560.

Kohn, A. (1990, May). The risks of rewards. *Health,* 28–29; 31; 78.

Le Shan, L. (1990). *The dilemma of psychology.* New York: Dutton.

Lewis, C. S. (1954). *The abolition of man.* New York: Macmillan.

McClelland, D. C. (1985). *Human motivation.* Glenview, IL: Scott, Foresman.

Machan, T. R. (1974). *The pseudo-science of B. F. Skinner.* New Rochelle, NY: Arlington House.

Mahoney, M. J. (1985). Open exchange and the epistemic process. *American Psychologist, 40,* 29–39.

May, R. (1965). Intentionality, the heart of human will. *Journal of Humanistic Psychology, 5,* 202–209.

May, R. (1969). *Love and will.* New York: Norton.

Merton, R. K. (1968). The Matthew effect in science. *Science, 159,* 56–63.

Moser, L. E. (1973). *The struggle for human dignity.* Los Angeles: Nash Publishing.

Nolan, J. D. (1974). Freedom and dignity: A "functional" analysis. *American Psychologist, 29,* 157–160.

Nott, K. (1977). *The good want power.* New York: Basic Books.

Perloff, R. M., & Perloff, R. (1982). Improving research on policies for peer-review practices. *Behavioral and Brain Sciences, 5,* 232–233.

Peters, D. P., & Ceci, S. J. (1982). Peer-review practices of psychological journals. The fate of published articles, submitted again. *Behavioral and Brain Sciences, 5,* 187–195.

Platt, J. R. (1964). Strong inference. *Science, 146,* 347–353.

Prochaska, J. O., & DiClemente, C. C. (1986). Toward a comprehensive model of change. In W. R. Miller & N. Heather (Eds.), *Treating addictive behaviors* (pp. 3–27). New York: Plenum.

Reisman, J. M. (1971). *Toward the integration of psychotherapy.* New York: Wiley-Interscience.

Roediger, H. L. III. (1987). The role of journal editors in the scientific process. In D. N. Jackson & J. P. Rushton (Eds.), *Scientific excellence* (pp. 222–252). Newbury Park, CA: Sage.

Rogers, C. R. (1959). A theory of therapy, personality, and interpersonal relationships, as developed in the client–centered framework. In S. Koch (Ed.), *Psychology: A study of a science.* (Vol. 3) (pp. 184–256). New York: McGraw-Hill.

Rogers, C. R. (1964). Toward a modern approach to values: The valuing process in the mature person. *Journal of Abnormal and Social Psychology, 68,* 160–167.

Rubenstein, R. L. (1971, September). Books: *Beyond freedom and dignity. Psychology Today, 5,* 28; 31; 95–96.

Sechrest, L. B. (1987). Approaches to ensuring quality of data and performance. Lessons for science. In D. W. Jackson, & J. P. Rushton (Eds.), *Scientific excellence* (pp. 253–283). Newbury Park, CA: Sage.

Shaver, K. G. (1987). *Principles of social psychology* (3d ed). Hillsdale, NJ: Erlbaum.

Skinner, B. F. (1948). *Walden two.* New York: Macmillan.

Skinner, B. F. (1953). *Science and human behavior.* New York: Macmillan.

Skinner, B. F. (1955–1956). Freedom and the control of men. *American Scholar, 25,* 47–65.

Skinner, B. F. (1958). Teaching machines. *Science, 128,* 969–977.

Skinner, B. F. (1961). The design of cultures. *Daedalus, 90,* 534–546.

Skinner, B. F. (1971). *Beyond freedom and dignity.* New York: Knopf.

Skinner, B. F. (1974). *About behaviorism.* New York: Knopf.

Skinner, B. F. (1975). The steep and thorny way to a science of behavior. *American Psychologist, 30,* 42–49.

Smith, M. B. (1969). *Social psychology and human values.* Chicago: Aldine.

Smith, M. B. (1973). Is psychology relevant to new priorities? *American Psychologist, 28,* 463–471.

Spence, J. T. (1990). Centrifugal vs. centripedal tendencies in psychology: Will the center hold? In L. Bickman & H. Ellis (Eds.), *Preparing psychologists for the*

21st century: Proceedings of the National Conference in Graduate Education in Psychology (pp. 25–29). Hillsdale, NJ: Erlbaum.

Spencer, N. J., Hartnett, J., & Mahoney, J. (1985). Problems with reviews in the standard editorial practice. *Journal of Social Behavior and Personality, 1*, 21–36.

Toffler, B. L. (1985). Commentary on the review process of "Occupational role development: The changing determinant of outcomes for the individual": The author's perspective. In L. L. Cummings & P. J. Frost (Eds.), *Publishing in the organizational sciences* (pp. 644–649). Homewood, IL: Irwin.

Weigel, J. A. (1977). *B. F. Skinner.* Boston: Twayne.

Willerman, L., & Cohen, D. B. (1990). *Psychopathology.* New York: McGraw-Hill.

Yalom, I. D. (1980). *Existential psychotherapy.* New York: Basic Books.

Yalow, R. S. (1982). Competency testing for reviews and editors. *Behavioral and Brain Sciences, 5*, 244–245.

Ziman, J. (1982). Bias, incompetence, or bad management? *Behavioral and Brain Sciences, 5*, 245–246.

Author Index

Subject Index

About the Authors

E. RAE HARCUM is Professor Emeritus of Psychology at the College of William and Mary. He is the author of *Serial Learning and Paralearning* (1975) and *Psychology for Daily Living* (1979), as well as numerous journal articles.

ELLEN F. ROSEN is Professor of Psychology at the College of William and Mary. She has published in numerous journals.